Praise for *Poss* ~~

"Susan is an amazing woman and her story is fascinating."
Cecil (Cec) Murphey, author, *90 Minutes in Heaven* and
Healing Hands as well as many other books

"For the real hunters, hunting is no hobby. Hunting defines
them, nothing less. Susan has put her own hunter's self-
definition on display in *Possum Cops*. Protection of the land and
the wildlife it produces became for her as much of a goal as
the pursuit of the as yet unseen buck that girdled the cedar."
Todd Holbrook, Deputy Commissioner, Georgia Department
of Natural Resources (retired); CEO, Georgia Wildlife
Federation (Retired)

"What a great read from an advocate for professional wildlife
management. It is a series of short stories on the early years of
deer hunting in middle Georgia. The book includes numerous
tales on how a courageous lady deals with poachers on her
property and many of her exciting hunting experiences. She
was one of the premier conservationists in those years. Any
hunter would enjoy her escapades."
David Waller, Director of Wildlife Resources Division of the
Georgia Department of Natural Resources (Retired)

"This book brings back many memories of a different time that
everyone should be aware of. I am thankful we had landowners
like Susan who would go the extra mile to do what was right.
Her book is a definite 'must read' for anyone who appreciates
our wildlife and natural resources."
Lt. Col. Bob Sires, Law Enforcement, Georgia Department of
Natural Resources (Retired)

"Susan Lindsley is a genuinely unique voice with a lot to say. Her prose is evocative and her stories wonderfully engaging. Anyone who loves the outdoors will be a fan. Her work makes me think of John McPhee, one of the finest nonfiction writers of his generation. Her writing is captivating and her storytelling imaginative."
Don Vaughan, Writing instructor, freelance writer and author of more than 1700 nonfiction articles and writer, co-writer, contributor to or ghost writer of 32 books. http://www.donaldvaughan.net

"First thing I knew about Susan Lindsley was don't poach on her land. If you were lucky enough to survive, you went directly to jail. Love her stories."
Eddie Whitmire, Georgia Trophy Hunter

Note: If you like this book and purchased it on Amazon or through Barnes & Noble (either online or in-store), please return to the site and add your review. Reviews count in this computer age, and every review could mean more sales for the author. Susan sends her thanks to each of you for taking the time to boost her sales.

POSSUM COPS, POACHERS
and the
COUNTERFEIT
GAME WARDEN

ISBN-13: 978-0-9972920-2-2
ISBN-10: 0-9972920-2-4

First printing, August, 2016
Second printing, October, 2016

In the interest of competitive pricing, this book has been condensed from its original version. The complete uncut version (with color photos where originals were in color) is available as a Kindle e-book for $9.99.

Front cover design by Elizabeth Kate Bramlett
Additional cover design by ThomasMax

Author's websites: yesterplace.com
                    susanmyrick-gwtw.com

Published by:

 ThomasMax Publishing
P.O. Box 250054
Atlanta, GA 30325
thomasmax.com

POSSUM COPS, POACHERS
and the
COUNTERFEIT GAME WARDEN

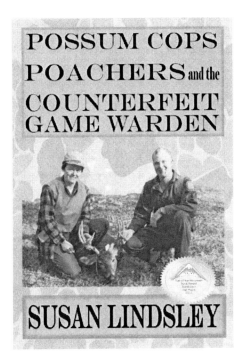

Susan Lindsley

ThomasMax

Your Publisher
For The 21st Century

ACKNOWLEDGMENTS

I must first thank all the rangers who came through my county for their support over the years and their willingness to let me share their adventures.

Many friends have pitched in with various aspects of this book: Pat Blanks for hours of typing and proofing and several line drawings; Phyllis Humphrey who also helped convert many pages of handwriting and old typing to digital format; Dave Waller, retired director of Georgia's Game and Fish Division; Todd Holbrook, Deputy Commissioner, Georgia Department of Natural Resources (retired); Robert (Bob) Sires of Game and Fish Law Enforcement; Jerry McCollum, retired CEO of the Georgia Wildlife Federation; the staff at the Game and Fish headquarters in Social Circle, Georgia; Lil James and Thulia Bramlett, sisters who always offer quality suggestions; faculty at the Southeastern Writers Workshops who have critiqued and evaluated numerous chapters; Amy Wethington (a.k.a. L. A. Patrick) for editorial suggestions; the *Union-Recorder*, my local paper, for allowing me to use their articles; Jim Chueh of Sprint Print in Decatur for his help with illustrations; Gail Cabisius for her encouragement for this and my other books and her hours of reading and helping with copy; Robert Preston Ward for help with indexing and other exacting details; Lee Clevenger for his care with the layout and production of this work; and especially Cec (Cecil) Murphey (author of *90 Minutes in Heaven*, *Healing Hands* and other books) for his encouragement and suggestions and for standing behind me in my mind as I write.

For Norman E. Simpson & John Wayne Barnes

World's best hunting buddies

TABLE OF CONTENTS

1. Introduction
    1. What would you do?
    2. Deer released on Oconee River (news item)
4. The nonpoacher
7. "So was it when my life began"
13. Typical possum cop
19. A bleak beginning
25. The year I arrested myself
29. The first buck scrape
33. More about scrapes
36. Beware the man who grants a favor
39. The poacher's buck
42. There's more than one way to get unlost
46. Laughter and Norman
49. Courting on persimmon ridge
53. The buck that thought I was a doe
56. Invasion: Government style
59. My noontime buck
65. Record keeping
68. The Silver Fox of Milledgeville
70. Dogging deer
72. Half a buck is better than none
80. Thank you, rewards and the "Bucky"
85. One ranger's first day
89. Bambi sentenced
91. The flat tire
94. When turkeys came to my county
97. My first turkey
102. The dEAr hunters
108. Turkey pictures
117. Action needed, hunter bids
119. A perfect ending
123. Memorable encounters
126. On hunting deer over bait
128. Teenage poachers
131. Blaze orange became the law
134. The day I got shot at

137. Other kinds of hunting accidents
142. The crime of poaching cannot go unpunished
143. Keeping records of poachers
146. The wonder of walking
150. More punishment for poachers
151. The sky-high stand
157. Letters about poaching
    157. She writes a letter to hunter she calls "louse"
    158. Reply: Hunting sport real victim
    159. Cooperation between local and state law enforcement
    160. Legal system not earning support
162. Shedding velvet
166. A turkey hunting weekend with a little fishing
173. Talking to the animals
177. Speaking of ticks
179. Project T. I. P.
182. Poaching is very serious offence
184. Wildlife ranger deserves commendation
188. The 1985 flap over deer season
    188. The flap begins
    190. Don't trim that deer season
    191. Special interests can't change hunting rules
    192. Going on the front lines: The Atlanta hearings
    195. The Macon Hearings
    196. Stancil and Me
        196. 'Gals' unfair at hearings
    198. Control of deer season
    198. Biologists should set game regulations
203. The new wildlife federation
    203. Personal view of GWF
205. Suggestions to State Senator Culver Kidd
206. My nonfights with Game Management
211. Deer pictures I especially like
222. James R. Darnell Outstanding-Ranger Award
223. The chufa patch
225. Ranger Marion R. Nelson
228. Morning at White Cloud Lodge of the 777 game ranch
231. Attitudes change with experience (Part I)
236. Attitudes change with experience (Part II)

243. A two-buck day
247. Broadus, Montana
256. The possum cop and the CB radio
261. Sharing makes for quality hunting
268. Impatience can be costly—or lucky
274. When the deer is on the ground
276. Hunters should kill does to thin herds
278. The nursing buck
279. Which comes first: The buck or the book?
282. Turkey roosts and decoys
288. Poachers stealing from each of us
289. Wayne and Norman: "The Boys"
300. Summer-time poachers
302. The long track
306. The raccoon-hollow buck
311. Other tracking ventures
315. Judge not
320. The fishing poachers
323. Waterholes and natural food
329. "Get up, Lazy Bones"
330. Me and Woot and the redbone hound
333, The great Peabody Possum Hunt of 1999
341. Funny things happened on my way to turkey hunt
347. Bearded hens
349. Spring poachers
354. Hunt by invitation
357. The parking lot toms
361. Under the spreading white oak tree
364. Two poachers named in GON
365. Opening week 1994
370. The buck on Larry's hill
375. Lost—again
376. The last doe
379. Time changes all
384. What lies ahead for the herds?
386. Why I did it, and why I keep on
388. The deer graveyard
394. My reputation
395. My possum cops

APPENDICES

399. I: Speech about hunting deer over bait
402. II: More about getting shot at in 1983
405. III: Letter from Rex Baker about T. I. P.
406. IV: Poacher article from local paper
411. V: Two letters re hunting seasons
415. VI: Speech in House Chamber
418. VII: Speech at the Macon, GA hearings
420. VIII: Two letters re control of regulations
424. IX: Letter re honorary membership in GWF
425. X: Complete letter to Senator Kidd, 1987
430. XI: Report of deer harvest, 1989
433. XII: Letter to Ledbetter re Nelson, 1985
435. XIII: Seasons and bag limits: A brief history
439. Index

INTRODUCTION

What Would You Do?

Battle zone. The dead lay in ditches. The dying fled into the darkness.

The killers roared up and down the road to seek victims. Bullets slammed into homes in the night.

No, this was not a war between nations or urban gangs, but the routine in rural Georgia each fall and winter in the 1960s when deer season opened and some illegal hunters decided to get a deer, no matter what.

I appointed myself captain of my civilian-only Poacher Patrol and set about helping the game wardens (possum cops) with the business of protecting the deer. After all, I considered the deer mine since they lived on my family's 2500 acres. For more than forty years I and my .12 gauge pump shotgun traveled the roads at night and hunted deer and turkey during the day.

I sat out at night in the cold, with coyotes circling me, to listen for gunfire. With my headlights off, I followed suspicious vehicles and waited for the culprit to shoot. I slept half-dressed so I could get out of bed and on the road before the shooter could pull his firearm back into his vehicle.

I spent many opening days of deer season at the county jail.

Having a poacher shoot toward me or a deer shot in my yard in the middle of the night, finding deer dead on the family land with only their hindquarters removed, hearing a poacher shoot a turkey every opening day of several seasons—even one such event was enough to generate my years of war against poachers.

During the mid-1960s, when deer hunting was new, our only communications with the rest of the world was with a ten-party-line telephone, sometimes off the hook for hours somewhere down the road and therefore useless.

A few people had seen a trophy-sized buck somewhere, and every man who heard about that buck wanted to hang it on his wall. Buck fever was contagious. There were no safety-hunter classes, no blaze-orange safety vests and no deer hunter's respect for private property.

Country folks had hunted possum, raccoon and rabbits for generations without regard to property lines. City folks had no concept of property lines. Early evenings, after work, some men took to the roads in pickups, one driving, one standing in back with his rifle or shotgun to shoot deer. Those who had no pickup would sit on the hood of the family sedan.

Up the road a ways, two campers loaded with hunters moved onto a farm where they told the owner they were there to deer hunt. The owner feared a forest fire and did not tell them to leave. But one of those hunters, a teenager, shot into a moving bush and killed his own uncle.

Some twenty years before deer season opened, when rabbit hunters shot from the road near our home, my father fought for and got a law passed to prohibit shooting from a public road.

So I reckon I came by it all naturally. I spent more than half of my life defending as well as hunting the wildlife, fighting for changes in game regulations and chasing down poachers.

Remember, it's the 1960s. Someone shoots at a deer, the *ka-boom* of the 30.06 semi-automatic rifle shakes the house and jars you awake. Your party-line phone is off the hook somewhere. It's four in the morning.

What would you do?

Hide under the bed?

Or do what I did—go give 'em hell?

* * *

DEER RELEASED ON OCONEE RIVER

Union-Recorder
Milledgeville, Georgia
May 2, 1935 (A year before my birth)

Solicitor General Baldwin Interested in Propagation of Deer in this Section

Middle Georgia sportsmen are watching with interest the propagation of deer along the Oconee River. Solicitor General G. S. Baldwin, Jr., of Madison, several weeks ago released thirteen young deer along the Oconee River. He released six in the swamp about three miles below Milledgeville, four on the Oconee River about four miles above Milledgeville near Oconee and Little Rivers and three in Jasper County near the big Georgia Power Company dam on the Ocmulgee River. Prior to that a large buck had frequently been seen in the Scottsboro community in South Baldwin. Several Grand Juries in this section have recommended a closed season for eight years to protect these deer. Sportsmen are making every effort to protect them until they get well started.

A large black bear has been sighted on the Oconee river a few miles above Milledgeville several times during the past year. Fox hunters are finding both red and gray foxes in large quantities all over this section of Middle Georgia.

A few years ago deer and bear were unheard of in this section and it was almost an impossibility to find a fox. However, the entire territory is rapidly becoming stocked with game of all kinds.

Local legend states that fox hunters imported coyotes into Middle Georgia as a substitute for foxes in the years foxes were scarce.

THE NONPOACHER

If the man took one step toward me, I would shoot. I gripped the pistol in both hands, my left supporting my right. I was rock steady, frightened and furious.

I had been on a two-mile walk across my land and was almost to the pasture gate when I stopped. I didn't know why, but I felt antsy. Maybe because no jay squawked danger; no crows declared an invader; no squirrels barked. But I had unsnapped my holster safety strap, eased out my .22 S&H pistol. It hadn't seen oil or a barrel brush in forty years, and the chrome finish peeled in spots. I pressed the release button, pulled the pin, and dropped the cylinder into my palm. The butt end of nine cartridges reflected sunlight. None of them had been fired—no indent from the firing pin. I huffed the lint off the inside of the frame. With the pistol reassembled and returned to the holster, I continued my walk.

I'd gone less than fifty yards up the trail when a man rose from the bushes. I snatched out the pistol, gripped it in both hands, wrapped my thumb over the hammer and my forefinger against the trigger, and yelled, "Who are you and what the hell are you doing on my land?"

Fear and anger trembled my voice.

He raised his hands, palms toward me. They shook.

Surely he couldn't be a poacher. No season was open for hunting.

This was midsummer. He was scared, and poachers weren't afraid when caught.

Poachers challenge and expect to walk away especially from a woman. Like those two men last deer season. The encounter in last November's bitter cold began as most did, with gunfire waking me in the middle of the night. I'd learned to sleep in my undies, with a tee shirt for a top so I could get dressed as fast, or faster, than a fireman. I simply slid into my jeans (with keys and wallet already in my pockets) and poked my feet into loafers. I grabbed a jacket as I ran to the door, and had it on before I reached my car. I had a loaded Remington pump .12 gauge and my .22 pistol in the car. The frigid November air bit into my bare ankles and my hands.

That night, I drove without headlights, my knowledge of the road and the light of the half-moon enough for my safety. Down the hill, across the railroad, and up the next hill. There they were, at the junction of my road and the state highway—a truck pulled crosswise and half off the road, its headlights revealing two men, in camouflage, walking into my woods.

One carried a Ruger .44 magnum, without a scope. The short barrel and iron sights were perfect for shooting from a vehicle. *Hope you'll both be deaf as the bed post.*

I pulled my car behind their truck to block it between me and the ditch.

I'd previously removed the bulb from my overhead light, so when I opened the door, no one could see who, if anyone else, was in the car. I stepped out, the .22 revolver in my right hand, held down by my thigh. "Got trouble?" I asked.

"No, thanks. We hit a deer."

Yeah, with that rifle. "Whatcha doing with a rifle if you didn't shoot it?"

"Look, m'am, this ain't your business."

"Oh, I think it is, since that's my land you're standing on. Why don't you just put that rifle in your truck and wait for the game warden? He'll be here directly."

They both started toward their truck, but then turned my direction. I stepped out into my own headlights, so they could see the pistol. "I think that's far enough," I said. My insides began to twist into knots. "Put the rifle up, sit down and wait."

The unarmed man said, "She ain't gonna shoot us. Let's git on the road. You move that-air car, lady, or we'll move it with the truck."

"Oh, I don't think so. I wrote down your tag number before I got out of the car. You don't want intentionally crashing a car added to the charges of night hunting and fleeing to avoid arrest."

They got in the truck, and I stood unmoving as the driver struggled to drive across the ditch, along the bank and juke his way back onto the road. They headed north, and I hurried back to the house, to the telephone, and called the ranger.

The men reached Nelson Road, some four miles north on the highway, and turned onto it. The ranger, who lived up that way, had reached the end of his driveway as the culprits drove by. He followed them, and when he turned on his flashing blue lights, they stopped. A deputy joined the ranger and took the men to the county jail.

The ranger and I found the doe they had shot; she died only a few feet across the fence. Had I been another ten minutes getting to the scene, they would have loaded her and been gone.

The State took away their truck and firearms, as well as a sizeable chunk of cash in fines.

This summer day, however, the stranger in the bushes couldn't be after game. He wore a denim work shirt with rolled up sleeves. His voice broke when he answered me.

"I'm sorry, m'am. I needed to go to the bathroom."

I held my pistol steady; he could be lying. "This is not a public bathroom," I yelled. "Get out of here and don't you ever even think of coming back."

He turned and stumbled as he struggled to pull up his pants while trying to run. I lowered the pistol and had to suppress a laugh.

I reached the pasture gate in time to see his truck, a logging truck stacked high with sawtimber logs. The name on the side of the truck was very familiar. The logging crew had cut the timber on this tract of my land only a year ago. And today, they were on the Lowe lands, about a mile north of me.

If that man was so desperate to go to the bathroom, why not go before he left the Lowe place?

After lunch, I drove up to the log yard to talk to the crew boss. He was the same one who had supervised the cutting of my timber.

"One of your drivers was on my land," I said.

"Yes, I heard. He didn't even deliver the logs, but came back, left the truck, and quit. I don't think you'll have a problem with him again." He laughed. "And not with any of the other men on my crew."

"SO WAS IT WHEN MY LIFE BEGAN"

Gunfire riddled three nights in a row that last week in October. After the ranger and I wasted those three nights hunting poachers, he asked me to sit stakeout. These were MY deer the poachers were killing, and, eager to catch the culprits, I agreed.

The ranger provided a pair of radio-telephones that were eavesdrop-proof so we could communicate across the mile that would separate us. I gave him the key to the gate a mile south down the two-lane State Highway 212, and I headed for the knoll overlooking the T junction of a local paved road and the highway.

When I opened my gate, I wrapped the locking chain around a tree to keep the gate wide enough for me to leave in a hurry, and then I drove a ways into the woods, turned around, and parked facing out. I figured a poacher wasn't likely to enter the gate, and I could drive out quickly to follow when someone shot.

I crawled into the truck bed, unfolded an aluminum chair, and had settled down by twilight, the time deer roamed in autumn. The peak time of the rut, when bucks pursue does, was only a few days away. I sat about fifty yards from a trail the deer had gouged in the road banks—a major deer crossing. From my high seat in the truck bed and the elevation of the knoll, I could see in all three directions: Both ways down the state highway, and back down the local road toward the railroad. I could hear a vehicle two miles away in the night's stillness.

The night crackled with cold. Even boots, wool socks and insulated gloves would not keep me warm for more than an hour; I'd have to get inside and run the engine and heater to thaw out. *I should have brought hot chocolate rather than a co-cola. Or maybe I ought not drink either.* I didn't want to have to drop my pants in the 20° cold and freeze my bottom.

When I hunted in mornings this cold, I could bear the temperature for the hour or so until the sun reached me and I thawed, but this was night, and the temperature would only drop.

Smoke from the cook fires at a hunting camp drifted toward me on the west wind, bringing with it the odor of frying meat and boiling cabbage. *Time for a snack, but I've been out less than an hour. Hafta wait awhile.*

Cars and trucks drove along the roads, but nobody slowed. A three-quarter moon crept westward and cast snake shadows of the tree limbs across my woods road. A fox interrupted the shadows, a dark silent figure searching for an evening meal.

A truck rattled up the local road. Sounded like the tail pipe was about to turn loose. The horn blared, tires squealed, the truck stopped, doors opened. No gunfire. *Maybe they dodged a deer.*

"Thank gawd we didn't hit it. It's a big un, woulda messed us up good. Let's git on down to the pool room." Truck doors slammed and the vehicle rattled and clunked on.

Something shrieked to my left, the something becoming a meal for a predator. An owl hooted, and the something cried again. Its captor hooted. *Owls. One has caught a meal and is inviting the other to come have a snack. Maybe they're mates.* The loud invitation continued. I gritted my teeth and my skin crawled. *Why doesn't the owl just kill the poor critter and be done with it?* The screams went on for another half-hour before the owl put supper out of its misery.

I stood up in the truck bed; I had to get my blood warmed up and moving in my feet. Stomping seemed to help a little. Flapping my arms warmed up my body just a bit, too.

Cars moved up and down the highway, some hurrying, others so slow I figured they carried courting couples wanting to stretch out their time together. An 18-wheeler sped toward me, a spotlight on the roof weaving over the shoulders of the road. I called the ranger. The truck would be on him in thirty seconds.

"It's going by now," he said. "I've seen this before. These truckers are afraid of hitting a deer and being late on a delivery. They use the spots for extra headlights. He's okay. Thanks for the heads-up. Anything else going on?"

I told him about the truck that missed hitting a deer and we signed off.

Time seemed to sleep it went by so slowly. I'd look at my watch, only to see maybe five minutes instead of an hour had passed. About a mile to the south, the train whistled, signaling its approach to the crossing at Harrison's.

Time to get up again and flap some life into my cold limbs. My teeth chattered. I needed to warm up. This time I stepped over the tailgate and onto the ground and walked down the woods road toward the wide-open gate where I came in.

The train reached its signal post almost in front of me, and the whistle set off the coyotes. Oh, they were close, right behind the truck. I didn't dilly-dally. I ran toward safety, the cold air searing my throat as I huffed through my mouth. Coyotes don't attack people, *somebody said*, but I didn't want to test them. Before I reached the truck, another pack complained about the train whistle. I jerked open the cab door, jumped inside, rolled the window half down, and listened.

The engine whistle died, the train rumbled through the crossing and the coyotes went silent.

I decided I'd had my last stretch-break outside the truck and my last time in the chair in the truck bed.

Movement pulled my gaze to the left. Moonlight caressed the golden-gray coat as a coyote trotted by. Then another. And another. I leaned away from the door and rolled up the window. I didn't care if somebody shot in the next few minutes. With the windows up, I wouldn't be able to determine direction and would be no good to the ranger.

Only silence kept me company for the next hour. Midnight came. No shooting. Sleep tried to creep into my eyes, and cold had numbed my feet. I needed out of the truck for a stretch break. *Surely the coyotes are long gone.*

I eased the door open and listened. Nothing. I stepped out. The night was as quiet as a bootlegger with the sheriff walking by. Overhead the stars spread glitter across the night. I leaned back on the hood and sought Orion. He stalked the heavens from the east, like the courting frog, sword by his side. The seven sisters still sat together.

The dippers marked the north. I thought of the photograph I had seen, a long time exposure of the North Star, that was bands of light as the stars circled Polaris. *Maybe some day I can take a night picture with the stars moving. Or maybe use a flashlight to write patterns in the dark.*

Time for a snack. I reached into the truck for my paper sack of goodies, got out my diet co-cola and a pack of M&Ms, and hoped the caffeine would keep me going another couple of hours. The co-cola was almost too icy to swallow. The M&Ms would have to do.

I would make them last—eat one and wait at least a minute. That resolution lasted all of a half-minute and I consumed the pack as if I were starved. Then the radio crackled.

"You about ready to call it a night?" the ranger asked.

"I reckon. Unless we want to wait out here for the early risers. They won't be around until about four. I'll be glad to call it a night. I'm having trouble staying awake."

"I'll be there in a couple of minutes."

He was. I returned his radio-phone, and we talked a few minutes.

"How many years have you been protecting the wildlife out here?" he asked.

"Forever, I reckon. I know they belong to the state, but I feel like they're mine, and I can't stand for somebody to ride along and shoot them. One of the first things that got me really mad with poachers was the fox they trapped. Right here. Actually, the trap was chained to that." I pointed to a sweetgum tree. "The fox was dead. I figured the trapper never came back to check. Then the next thing I knew, a poacher put a bullet into the Harrison's house."

"Well, you need to be more careful," he said. "Just call me instead of running after them. You could get hurt."

"Okay," I replied, but knew I wouldn't pay him any mind.

"You go on and I'll lock up the gate," he said.

We then said goodnight, and as I pulled through the gate, I thought about his question. Not forever, but I'd been fascinated with deer for some twenty years. Well, not just deer, but all wildlife on the farm and everywhere I happened to be.

I took all my vacations to hunt; I meddled into Game and Fish business of regulating seasons; I struggled to halt poaching and pushed the legal system to issue harsher punishments, and I challenged every man who dreamed of shooting into my yard or along my roadways. Game and Fish had even released wild turkeys on my land because I would protect them.

Who would have thought that one event when I wasn't yet ten years old would lead me to chasing poachers, drafting wildlife laws for the legislature, and getting bag limits changed even after tags were printed and distributed? It all began that morning when Dad yelled up the stairs at us, "Wake up! Hurry! Get dressed. Come on! Hurry!"

The sun hadn't gotten high enough to creep into my window, but the urgency in his voice was greater than if we were about to miss the school bus. I hurried. Into jeans and cotton shirt and ankle-high Keds. All three of us girls dashed downstairs.

"There're some deer in the meadow," he said. And almost ran us down the hill and along the path to the spring. There, we stopped, and he cautioned us, "Be quiet. No talking. Walk soft."

We hushed and walked soft as we stole up the incline to the road going to the meadow.

The only deer I knew about were Santa's herd. And Bambi and his children. But Felix Salten's *Bambi* and *Bambi's Children* lived in Germany. There were no deer in Georgia.

We slipped to the edge of The Meadow. Two bucks and a doe fed in the dry ditch near the middle of the field. A mature whitetail Georgia buck stands three-to-four feet at the shoulder. In summer, velvet antlers look much larger than in fall when the velvet has dried and the antlers hardened. To my child's eyes, these deer were ten feet tall, their antlers bigger than any in Christmas books or Salten's books. When one of those bucks lifted his head, antlers rose to the sky. He turned and looked our way.

King of the meadow

The other two looked up and froze themselves onto the scrapbook of my memory forever.

"So was it when my life began" is from William Wordsworth's poem "My heart leaps up when I behold."

TYPICAL POSSUM COP

Cows out! The two most dreaded words for a farmer, especially when brought by a neighbor. We hurried down the road and found at least a dozen cattle feeding along the fence. The gate stood wide open.

After we herded them back inside, we followed vehicle tracks to the hay barn and empty tenant house.

The lean-to against the barn had been pulled down and two yearling bull carcasses lay on its roof. The hides had been sliced down the middle of the backs, pulled aside, and the back straps cut out. Also gone were the hindquarters.

"Rustlers?" I asked Dad.

"No. They'd have taken them alive and home to butcher. Probably hunters after the few deer we have. I'll go get the sheriff."

The deputy who came out agreed with Dad. "Let me call the game warden," he said. "Looks to me like somebody shining for deer. He'll help you."

The game warden drove into our yard in an official truck with radio antennae waving as he stopped. After introductions, Dad and I went with him to the pasture to show him the dead cattle.

Bending over the carcasses, the officer pointed to the bullet hole in each head. Between the eyes. "These were most likely killed by men looking for deer."

"We don't have many deer around here," Dad said. "And no deer season."

"True. But some people don't care about the law or seasons. They want a deer head. Cow eyes shine just like deer eyes. But since they took only the hindquarters and back straps, I'm right sure they weren't rustlers. I'll hang around out here tonight and tomorrow night to watch for them to come back."

That incident began a life-long friendship between my family and game wardens, although we never did catch the cattle killers.

When deer season did open in our county, hunters appeared up and down the road from who knows where. Strangers parked alongside the road and wandered over our lands with no concern about who owned the acreage or who else might be in the woods.

My father had died in 1963, and Mother lived alone. Cars and pickups parked by the road let her know that poachers were everywhere. Men driving up and down the roads, with shotguns showing out the windows, kept her worried about going anywhere on the land.

One Saturday morning we stopped beside a parked car with a Bibb County tag, and I honked several times. A hunter came out of the woods and said he had been told to come here to hunt, that no one owned the land. He was a middle-aged physician. How in the heck could he believe land didn't belong to anyone?

The game warden suggested we lease the land to hunters to keep out the strangers, so Mom and I decided to collect rent from the men who were already hunting. We were on the road by daylight to check on parked cars and trucks. The family property was scattered around northwest Baldwin county, some tracts as far as five miles away from the house.

We waited near a car for the owner to return. One by one, we offered them a chance to hunt legally for a fee, or to be charged with hunting without permission if they ever returned. Most wanted to keep on hunting and were willing to pay the fee. Some wanted sole rights, and they formed the early hunt clubs.

Mom and I drove up on a group of four men standing next to two campers on Stiles Cemetery Road, beside land where my mother was reared. They were dressed for the hunt. We stopped to talk to them and learned they planned to pull their campers onto the land and hunt for the week.

Mother explained that this was private land and they were not to hunt there. One of the men said, "We hunted here last year and we're gonna hunt here this year. Who's gonna stop us? You?"

"Yes. Us and the game warden."

I turned to Mother. "Go call him."

Hilda, Mother's German shepherd who was attack trained, was trying to tear her way out of the back seat while barking her fury. I went to the car, put her on a leash, and brought her out to stand with me about fifteen feet from the men. I had a pistol on my hip.

Mother roared off—a surprise to me. I always thought Mom was a sedate lady who never got ruffled. Too softly for the men to hear, I whispered to Hilda, "Sic 'em," and as she lunged I pulled her back down. Confusing for her, but she was a trooper and let the men know to stand back.

They all smoked. One held out the stub of his unfiltered cigarette and said, "Be a shame if somebody dropped one of these in your woods."

"Yes, it would," I said. "It'll also be a shame if lightning struck and set a fire. Didn't you notice we got your tag number? You'd be the first one arrested for arson."

They had no more to say.

Where is a ranger when you need one? Right up the road, headed your way.

Mother hadn't been gone five minutes when the game warden drove up, Mother behind him.

He slipped out of the Law Enforcement truck and walked over to me.

"Sit, Hilda," I said, and she sat.

"You and your mom go on. I'll take care of them."

We left, and he did.

That fall I began my life-long war against poachers.

By the next season, the officer had helped us cull the hunters to a few good men who wanted to lease land and form a club. We still lease to clubs, but over the years have dropped groups for various reasons, such as hunting over bait and leaving a child under sixteen unsupervised to hunt alone in a stand with a high-powered rifle.

The third year I hunted, I had to spend part of opening day at the county jail. That morning, as on opening day for the previous two years, someone across the railroad from my stand shot. I just knew it was Sonny—and Sonny just knew it was me.

On the way to town, I met Sonny at the railroad crossing, standing beside his brother and three vehicles. Two men, three vehicles.

I stepped out of my station wagon and said, "Congratulations to whichever one of you got the deer."

"We didn't," Sonny said.

"I heard you shoot."

"Didn't either of us shoot. I heard you, though."

"I didn't shoot. Whose truck is that? Maybe he got one?"

"We don't know. If you didn't shoot, then somebody was in between us."

I looked north down the tracks. Far in the distance was movement. "Maybe that's who shot." I pointed. Squinting, I made out what looked like two men.

Jimmy, Sonny's brother, was a GBI agent, and although not on duty, he was adamant that we'd tend to the men if they were hunting. We waited for them to approach. Each pulled a deer with one hand and carried a rifle in the other.

When they reached us, they dropped their grips on the deer and looked from one to the other of us.

"You were hunting on my land," I said. "I heard you shoot, and so did they."

"We've been hunting here for three years. Nobody ever said we couldn't."

"Nobody ever said you could, either," I responded.

So I had the two men arrested for trespassing, and had their deer seized. The deer wound up in a cooler some twenty miles away for the weeks until the men faced state court. They entered a guilty plea, and when they paid the fines, they were allowed to have their deer back. I wrote the Department of Natural Resources (DNR), Game and Fish Division, and asked why they were given the deer when they had been killed illegally.

I received an explanatory letter from Robert Baker, coordinator of Special Services of Game and Fish.

He enclosed a copy of the Georgia Code that dealt with the laws about hunting without permission which give the rangers authority to seize illegal game.

I had made the mistake of charging the men with *trespass* rather than with *hunting without permission*. He stated:

Since trespassing is not considered a wildlife law violation, there is no way game taken as a result of this violation could be seized by our personnel.

A technicality, but at least I began to learn what I needed to do to protect my wildlife.

The poachers got their deer, but the meat was no good—the deer had not been field dressed, and dragging them along the railroad had infused tar from the crossties through the hide.

Neither man ever returned.

* * *

What I like best about these wildlife officers is they didn't care who you were or what political office you held. You poached, you paid.

One officer caught a county commissioner. He paid.

One caught a former state representative's brother. He paid.

Unfortunately, some politicians didn't like the officers who brought charges against family members or special friends, and they in turn used politics, or the judge's bench, to serve up revenge, a plate they never let get cold.

In 1975, I received a note in the mail from my local ranger. It has become a treasure:

Dear Sue,

I had hoped to catch you at home and personally thank you for your interest and stand in behalf of myself and our Dept. This was greatly appreciated, more probably than you will ever know.

Until I can tell you personally, this will have to be an expression of my thanks to you.

One winter, I didn't get to the family home for several weeks; the house stood empty. That is, until some teenaged boys decided to enter and empty it more. The owner of a pawn shop called the sheriff about some items these boys were trying to sell, and the youngsters admitted the items in the trunk of the car were stolen—a chainsaw, a case of potted meat, and other items that had not been reported missing. The boys didn't say where these things came from, so the items were stored.

When the possum cop conferred with the sheriff on some matter, my things were laid out in the office. The ranger told him it was my stuff. I hadn't heard about it, did not even know someone had broken into the house, until the warden called me a few days later and asked if I had picked up my things from the jail.

"What things?"

The next Saturday I was at the jail, asking about my stuff—I had been to the house the night before and listed everything that was missing. I handed the list to the deputy on duty and he said let him check. He came back empty-handed.

"Sorry, Miss Lindsley. None of these are here now. They've been sent to storage. Can you come back next Saturday? We'll get them out for you this week."

I wondered why they had not called me or made any effort to reach me. Included in the items were some prescription medications that were issued to my mother, left in the medicine cabinet—her name still on the bottles.

Next weekend, I made another trip from Atlanta to Milledgeville and to the jail. This time, my items were available—except half of the potted meat was gone. I didn't mention that. I reckon whoever had taken my things home had eaten some of it. Probably hated to part with all the good stuff, too. Besides, he'd sharpened the chainsaw.

Possum cops are special. They not only chase the bad guys, but are everyday friends and neighbors.

A BLEAK BEGINNING

I swore off deer hunting after being in a stand for about a half-hour. I shook with cold. Frost settled on my shoes. The stars seemed to brighten, not grow dimmer. Time didn't drag—it slept. Even the tree shook itself with the cold. Finally, the sky brightened in front of me, but long before the sun reached me, the breeze came up to intensify the cold.

I hadn't been that cold when I lived in Boston and walked through eighteen inches of snow to the grocery store. But then, I had snow boots and long wool socks. In middle Georgia, I had only a pair of jeans over some flannel pajamas and a couple of cotton shirts beneath my leather jacket. No one told me that frost degrees in a deer stand were the same as below zero even before the dawn breeze begins to shake the icicles from you. When I shifted the borrowed 30.06 bolt action rifle in my hand—gloveless—the metal was so cold it almost froze to my hand, the way the pitchfork did once when I was a child feeding cattle. I swore I'd never waste my time freezing on a deer hunt again and my neighbor E. D. could have all the bucks in the county if he wanted them. Why had I let that friend from work *talk me* into *talking my neighbor* into taking us on this hunt?

I thought about the fire back at the house and could almost smell my mom's cooking when the breeze drifted a little from that direction.

Lights from the house showed through the leafless trees and might have been fifty miles away for all the good the fireplace or electric blanket could do me now.

If this were hunting, I wanted no more of it.

Until 8:00 a.m.

I was nibbling on an apple and happened to see a form take shape across the meadow. He lifted his head to show me antlers, and then dropped his nose again to nibble at something. Before I could move the rifle to my shoulder my heart was pounding loud enough for that deer to hear it and I shook—far worse than ever from the cold. I was not cold now. Sweat ran down my face and back—like a hot flash from my future.

The end of that gun barrel wobbled around, across the deer from his shoulder to his rump, and from his feet to the tree tops behind him. Try as I might, I could not hold it still. I did not know to take a deep breath and hold it and then release it slowly; I did not know that every time my heart pumped with enough energy to drive the generator at a power plant I was moving that rifle because my heart was moving my whole body. When I finally jerked the trigger, the deer simply lifted his head up, took another step forward and returned to feeding.

In the next five seconds I wondered many things—Had I really beaten a local law officer in a private shooting match? Had I missed that deer? Why didn't the deer run? Why didn't the other hunter down the meadow shoot? How do I get another shell into the chamber of this rifle? Howcome he didn't show me— "You won't need but one bullet," he had said. Why do people make guns right-handed anyhow? Don't they know bunches of us are left-handed?

By the time I figured out the bolt action, the deer had moved only another couple of steps. But I was shaking worse than before, my level of confidence was way down and I again jerked the trigger. I thought I missed and cursed myself when, tail up, he leaped skyward and then loped off, out of sight to my left. The echoes of my shot were still in my head when Annelle Harrison, E. D.'s wife, shot.

I did not know until we gutted that deer but I did hit him, right in the gut.

I was hooked in spite of the cold and the bad shot. My co-worker, who saw no deer and also nearly froze, never wanted to hunt again.

Anyone who tried to keep me from hunting after that would have found it easier to plow with a dead mule.

The next weekend I had another shot from the same stand, this time over my right shoulder, a perfect shot for a left-hander. Again, I had the shakes and again I jerked the trigger, but I watched the deer fall and I knew he was dead. I whistled for my neighbor to come help me. (Actually, he was going to have to do it all because I knew nothing, absolutely nothing, about what to do with a dead deer!) Down I went and rushed across the field and into the woods. The deer was gone.

I began to shake harder than I had when I shot. The evidence of what happened almost made me cry, with bone slivers and massive bleeding telling me that wherever he was, that buck was very close to dead. I followed the blood trail a few yards and then returned to the meadow to wait for the other hunters; all three usually dropped their game instantly and I read dismay in their faces when I told them it had run off.

We tracked, and for a while blood sign was heavy and tracking was easy in spite of the bright autumn-colored leaves thick across the path. The deer had crossed the fence line into other property and only my coaxing took my hunting companions across that land line with me, for, although it was my family's land, we had heard a poacher shoot there that morning. But the trail dropped into a hardwood hollow blanketed with red leaves and the bleeding stopped. Three of us looked for another drop of blood while the other scouted ahead. Suddenly the buck was up and running but no one had a chance for a shot.

Today, I know it was my buck that dashed off; today, I would follow that deer until darkness trapped me in no-where land; but that day, my companions decided that the deer would survive and it would be easier to get another one. They went home. I lacked the courage to go it alone—then. Three days later, another hunter reported finding that buck, dead, about 200 yards from where we quit tracking.

I had one other shot at a deer that year and again I used the borrowed bolt-action 30.06 with 2 ½ x scope. When the buck loped along the trail headed directly for me, I began shooting. The buck hid himself halfway into a clump of brush and stood broadside at seventy yards, a perfect shot. This time, I *almost* managed to stop the shakes and to set the wobbling cross hairs on the deer's shoulder. I missed three shots, one after the other. I had to shoot slowly because it was a right-handed bolt action so I took it down from my shoulder each time to crank in a new shell. The deer did not move until I fired the final, fifth shot. He leaped, spun, and loped through the woods.

I scrambled down and began to search for my deer. Although I was reared in the country, I had never tried to track an animal and could not tell where the deer had run. This time, there was no bleeding, no trail for me other than a few scruff marks where he had plunged into the woods—and I had seen him farther off than I could find the trail. So I sought the help of some experienced hunters who combed the ground and followed the trail for almost a mile. We found only one small drop of blood—today, I know that such a trail means a gut-shot deer that might take a day or more to die. Then, all I knew was that I had injured the animal and had not killed him mercifully.

I had a lot to learn. And no one to teach me how to track. If only then I had a teacher like Tom Brown, Jr., I could have learned how to track a mouse across a grassy meadow. But Brown was far away and unknown to me. (He still holds classes on how to track and to live and survive in the wilderness. His teacher was Stalking Wolf, the Lipan Apache grandfather of his childhood best friend.)

Every hunting magazine that carried any article about deer came into my home for reading and study.

Opening day the next year, I was back in that same stand but not freezing; I had learned about dressing for the cold and was bundled in an insulated jumpsuit over layers of longjohns, flannel and denim. Fleece-lined gloves warmed my fingers. Two pairs of socks—cotton against the skin and wool against the boot—kept the cold to a faint numbness in my feet. I stayed warm for my before-daylight nap, with my feet resting on a board and the rest of me lying straight back, rifle wrapped immobile against me so it would not fall into the darkness.

As the first light faded the stars, I sat up, stretched myself awake, and loaded my new rifle. This one I had gotten to know. A 30.06, semi-automatic, Remington Model 742, with a 2 ½ X scope, fitted me well. I had zeroed it myself, carefully, under the directions of the neighbor who had introduced me to hunting. We both learned that day that a rifle zeroed for one person is useless for somebody else—he could put five shots so close together a half-dollar would cover them all, and with my new outfit I could too.

But with my rifle, the scope sighted for me, he missed the bullseye by more than eight inches. He clustered the shots some, but they were not close enough for a pocket full of change to make them cousins. We never swapped out on firearms again.

So that opening day I was confident. I knew I would be able to hit my target. For some reason I felt I had gotten over the wild attacks of buck fever that had ravaged me the year before.

I was to know soon enough. Daylight came after 6:00 a.m. and by 7:00 I had my chance. I heard the buck first; running in a gentle lope, he came up almost silently from behind me to my left, an impossible shot for a left-hander. Then he slowed, stepped into the edge of the meadow and stopped about ten yards away, almost directly in front of me.

The range was almost too close for the scope. I found hair, moved the rifle around until I found his backbone, his shoulder, his neck. This one dropped. I sat still, determined that if he got up to run off he would have to outrun the other four shots still in that rifle. Not even his eyes blinked. I squinted to see if he were breathing. He wasn't.

With the chamber unloaded, I slipped down, reloaded and cautiously crept toward my deer. Like a cat checking its prey, I circled him and poked him gently with the gun barrel, ready to leap backwards if he moved. But only a faint *whoosh* answered my punching as air escaped the body cavity.

I had my first deer, a heavy eight-pointer, and the hunting bug bit even deeper. But I had no idea what to do next.

I whistled victory and my neighbors came to teach me about field dressing a deer. They suggested I have it mounted since its antlers were wider than the buck's ears (in hunter terms *outside the ears*). "It's a trophy," they told me.

I had it mounted and it hung above my fireplace for many years—until a local artist borrowed it to use as a model for a painting.

Unfortunately, he moved away, and the mount went with him. A lesson learned.

Since then, I have averaged at least one deer per year in the freezer and probably have watched five bucks per year walk by—why not let them walk for another hunter if I had enough meat already at home. I *usually* took the first legal deer I saw and would by-pass others until everyone in the group had filled one tag. *Usually* here means except when the monster of monsters came by, I would take him if I could.

I have not forgotten those hard-learned lessons—I take care of myself, staying comfortable, no matter the weather. I get familiar with any new firearm so I know what the two of us can do together to ensure a quick kill. And I never quit a trail until I know there is absolutely no possibility of locating the animal.

It may be easy for a hunter to find another buck but it is not easy to let a buck wander off, wounded, to die a slow death. I learned to track the hard way—by doing.

That first deer seemed a long time coming, but I learned to ask and to read. Some information was weird, some helpful. I musta gained some knowledge, 'cause by my fourth or fifth year hunting, others were asking me about some of the basics of deer hunting. I had graduated from *hopeful* to *hunter*.

My first deer, 1967.

The negative was so overexposed it was not printed back in the '60s, but left in an acid-paper envelope. My modern-day scanner was able to produce this picture from the damaged negative. I'm clad in my first hunting outfit—bright red jump suit, red cap and Ted Williams kangaroo boots.

The visible holes in the picture are from the acid in the envelope.

THE YEAR I ARRESTED MYSELF

It was a lesson I learned the worse way possible, and one I will never forget. That event toughened me into *if I punish me for that, I'll punish everyone else*. I was careless. Not just careless but horrendously careless. I shot the wrong thing.

And had to have myself arrested.

Oh, how it had rained all night and into the morning. Not just too wet to plow, but too wet to even go hunting until almost noon when the clouds finally quit dumping on us. Rob was visiting. I met him through his wife who worked in the same office I did in Atlanta.

After my mother died, although my sister had inherited the home place, I was able to continue to stay in the house while I hunted or attended to family business at the farm. With enough room to sleep fourteen people, there was never a problem of crowding in our *camphouse*—a columned plantation house. One bedroom belonged to the gals, one to the guys and one to the couples.

Rob and I decided to take a walk into the woods that morning after the rain stopped. At least we had ponchos and we certainly wouldn't make any noise walking on the sloppy land. The dripping from trees would be louder than any noise we might make.

I wanted to get out into the woods something fierce. My fourth year to hunt. My vacation week was already into its fourth day, and I hadn't seen a deer. I didn't care how wet it was—my boots were waterproof. My camouflage poncho would cover me and my shotgun. I just wanted into the woods.

I suggested we each take one side of the pasture—he took the west edge and I took the east side. We'd be close to a half-mile apart. Walking north, we could sneak, or in hunting terms, *still-hunt* our way to stands near the back fence. (For you nonhunters, *still-hunt* means walk so slowly you are almost still; some folks call it *stalking*, but you can't stalk if you don't have your prey in sight.)

Shotguns would be a lot safer than rifles, and buckshot would help in the thickets we would both look over when we reached our stands.

Rob had hunted for several years with a club just north of Atlanta and I was a definite newbie, but at least I'd learned about *still-hunting*.

Actually, my first lessons came from a childhood game my sisters and I played, called *guard*. One of us would guard the front porch. Her job was to catch the others as we tried to get onto the porch. The game began at dark. Only moonlight and starlight and the night callers. The guard could stand silent, and noise by the others was a dead giveaway and got us caught. And noise by the hunter would benefit the deer in the woods.

The rain provided silence, but movement was on the deer's side in spite of the mist that thickened to the consistency of potato soup. I had to be *still* while walking—one step, stop and stand. Look for the curve of an ear, the water's glisten on an antler. Be still. Be still. Be still. Take one step and repeat.

I took almost an hour, slipping along the edge of the woods, to reach the half-way road that ran across the patch of timber from my side of the land to a large meadow on Rob's side. I stood beside a sapling wrapped in honeysuckle and looked down the road.

Nothing. I took a step. A buck cantered out of the mist, skidded to a stop and leaped into the brush.

I gripped the shotgun until my fingers ached. I tried to swallow, but the spit dried out in my mouth. My whole body shook. His head and massive antlers rose over the brush. He looked at me. In my brief weeks of hunting, I had never seen such a deer. Or suffered a worse attack of buck fever.

Do I dare move? The shotgun pellets will go through the brush. Will he run if I—

I eased the shotgun to my shoulder. From the antlers, I moved my aim down and back to where his heart and lungs should be, pulled the shotgun as tight as I could to my shoulder, and eased down on the trigger. Down went the antlers. I whooped and ran over.

And found a dead doe.

No buck anywhere. Where had he gone? Where had **SHE** come from?

Oh, gawd. What have I done? She musta been in the bushes and he stopped behind her and her body was where I thought his was.

Does were sacred. It was not only illegal to kill one, but terribly wrong if it wasn't the doe day at the end of the season. Does were the future of the herds.

Rob trotted up while I stood there crying. One look and he knew why.

"What do we do?" he asked.

"I have to call Jim," I said. "I just have to."

"Who's he?"

"The game warden."

"You mean…?"

"Yes. I have to. It's the law. I have to. Oh, gawd, Rob. I hate for him to know what I've done. I'm just sick."

Rob hugged me. "I'll stay here. You go on," he said.

Jim was home. When he answered his phone, he sounded rushed.

"I need you here, Jim."

"I'm on my way out the door to Macon. What is it?"

"A doe's been shot." I couldn't say I had shot it.

"Where?"

"In the front pasture."

"You know who did it?"

"Yes."

"I'm on my way. You at the house?"

"Yes."

I stood in the yard to wait for him. He drove up in less than ten minutes, stepped out of his truck, and asked, "Where's the deer?"

"In the pasture," I said and nodded in that direction.

"Who shot it?"

I started to cry. Thirty-something years old. I stammered, "I did."

I don't know who was more embarrassed.

He waited for me to calm down before he asked me what happened. I explained as best I could. He said, "You know I have to charge you. And take one of your tags."

I nodded. While he wrote out the charges I reached into my pocket for my hunting license and tags. My hands shook as I handed them over. He removed a tag and handed the rest back to me. Along with a copy of the ticket.

"I have to take the deer."

"I know. I'll show you where it is."

When we arrived at the site, Rob had already field dressed the doe and she was hanging from a limb.

I introduced the men. Rob helped load the deer and we all rode back to the house. Jim thanked Rob for his help and drove off.

I was sick with humiliation all day and couldn't even eat, although Rob tried to buck up my feelings, and even cooked up bacon and pancakes. I could only nibble.

Rob discovered he'd left his knife in the woods where he dressed the deer, and we searched for it. We searched everywhere except into the gut pile before we gave up an hour later.

After the lunch that I didn't eat, Rob asked me to go with him into town to replace the lost knife. We went to the Army-Navy surplus store. When I walked in, several men turned to look at me. The owner greeted me with, "I hear tell you got your own self arrested today. Man, I would-a just left that doe in the woods and been done with it."

I'd never considered leaving her in the woods and lying to my ranger friend with silence.

Several weeks later, the ranger called to tell me he had taken the case to the grand jury, an unusual procedure, and explained to them I had turned myself in and he would appreciate their returning a no-bill. The grand jury obliged him—and I have been forever grateful.

I have never gotten over the stupidity of shooting at a deer's chest when I didn't see its chest, only its head and antlers.

The only good thing about the incident I realized several years later: Poachers stayed away from my neighborhood for a long time. Word around the county was, if I'd have myself arrested, what would I do to them?

They learned: If they survived, they would go to jail.

MY FIRST BUCK SCRAPE

"If I even thought it *might* be a scrape, I'd hunt it," the wildlife ranger told me when I described a pawed up spot near a creek crossing.

The spot was only three hoof marks, but a limb hanging over it had been thrashed. With the ranger's words to encourage me, I decided that was the spot to hunt.

But how to hunt the site became the question. The scrape was on the south side of the creek, just up from the old cow path, a good ten feet above the creek bed. I'd read enough articles in various hunting magazines to know not to get too close to a scrape or my residual scent would spook off the buck. So, crossing the creek where the cattle had, to take a stand on the uphill side, was not an option. Nor was circling downstream possible because I'd have to cross the land line—the scrape was only two or three feet on my side of the fence. Nobody was allowed to hunt over there, and I wasn't about to violate my friendship with the owner.

This was my third year hunting, and I had learned a little about scents. Only fox and skunk scents were available. Before her death, Mother had run me out of the house when I came home with skunk scent on, so I had abandoned that one in favor of the fox, which was bad enough. At least I knew we had lots of foxes on the land. So I dropped a bit of fox scent on my boots, just in case the wind drifted from me toward the scrape.

I pictured the near side of the creek in my head and remembered the fallen oak, with almost a three-foot diameter trunk that lay over the path to the crossing. Its butt end rested on the tall stump it angled from. Honeysuckle grew up the limb stubs. I'd sit beside it and hope it would give me enough cover.

The log was too high to see over it if I sat on the ground, so that afternoon I walked down the old cow path with my 30.06 slung over my shoulder, a folding chair in one hand and a lopping tool and cushion in the other. I would clear out the brush to have a clear shooting path to the scrape, and I would be comfortable. It'd be a long time from 2:00 p.m. until dark—about 6:00 p.m. It was also quite a long distance for me to tote that load.

I cleared a shooting lane through the vines toward the scrape and pulled up the chair, facing the log. Wouldn't work. I couldn't lean forward far enough to rest my right hand, supporting the rifle stock, onto the log.

Which way to face? The creek flowed west to east, but just as it reached the creek crossing—and the scrape—it turned 90° to the north. On the long west-to-east stretch, the deer had worn several paths down the steep banks as they crossed the stream. Suppose he came down the hill on the other side of the creek? Suppose he came from the neighbor's land behind that stump?

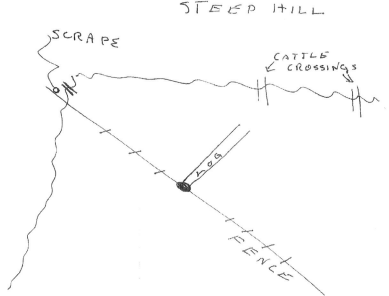

I decided to face the straight-away and turned the chair sideways to the log, the major crossing and the scrape. Not the best angle for a left-hander, because now I would have to sit with my left side toward the scrape. I had never shot from my right shoulder and didn't want to start here. I would have to wiggle around some but I'd have a good view of the straight-away and the paths across it. No telling where that buck would come from.

If he did come along.

Oak trees lined the fence and the creek bank. I settled down, got comfortable and still. The squirrels ignored me and chased each other up trees and across the ground. Small birds twittered and fluttered. The wind rattled a few branches as it slipped by, and I listened for any sounds that might be deer.

An hour passed, and I fought sleep. I wanted to turn toward the log and put my head down, but knew that as soon as I did, a dream buck would trot up, see me as I rose from my nap, and be gone before I got the safety off. I tried to be still, but after awhile my backside began to feel as if I sat on concrete rather than a cushion. I shifted around as slowly as I could. Time dragged her skirts.

I faced south, and as the sun moved westward, it seemed to find pathways through the trees to aggravate my eyes. Slowly, oh so slowly, it moved toward the top of the hill in front of me. The wind stilled. Birds roosted. Squirrels scampered upward to find their beds for the night. Bullfrogs at the lake way up the trail to my right began to call.

Leaves rustled in front of me, where the creek ran east to west. I eased the safety off and squinted. Nothing in sight. But something splashed its way downstream. I looked to my left.

A dark shape trotted up from the darkness of the creek bed into the light of the opposite bank, antlers first, then massive shoulders and body.

While his back was to me, I turned in my chair, leaned my right hand on the log. He reached the scrape, faced three-quarters away from me and lowered his nose to sniff the scrape. I put the crosshairs on his chest and squeezed the trigger.

My 30.06 150-grain Core-Lokt® entered just behind his left shoulder and exited midway in his neck.

He was so big I had to call some hunter friends to drag him across the creek and over the oak log to their truck. I decided to get myself a woods-going Jeep.

My new faith became scrape hunting.

MORE ABOUT SCRAPES

My first year hunting, I wandered all over the woods, tromping here and yonder, making enough noise to frighten off a battalion of Marines. Naturally, I did not see a deer in my roaming, but I did see a scrap, a huge one. Just didn't know what it was.

Hooves had scratched the ground from several directions, had flung dirt a couple of feet onto leaves and rubble alongside the trail. Droppings lay in piles and were also scattered over the scrape and outside the pawed area. I smelled the strong odor of musk and urine. The limbs overhead had been slashed.

I just knew I'd found the site of a major buck fight. (At least I didn't think the deer were digging for salt, as one hunter did—and filled the scrape with twenty-five pounds of rock salt.)

Where were the wanta-be kings who fought here? They had to be nearby, especially with those urine splotches still wet.

I had not yet learned that bucks urinated down their own legs and pawed the moist ground to leave a scent trail for a receptive doe to follow. I didn't know the buck would stay with a doe for about three days, or that she would be receptive for only about one day, that he would then return to re-issue his invitation to another doe at the same scrape and scrape line itself, which might include a half-dozen or even a dozen scrapes.

I have seen scrapes along ridges, along paths in bottom land, scattered along trails that parallel ridges in hardwood hillsides, on logging roads and on trails between food plots. As younger bucks mature, they take over scrape sites from older bucks. I've seen scrapes freshened under the same oak for more than ten years.

One morning, I perched in a platform stand high in an oak that overlooked a ten-acre field, and watched a heavy-bodied buck enter the field, scrape under the limbs of a small oak, gallop across the field, and, at the edge, make another scrape. Later that day, I went to the second scrape and followed the path downhill. His scent pervaded the area. He had hit a dozen scrapes along the sloping path and continued down the hollow toward the land line.

I never was able to collect that buck. From his size, I figured he ranged over a large area and my persistence in hunting him probably left my scent along that trail. He never freshened those scrapes again.

The success of that first scrape hunt and a year of reading every hunting magazine article about deer and deer hunting had me eager the next year to hunt over a scrape. I had a week's vacation, and instead of just sitting for a couple of hours, going home to eat and lollygag with the other hunters in my group, I spent my first three days of vacation slipping up and down Jeep trails, half-grown-up logging roads and old cow-paths-turned-deer paths in search of fresh scrapes as I worked my way to my afternoon stand. On the third day, success. A scrape fresh, wet, and littered with wet droppings.

Like the first one I hunted, it was scrawny, in a hollow, and at the edge of an artificial opening—a logging road. But enthusiasm was not catching me—farther down the hollow I'd seen numerous bushes and saplings, and even one six-inch tree with fresh sap running from cuts made by antlers. I had two choices; the area around the scrape didn't offer much cover with a view. I considered the site of the horned trees.

But after lunch, I felt the lure of the scrape. About three-quarters of a mile stroll. I strapped a folding stool on my back and headed out with Ole Betsy, my dad's 1913 Stevens .12 gauge single shot.

Camouflage in those days was a simple green-on-green or green-and-black-on-green that really did not blend in well, certainly not like the Real-Tree, Mossy Oak and other patterns available to hunters in the twenty-first century. When I approached the site, I picked out a nest of sweetgums. Growing in a semicircle, they provided climbing posts for honeysuckle and sawbriars (a vine with such sharp thorns that if you pull it with your bare hands, it will saw your flesh as surely as the blade of a crosscut). I unfolded my stool and placed it by the middle tree. My camouflage wasn't going to blend in with the other leaves, but at least I had some cover from the vines and from a pine top on my right that had been left by the loggers.

Four o'clock. Perched on the stool. Feet on a half-rotted stump. Ole Betsy loaded and ready. Head and back rested against the tree. Eyes closed. Ears alert.

Fifteen minutes later, right on schedule, the daily flight of SAC bombers from Robins Air Force Base thundered low overhead and shook the trees. I coulda set my watch by those planes.

When the world around me quit trembling, the woods seemed to come alive, as if all the critters had been waiting for those planes to go by before they moved. A blue jay squawked. Small birds flitted and tweeted. A chipmunk scampered by. A fox squirrel bounced across the hollow, a snack in his mouth, and scratched his way up to his nest. Back and forth he came as he prepared for winter. Crows cawed as they dove at a hawk that tried to outfly them.

I thought the fox squirrel was the noise maker behind me, stirring up the leaves, coming back down the hill. I paid no mind to the noise and glanced at my watch. It was almost half-past five; the sun had moved so far down that it was shining on only the tree tops. Shadows deepened on the ground.

The sound behind me changed. No bouncing sounds, just steady hoofbeats, trotting toward me.

Somehow my feet came off the stump, Betsy came to my shoulder, the hammer came back soundlessly. The buck had his mind on love-making, not on me. He trotted by, reached the scrape, turned sideways as if to look back, and Betsy put him on the ground.

My second scrape buck. He would not be my last.

BEWARE THE MAN WHO GRANTS A FAVOR

When I bought Nellybelle the Jeep, two of my hunters started out from north Georgia to Milledgeville, one driving the Jeep and the other following in his family's pickup. Nellybelle was a 1948 CJ, with a metal body and a double set of gear shifts.

She made it about thirty miles before she died plum dead. The boys, fortunately, had a trailer hitch on the following vehicle, and the Jeep had a tow bar. They towed her back to my mechanic.

When she was ready to go to the farm as a running vehicle, a cousin of one of the fellows said he'd take her down on his flat-bed truck. "How much?" I asked.

"Oh, nothing. I'm doing it for my cousin since he hunts with you. You don't owe me a thing."

I argued a little, but finally relented since he insisted it was a favor for his cousin. Off he went with the Jeep on his flatbed wrecker, his cousin riding down with him.

Ah, but come November, he called.

"I want to go deer hunting," he said. "Remember me? I took your Jeep down for you. You owe me."

Mad? I was furious. That favor was gonna cost me more than if I'd paid him. Which, of course, was his idea to start with.

What to do? It became a matter of honor for me, so I invited him down for the second weekend of the season.

He came prepared, with his camper truck and a friend, whom I had never met, and with a bottle of hooch that they cracked Friday night. But they were up by the time my gang and I were, and ready to head for the woods. I drove them in Nellybelle and dropped his buddy off at a stand, with strong orders: "*Do not* get out of that stand, even if you shoot a deer, until I come for you."

I gave them both an empty 30.06 shell and explained our signals: One whistle after you shoot means you got the deer. Two blows when you haven't shot means you're ready to leave the woods and want me to come pick you up. Three means you need help.

I dropped off the wrecker man, with the same instructions, at the three-legged turtle hollow—so named because Norman found a three-legged turtle in the wetlands there. The stand was four feet by four feet, and I told him, "If you get tired before I get back, stretch out and take a nap, but whatever you do, *don't* get out of that stand. You could run off all the deer from everybody else or you could get shot."

It was during the years no one wore orange safety vests.

I left him and went to my stand.

No one shot that morning. At 10 a.m., I drove to the three-legged turtle hollow to pick up the visiting hunter. He wasn't there.

Furious? Yes. No wonder none of the gang had shot. The idiotic bumpkin had probably run every deer in the neighborhood into the next county. And where was he? I not only whistled with the rifle shell, I yelled. And I yelled. No answer.

After fifteen minutes, still no answer and no hunter.

I went to pick up his friend. He had better sense. When I drove up, he unloaded his rifle, tied it to a pull-up rope, and lowered it. Then he clambered down.

"Where's Buddy?" he asked.

"Who knows? He took off for somewhere. He never answered when I called. He can find his own way out. I'm going to the house. Get in."

Neither of us spoke on the way to the house. The others in my gang were there, and they too asked about Buddy. His cousin was, needless to say, rather upset.

Two hours later, Buddy arrived. By truck. He had walked east, down the hollow, some thirty yards from another hunter at the land line, crossed onto the neighbor's lands, and kept going until he wound up on another state highway.

There, he flagged down a local, who knew me and drove him to the house.

I didn't give him time to make excuses. I invited him off the land, "Right now. Go and don't stick around here. Get out of the county and don't come back. You could've killed somebody wondering around like that."

He hemmed and hawed but I kept shaking my head. "I don't want to hear it. You violated the basic rules of the group and wandered all over creation. You trespassed on the neighbors and hunted their land without permission. And they don't give permission to *anybody*, not even me, to hunt. Get out!"

Well, Buddy and his friend left. I shoulda followed them to be sure they went north. Funny, however, his cousin decided to go to town for some beer and found their vehicle parked on the side of the road, and both men, with rifles in hand, halfway across the railroad and headed for my land again.

He didn't just invite his cousin to head north—he demanded they go home and followed them to the county line and beyond.

So now, I beware the man who wants to grant me a favor.

THE POACHER'S BUCK

I had been up since 4:30 a.m., and had perched in a climbing stand overlooking a dry hollow for four long hours after daylight. Time to call it quits, in spite of the squirrels running in the oaks and the hawk overhead telling me the animals ought to be at their table.

The heater over my kidneys had stopped the shakes about an hour ago, and frost had melted from the grasses and the toes of my boots. But my feet still ached from the cold. The oak leaves that clung to the twigs had given up their silver glaze to dripping melt.

Let'em have another day, I decided and went to the house.

But not for long. Just as I stepped out of Nellybelle and one of the other hunters came onto the porch to see if I had a deer, somebody shot. Down the hill, just a bit to the east. On our land?

"Call Marion," I yelled and jumped back behind the wheel.

Down the hill I went, around the pond to the edge of the woods, where I crawled out, grabbed my shotgun, checked the load and safety, and slipped off down the path to the back line.

The path was narrow, only wide enough for cattle to walk in single file. We had not yet opened it into a Jeep track. Oak and sweetgum trees draped limbs that invited bucks to scrape, and I trod carefully to avoid stepping in them. One contained fresh droppings and stank of musk. Urine darkened the ground he had pawed.

I'll come down with a climbing stand.

The squirrels that lived here, along the branch, in these oaks, were quiet. No jay yelled. Even the smaller birds remained silent. Too quiet.

Where was the poacher? He probably didn't have on a red vest, but I did. No way was I going to risk being shot. I didn't have on my camouflage—I'd taken it off when I left the stand and reached the Jeep. The day was warming fast and I wore jeans and a wool green plaid shirt under the orange vest.

Although I was walking eastward, I was in a deep bottom and headed toward a high ridge, and the sunlight had not topped the trees. So I was not sunblind.

And fortunately not deaf to the approaching footsteps.

I eased behind a short sweetgum brush and waited for the poacher.

But the footsteps approaching were not human—something, some animal, was running, not hard but steady. A deer? Or a dog?

If a dog, it was trouble—we had something like a dozen feral dogs roaming in packs at any time, and they didn't run from people. I clicked off the safety, just in case.

The buck cantered toward me, jumped the fence, and slowed to a walk.

I gulped, unprepared for this near trophy instead of a poacher.

He came on. At thirty yards away, he stopped, turned sideways, and looked back toward whoever had spooked him.

Resist? Not on your life. I had two deer tags.

Seemly without any effort on my part, the shotgun rose to my shoulder, lined up with the buck's chest, and fired.

He jumped and ran off. I heard him fall.

Behind me, somebody came running.

"Are you all right?"

Marion had arrived.

"Oh, man, I can't believe it! The poacher musta run the buck to me! I just shot a really nice buck."

Marion asked, "What about the poacher?"

"I hope he's gone now, but in case he's not, I gotta get my buck out of here before the poacher thinks he might come get it."

Wildlife rangers are more than just *possum cops* or *rabbit sheriffs* or *fish fanatics*. Each one is a friend to landowners and legal hunters, even the ones they have not yet met. Every ranger I've known has stepped up with help when the situation asked for it. Marion didn't wait for me to ask—he helped pull that buck out of the thickets and loaded it onto the Jeep.

Me with the poacher's buck and Ranger Nelson.

THERE'S MORE THAN ONE WAY
TO GET UNLOST

I became restless as the fog thickened and the ache in my bottom increased. Two hours seemed more like half a day, and I still waited for one of the other two hunters to shoot. I'd left them up on the ridge, where a buck had horned every cedar along the trail. Some trees had a diameter of more than ten inches and seeped sap where the ear guards had raked the front and other tines had scarred both sides. He had to be a big one to get his rack around a trunk that size.

Maybe he passed by before daylight and slipped into the deeper swamps. Whatever. I gotta get up from here.

I stood in the thicket of pine limbs I had selected for a hidey-hole. *If I ease along the south edge of the ridge I can drop down into the swamp and maybe drive that old buck uphill to one of the others.* My boots fell silent in pine straw and leaves damp from fog. Trees reached black ghost fingers toward me as the fog swirled.

I thought back to another foggy morning a mile away. I had spent three hours perched in a sweetgum tree stand, a lot more comfortable than the damp ground under me this morning. There, I had a cushion between my bottom and the plywood; I had a foot rest the perfect distance from the stand seat. I had two tree trunks to lean against, one on either side. Time that morning was comfortable, even if slow-moving.

My view then extended across a meadow scattered with broom-straw and centered by an apple tree. Deer had plucked the low-hanging apples before they ripened, and the last of the high-hanging ones had long ago fallen to the deer.

No buck had sashayed into the field but several does entertained me. Dreamlike dark shadows emerged from the fog and vanished without a sound. That morning I learned the meaning of *silent as the inside of a grave.*

I had finally decided to head to the house and coffee. I checked the safety again, lowered the 30.06 on the pull-up rope and clambered to the ground. With the rifle slung over my shoulder, infantry style, I strode off as if there was not a deer anywhere in the world.

I had been wrong. A buck had appeared from nowhere. We stood face to face in the rising fog. Neither moved for at least a minute. He wondered what I was, and I wondered if there was any way to unsling that rifle, flip off the safety and put him on the ground.

He had allowed it was time to go and bounded off, his flag waving goodbye. I did not collect him that year.

This morning, I didn't want a repeat of that earlier foggy morning. If I should walk up on a buck and be able to get within range, I'd have Ole Reliable at the ready. She had been a good weapon. She was almost as lightweight as a .22 rifle. I could ease the safety off while I kept a light pressure on the trigger, and have her ready without a sound. Together, we had walked miles.

And already this season, on day one, she had put down an eight-pointer on a bright, cold afternoon. But today the world was silence and fog. A buck could be only yards away—and silent as a ghost.

I slowed to almost nonmovement. One step. Stop. Wait. Look ahead. Look over the left shoulder. Look over the right shoulder. Look ahead. Wait. One step. Stop by a bush. Both feet solid on the ground. No sticks underfoot. No strain on either leg. Wait. Look. Is that thicket hiding a deer? Is that movement a deer? No, a bird flitting by to haunt the morning.

I was unmindful of time or distance, and in the silent grayness I was even unmindful of my whereabouts. The train rumbled some-where ahead of me and carried on to my right and circled behind me. The sounds were wrong. *Have I crossed onto my neighbor's where the fence is down? No, I don't think so.* I tried to orient myself and discovered I couldn't. Where the heck was I?

Off to my left, the land dropped down, toward the swamp. *Okay. Now, if I go straight ahead, I'll be back at the highway.* For the moment I forgot to hunt; I wanted only to get my bearings. I stepped out briskly a few paces and the fog broke. Halfway down the ridge, a buck browsed in a small opening. His head down, he stepped to one side and then the other, not alert, not even raising his head, totally unaware.

Two tines, two middle tines, stood tall. Only one side of his rack, but it was enough—the fever hit.

I began to tremble. Heat poured over me. My heart beat louder and faster and throbbed in my ears.

I tried to calm myself. *Take a deep breath. Again. Concentrate. He's too far away anyhow.*

Seventy-five yards away, out of range. Feeding, he angled away from me but also up the ridge I was coming down. I studied the land. *What would hide me?* A large pine half-way down the hill and to my left would block me from the buck's sight if I could just move over so it was in line between us.

Watching to be sure he kept his head down, I stepped to my left until the tree hid me. I tilted my head from side to side to look around the distant pine serving as a blind. Out of his sight and watching for sticks, I hurried to the pine. I peeked around it. He still fed.

The rack grew taller as I got closer. My heart throbbed. He was big all right. He ambled forward and put his head behind another pine and gave me a chance to get closer. I stepped around my shield and strode forward again while I tried to watch the buck's hind end and the ground. I placed each boot carefully, tested the straw to be sure no stick was hidden.

When I reached the second pine, I lifted Ole Reliable, moved the trigger slightly as I slid the safety off to cut off the giveaway click of the cocking mechanism. I took my finger off the trigger to be sure I didn't fire accidentally. I raised the shotgun, leaned against the pine, put the bead on his shoulder, took a deep breath, held it, and squeezed the trigger.

The sound and the cordite almost cleared away the fog as the buck went down, unaware of what had happened. I whooped. My voice echoed from the hill. I ran to the deer, knelt beside him, patted him on the shoulder and thanked him for his donation to my freezer. I was still admiring his rack when the other hunters arrived, both out of breath.

The fog swirled overhead as it lifted.

"I'm sorry," I greeted them, "but I couldn't let him go."

And they thought it was hilarious when I asked, "Can either of you find the Jeep?"

One went for it while the other helped me field dress the buck. But to this day, they still tease me about the buck I killed so someone would come help me find my way out of the piney woods.

Before delivering the deer to the butcher, we drove up the road to a big buck contest we had heard was being held at a mama-papa type convenience store.

At least twenty men in camouflage were hanging out, swapping hunting tales and bragging on their past adventures, when we drove up. They saw my deer and came over to admire it. They all patted Rob on the back and admired his buck.

"Oh, it's not mine," he said and pointed to me. "It's hers."

A couple of whispered curses, and "It's not fair." "A woman?" "Ain't no justice."

I said, "But guys, my first one was a lot smaller."

LAUGHTER AND NORMAN

And then there is Norman. One of the nicest guys you would ever want to go hunting with. And a lover of fun.

I was bow hunting in a pine at the edge of a field. Norman was about fifty yards away, in a platform stand overlooking the crossing of several trails—two met about twenty yards in front of his stand and another path ran along behind him.

That pine tree saw many strange events.

Four does materialized from nowhere and Norman rose to his feet, ready to become Robin Hood and slay the deer.

I couldn't see him or the deer, but I heard the shooting. *Twang* of the bow string. *Thunk* of the arrow hitting something. But no sound of deer running or of one falling and thrashing. Again, *twang-thunk*.

And again. And again.

Then Norman's voice.

"Somebody bring me some arrows!"

I hollered back. "I've got some, but I'll have to run your deer off."

"That's okay. I can't hit them anyhow."

Moments later, Norman walked out of the woods.

"Sorry," he said. "I killed two of your pines. One of them is plum dead, sliced in two."

I didn't charge him for the dead pines.

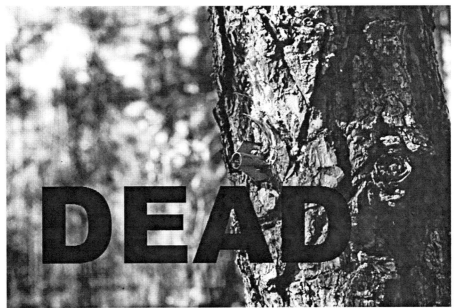

The A points to the fatal arrow.

* * *

Another day. Same stand. Same hunter. Norman spent all morning listening to the little birds fuss and the jays squawk at him. He watched a hawk circle. An owl perched a few yards away. His buddy Larry hunted the field where I had hunted the day Norman became the tree-slayer.

At 10:00 a.m., Larry whistled the *let's go* signal, and Norman whistled back. He laid his rifle down and stood, which wasn't easy since he had a cast on his right knee. Deciding that it was best to have an empty bladder before he began the descent, he had his fly open and the plumbing going when seven deer appeared in front of him and stopped to sniff the air.

Norman swore he had the faucet turned off when he reached for his rifle and put down the largest doe.

Larry yelled behind him.

The faucet was not off.

I was at the house, with several guests, and we all heard the shot.

At 10:30, no Norman and no Larry. Should we go check on them? Maybe they needed help if they were tracking.

No, we decided, maybe they're field dressing the deer.

But we all knew neither of them had ever dressed out a deer. And both of them tended to vomit when they helped me and I opened up the abdomen.

Another hour passed before they came in, their bloody hands evidence that they had cleaned a deer.

 Two years later he got his first trophy from that stand. We were field dressing it when another buck came up to see what was going on—and it too was a trophy. He didn't stay long after catching sight of four humans.

When that visiting buck sashayed off, Norman told the story of the day he and Larry field dressed his doe to have an excuse to stay in the woods while his pants dried.

COURTING ON PERSIMMON RIDGE

I woke to a room almost freezing. The small heater was turned too low for comfort. I hurried to the heater and turned it on full blast. I grabbed my longjohns and pulled them with me as I crawled back under the covers. It wasn't my first morning to dress in the bed.

Growing up in an unheated house, I had experienced a lot of cold mornings.

Norman's alarm clock sounded off in the next room. I yelled, "It's freezing out."

"In here too," he hollered back.

Dressed for the outside cold, we met in the kitchen and had Bear Claws and instant coffee before we headed into the predawn. We decided to go to Persimmon Ridge, where he'd perch in his new home-made hanging stand in an oak overlooking the trail and the persimmon trees.

I'd go along the ridge top about 200 yards and drop down to my (also home-made hanging stand) oak tree half way down to the hollow.

Trusty Nellybelle cranked right up in spite of the cold, and we attached the removable doors to keep some of the wind off. I drove us—Norman would be the navigator and the gate man.

Ice crunched beneath us as we crossed the two mudholes in the Jeep road approaching the ridge.

"If you get cold, just blow twice. I'll be ready to go," I said as we scrambled out of the Jeep.

Norman lit one of his unending supply of cigarettes. "These'll help me stay warm. You just let me know when you're ready to go."

"You know smoking runs off the deer. Put that thing out!'"

He took a few more puffs while I dug into the bucket in the back of the Jeep where we kept a variety of supplies.

"At least use some of our pine scent," I insisted as I dabbled some on my boots and on the hems of my camouflage pants.

He did so.

Our camouflage was not the fancy choices of the 1990s, but the simple greens and blacks on green, the design common in the early 1970s and similar to the earlier greens on green.

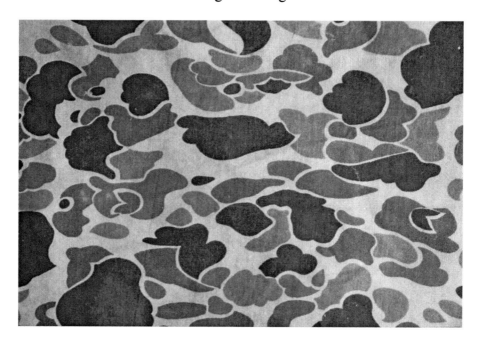

We had donned our orange vests before we left the house. Once we were scented up, we gathered our weapons and headed northeastward along the ridge to our stands. We reached his first, in a small oak on our left. I had seen a fresh scrape under an oak limb across the trail from the stand two days before. He climbed up, settled in and fastened his safety rope. I passed his rifle up.

"Good luck," I whispered. "And don't smoke."

He chuckled. "Okay. Good luck to you. Whistle if you need me."

I left Norman in his stand, where I was sure he had already lit up a cigarette, and strode off at a more rapid pace than ours from the Jeep to his stand. The east showed approaching dawn. I didn't want to spook anything, and was grateful for the frost that dampened the leaves so I could step out without breaking the wood's silence.

My gloves didn't stop the cold, and I worked my fingers to increase circulation. *I won't last till the sun hits me. I hope something comes to the persimmon trees early.*

Twenty yards from my stand, I spooked a deer. It crashed through the brush and snorted a warning to every critter in a quarter-mile.

I went on anyway, climbed into the stand, fastened the safety belt and brought the rifle up with the pull-up rope. I checked that the safety was on, inserted the clip and jacked a cartridge into the chamber. At least I'd be ready if another deer came along.

The woods remained quiet. The sun highlighted the pine tops uphill. Crows talked back and forth. A hawk drifted by and flapped to rise higher on the thermals. The crows saw it and began their harangue at the larger bird.

They drifted off, the crows screaming and the hawk rising higher to escape.

The day did not go dull, just colder. I snugged the rifle close to my belly and stuck one hand under my armpit.

A squirrel spotted me from another oak and barked. His tail flipped an S-shaped warning to all in sight.

Birds Norman called *alarm birds* joined the commotion.

Movement ahead of me, to my left, coming up the path.

Coyote. I eased the safety off and the rifle to my shoulder. Not easy enough. He spotted me and loped into the thickets.

A 30.06 *ka-boomed* behind me. Up the ridge. Close enough to shake my tree.

Norman.

The echo still bounced back from the next ridge when I heard his whistle. One long blast. One for "I got him."

At the time, those empty 30.06 shells were the only means we had to communicate.

Down I came, and back up the hill I went. What did he get? How big was it? Was it in the persimmons? Was it at the scrape?

I was puffing pretty hard when I reached him. Norman's buck lay across from his stand, his body flat out across the scrape. A nice eight-pointer, in full rut. His neck was massive. And broken with that one shot.

"He's a beauty," I said. "Did he come from the persimmons?"

Norman still suffered the after-effects of his attack of buck fever. But he told his adventure while he waved another cigarette in the air to emphasize points.

"I know you told me not to smoke, but I was so cold I had to have a cigarette. I hadn't any more lit it when I saw a doe over under the persimmons. I had to cup the cigarette in my hand and put it out on the stand. It almost burned me."

He showed the red spot on his palm and continued his story.

"She came out of the woods right there and went to the scrape and it was just like you said. She sniffed at the ground and peed in it and then stepped in her own pee. And walked back into the trees to eat.

"It wasn't ten minutes later that the buck came right up the road where we did. I guess he came from—I don't know—maybe he came from across the road. He wasn't in any hurry. He just sorta ambled along."

"Why did you wait to shoot him over the scrape?"

"Well, I'd watched the doe, and I wanted to see what he'd do. He came on up to the scrape and sniffed it and pawed it. And then he turned and saw the doe and his head came up and his ears flipped forward. I shot him."

"Why, Norman, you let him get all het up first. Shame on you."

He laughed. "Well, at least he died happy."

THE BUCK THAT THOUGHT I WAS A DOE

Some say whitetails are smart; some say they are stupid; I won't say which, but I do know that they aren't all that smart. I won't say he was stupid, but I met up with a buck once that needed some educating. He didn't know me from a doe.

It was November, with leaves tumbling and frost coloring the air crisp, but in Georgia's central regions the afternoons felt like early fall way into November. Afternoon temperatures climbed into the upper 70s. Deer had returned to their summer trails after a short cold spell late in bow season, and we were all trying to outthink at least one buck.

I left the house right after lunch and walked into the woods to scout for a place to hunt. When I found a valley trail cut with tracks, speckled with droppings and bordered with scrapes that early afternoon, I hurried back to camp for the others who had planned to hunt another area. They were just loading themselves into the Jeep and I joined them to bounce back to my hollow.

I placed them on cross trails all along the valley and moved out of their way, into an area I had not even had time to explore—an open area with little underbrush beneath the tall sycamores and poplars, in sight of the fence line. A wet-weather creek slid silently down the hollow and under the fence.

Where to sit and wait for someone to shoot and signal a kill? With three people between me and the upper end of the valley, someone would get that buck before he reached me. Each perched in brush or in a climbing stand overlooking a scrape. Nowhere for me to sit to pick off a deer. Just wide open space between me and the fence line, and thickets everywhere else.

I selected a fat poplar that would give my back some protection. If a buck were dumb enough to come into this open space with my hulk in full sight, he was either sex-crazy or just plain stupid.

I began to get settled.

Getting settled consisted of loading the shotgun, laying it a safe distance away, setting up a folding stool so I could lean against the tree—frankly, I'm a lazy hunter—and kicking leaves away from where my feet were to be so I wouldn't make noise and scare off my buck, if he should make it by the other three.

While I sat on my stool, kicked dead leaves for all I was worth and tried to figure where to stash my tote bag, something off to my right made more racket than I did. That *something* trotted toward me, from across the land line.

I had made enough racket to hush all the birds and squirrels, but apparently that smart old buck trotting toward me must have thought I was his lady friend kicking at those leaves and he didn't believe in keeping a lady waiting.

I had done something stupid, though, myself. Here I was, sitting, knowing that only a deer would be making that kind of noise, and my shotgun was lying almost three feet away, where it would be safe from the flying leaves.

Somehow I wobbled my stool half-over and got that shotgun into my hands and brought it up to my shoulder. He solidified and rose over the fence. When I saw his rack, sweat erupted all over me. My heart raced.

Birds and squirrels watched but gave no warning. I managed to swallow my heart back down and lean my right elbow on my knee and get my hands steady again. I waited. Would he see me, my sleeves rolled up to reveal my bare arms, my face a white blob, my eye glasses and red vest catching sunlight and flashing danger? The eight-pointer never hesitated, never even lifted his head to nose the air, never looked around for danger.

He came directly toward me. Would I have to shoot him in the face with buckshot? Or should I let him go up the trail to one of the others? *Naw, I'm not that generous. I'll take whatever shot can put him down.*

He stopped, half hidden by a sapling covered with honeysuckle. I thought he was looking right at me.

Come on, come on.

He came on. Just ambled down the path until he wasn't more than thirty yards away. And stopped again, turned his head to his left and seemed to study something—I later discovered it was another scrape.

He practically posed to give me a perfect shot at only thirty yards.

My shot put him down

Was that buck very smart? He wasn't even smart enough to be spooky or the least bit cautious.

* * *

My shot also brought my friends down. One was still un-strapping his feet from his one-part climbing stand and *oops*. He forgot to keep his feet flat, and when he tilted his toes downward he was unable to hold the sudden shift of weight. His response was normal—grip the tree with your knees. But doing so kept his toes pointed downward and the stand would not grip the tree. Down he came. He got himself a raw belly and understood the nickname *belly scrubber* for the stand.

INVASION: GOVERNMENT STYLE

The NRA is probably right—we all need firearms to protect ourselves from our own government. One hunting season, I faced an invasion that appears even today to have had the support of Georgia's bureaucrats.

Opening day of deer season, as I reached the house after a fruitless three hours in a stand waiting for a deer or darkness, I was greeted by a deputy. "Hurry," he said. "You're needed." He described where to go.

I went full speed ahead in my station wagon, an all-white vehicle that I never took into the woods for fear of scaring off the deer. I'd had problems at this gate a couple of times before; once, a station wagon load of guards and prisoners from the Training School for Delinquent Boys was parked there, with several men and boys out on our land. Another time, I found the gate pulled down and heavy traffic going in. I had followed the tracks and found two Georgia Power trucks almost a half-mile in the woods.

Georgia Power did not provide electricity to anyone out there— our electricity came from the REA. One truck was stuck and had gouged deep ruts. The other truck was rigged to pull it out of the ruts. A cable wrapped around a large pine was gonna kill it.

I ordered the Georgia Power men to walk off the land—"No, you cannot take the trucks. You have to walk," I told them. "And put the gate back up." I also forbade them access to the land. I impounded their vehicles and sent them hiking back to their office. A couple of days later, I relented and didn't charge them with trespassing—that supervisor learned his lessons, and so did the rest of the power company crowd who worked in my county. They never trespassed again.

What, I now wondered, could have happened this time?

When I drove up to the gate this night, a deputy stood guard and waved me through. At the first fork in the Jeep trail sat a State Patrol car, its lights flashing blue into the night woods. The officer jumped out and pointed down one arm of the fork.

On I went through the night. I bounced in and out of ruts and dodged around low-hanging limbs that others had already slashed into. At the field we called the High Meadow more lights flashed from a sheriff's vehicle and another state patrol car. A crowd had collected at the opposite side of the field. About ten were in camouflage; all others in law-enforcement uniforms.

I recognized most of the men in camouflage: They were my hunters, who had a lease on this land. But four were strangers.

It took some talking back and forth to learn what was going on. Merle, the lease holder, had called the law when he found the unknown vehicle parked there. The four illegal hunters arrived back at their vehicle about the time the law appeared.

The culprits insisted they had permission to hunt. Of course, they did not. But, oh yes, they did, they said. They were hunting across the fence, on the state land. On state prison land. The wife of one of the men—she worked for the State—had gotten them permission from somebody. They had just parked here on my land, not hunting it, they kept insisting.

None of the men were local, but came from northwestern areas: Villa Rica, Douglasville, Lithia Springs, and Winston, Georgia.

While all this discussion went on, Ranger Vernell Jackson, who lived up the road about two miles from my place, and Ranger Steve White, stationed in Dublin, got to the battle scene. They'd been on a project in another county and had sped to the location as quickly as possible.

I took their advice. They gave each man a warning, and I did too. They were never, but never, to come back to my land, no matter what.

Then I went to war with the state of Georgia—with the governor and the Department of Corrections. The state was allowing armed men onto the lands of the boys' *redevelopment* (state prison) center.

The boys who escaped sometimes committed horrendous crimes. One group shot and killed the former sheriff who was standing beside his grandchildren, preschoolers who witnessed the shooting. The local story was that since there was no fence and the boys could get out of their cottages at night, they were forced to sleep naked. Without drawers or shoes, they couldn't escape. But they did.

The Center personnel finally accepted reality, that the boys, their "nonprisoners," did escape and did cause harm, so they erected a fence topped with rolled barbed wire around the boys' prison.

As a youngster who rode the school bus that picked up employees' children on the grounds, I saw two staff members holding one of the prisoners while a third man beat him. Wonder what went on when there were no witnesses.

I wrote numerous letters about the illegal hunters to the State of Georgia, but state officials refused to acknowledge any responsibility for such behavior. I received letters that reminded me of the world's greatest lie: "I'm from the government and I'm here to help you."

Governor Busbee's legal assistant just said for me to call the game wardens.

John Hunsucker, the Director of the Division of Youth Services, wrote:

While we do not actually grant anyone permission to hunt on Youth Development Center property, the extended lands are not posted or patrolled to prohibit hunting.

Typical government "good if you do, good if you don't."

MY NOONTIME BUCK

Sweat trickled down my back and I wiped my face with my sleeve as I breathed deeply and leaned against a hardwood tree. Here it was, middle of opening week of deer season, and I was experimenting with a noontime hunt, roaming the ridges and valleys to settle a puzzle in my own mind.

When I first heard of John Alden Knight's theory about animals' feeding schedules, I'd chuckled and shrugged it off as another superstition of another desperate hunter. But the idea, like an unkept promise, lurked behind every bush and seemed to wink at me from the dew while I waited for the buck that did not come. But then, a friend introduced me to Knight's book *Moon Up, Moon Down* and I thought maybe there was something to the idea.

Besides, last summer's events convinced me—because of a ranger's comment:

"If the cows lie down," the ranger said, "I quit hunting because the deer are bedded down, too."

Since all the other advice from rangers had paid off, I knew that statement was valid, too. But was John Alden Knight also correct? I decided to investigate for myself during my vacation week.

Smart deer are supposed to spend the summer in the shade and deep in the swamps where it's cool and food is plentiful. Maybe my deer weren't smart last July—because they were in open fields every day, no matter the temperature or weather conditions.

The only visible factors that affected their presence were the two bulls pastured there. Like a barometer, the bulls predicted the deer's behavior—if the bulls fed, then the deer fed; when the bulls bedded down to chew their cuds, or were not in the meadow, deer did not show up in the field.

Armed with camera and binoculars, I crawled into a high oak stand at first light every morning that July. The field runs west to east along a ridge top. Grasses included lespedeza and coastal Bermuda. A host of briars (sawbriars and blackberries), bushes and weeds speckled the field, as did a jumble of young trees, mostly pines and wild persimmons too small to produce fruit.

A thicket of wild crabapples stood about half-way down the field, on the north side.

My oak was at the west end of the fifteen acres. To my left was another meadow, also speckled with waist-high persimmons; part of this field was blocked from view by a half-fallen barn and its guard of briars, blackberries and brush.

Every evening, I checked over the Solunar Tables in *Field and Stream*. By the end of my week's vacation, I was convinced. The bulls and the Solunar Tables agreed—the deer fed with the bulls and the tables. Other times of day, no deer and no bulls.

Summer, with consistent weather and no people around to spook the deer was one thing, but what about fall, deer season, woods full of people, and the deer in rut?

So I was hunting in mid-day, opening week, on a hot November day.

The deer had gone crazy those first two days of the season, with the woods full of opening day hunters, but by Tuesday the countryside was again quiet with the last weekenders gone home and only serious hunters left. We talked of the need for a cold snap to get the rut in full swing again, the need for clouds to cover that bright moon at night. But I needed patience to wait it out in my stand instead of letting restlessness drive me to camp after a couple hours of sitting.

The fellows laughed when I mentioned the Solunar feed tables, but I continued to let the idea gnaw at me until it finally drove me from the house at midmorning that Wednesday. I knew the fellows were right—sensible deer feed at dawn and twilight, or all night long if the moon was bright. So with the temperature pushing into the 80s, I didn't expect the tables to be right.

I thought back to deer I'd seen last summer—two bucks, together, ambling along a trail, and that same afternoon with the mercury over 95°, two fawns and a doe feeding in midfield under the glaring sun. They did feed at noon.

Maybe, I promised myself—the same *maybe* that lures us all into the field year after year and keeps hope alive in Chicago Cub fans.

But, because I didn't really expect to see deer, I did the things necessary to fulfill my expectations. I tromped over the ridges and through dry leaves as if I were driving cattle, until I was puffing and sweating. My attention had been on the ground as I studied sign—my excuse to the fellows for being out at that senseless time of day. I worked my way down a pine ridge, the ground deep in straw that muffled my boots in spite of my carelessness.

So when I stopped to catch my breath and lean against a tree, I'd been walking quietly for some minutes. The bottom spread out for more than a hundred yards before giving way to a mixed pine and hardwood ridge. It housed a wet-weather stream that meandered eastward, to my left, and slid out of its banks on any excuse, so everything was usually soggy except in late summer's dry spell.

It was after high noon, time for the major feeding period to begin. According to the tables, I should be seeing deer if I was in or near their feeding grounds. Somewhere a bird scratched in the leaves and a small critter made enough noise to be a herd of deer in the thickets. My long-sleeved tee shirt was soaked. My shady spot didn't do much to keep me cool. I eased the shotgun butt onto the ground and listened.

Cracking sticks and crunching leaves like cornflakes, a deer trotted down the ridge. I eased behind the tree, kind of rolling back against my shoulder as I lifted one foot and put it oh so slowly down, toe first, wiggling it into the leaves and then easing the heel down to silently shift my way around the tree. I then froze and watched.

A doe broke out of the brush and stopped broadside to me not more than fifty yards away. Ears forward, she looked off toward her left, directly uphill. My hands wrapped around Ole Betsy and my heart began to thump louder—other hunters had told me when a doe looks back she's waiting for the buck to follow her. I waited too. My thumb eased back on the hammer of that single shot; my forefinger nestled against the trigger; I could almost see antlers in the branches behind her.

Nothing moved.

She turned and looked at me.

A deer has unlimited patience. I don't, especially when I'm being eyeballed by a deer and don't dare move. I stood so still my body shook with each heartbeat. I expected her to throw up her tail and depart.

Instead, she angled to my right, toward the thickets. She paused again, surveyed the swamp, and then plunged down the last few yards to disappear behind a still-green bush shrouded in honeysuckle. She browsed for long minutes out of sight, ambled almost silently in the leaves. I'd hear a slight sound repeated two or three times, then silence again. "Walk one or two steps and stop," Rob had told me when he was discussing *still-hunting*. "That way, if a deer hears you, it'll just think you're another deer." That deer was proving Rob's words to me.

She also proved that deer dine at noon. Had she been bedded down along the ridge top? Did deer bed down high in the mornings and feed low at noon? Maybe then they'd work uphill again at dusk. I'd seen them both high and low at twilight. But I had little time to ponder their afternoon habits while that doe fed; her footsteps got closer.

Squinting did not help me see through the honeysuckle and thick leaves that defied winter by clinging, still green. I figured if I couldn't see her she might not be able to see me, and I glanced at my watch. She had kept me pinned down for almost ten minutes.

Sweat teased down my face. If I moved she would spot me and I did not dare raise my hand to wipe it away. Slowly and awkwardly I managed to wipe my eyes with my sleeves. My arms were beginning to ache from holding the shotgun at near ready; one leg had gone numb. I had to shift around, doe or not. I told myself there was not a buck within a mile and put my weight onto the one leg I could feel. No deer flushed from cover; no flash of white waved goodbye. So far, so good. I leaned against the tree and eased the shotgun down, butt resting on the ground, muzzle skyward and away. Then the doe came into view, and I decided to settle for what comfort I'd been able to establish.

She nibbled at a bush, so close I saw her jaw muscles rolling as she chewed; a few mulberry leaves went next; then her ears were up, head lifted, as she looked off down the swamp for a few seconds. With a flick of her tail, she dropped her head again, ambled a few steps, and nibbled again. A bit of honeysuckle, a nibble from a bush, and she moseyed on, putting brush between me and her head. Not once had she looked my direction, although she had almost circled me since her descent from the ridge. My *Smell of the Woods* pine scent I had used this morning had certainly passed a critical test.

I, too, had passed a test by standing still enough for her to walk by without seeing me, without my moving enough to attract her attention. The blaze-orange vest glared at the corners of my eyes, but to her, it was only a splash of noncolor broken up into a nonpattern by the shadows that covered me.

When the doe moved again, only her back leg was visible. Even this brown-gray evidence disappeared when I blinked, and I had to stare hard to locate it again. I am in awe of how nature's colors can be so distinct and so alike. The doe moved on down the swamp into silence and I finally relaxed my tense muscles, sure now that no buck was around. She had kept me pinned against that tree for more than fifteen minutes—although it seemed more like two hours. After my long walk, I was glad to sit. I perched my butt on the edge of a log and leaned against a limb that didn't want to hold me up. It gave way when I leaned back.

After resting a few minutes, I eased across the swamp and started upstream, along a deer path at the base of the knoll. Ahead, on my left, the knoll curved away to another hollow. My every step on the leaf-strewn pathway sounded like a marching troop of soldiers in the stillness. I resorted to *still-hunting* tactics and managed to quieten my footsteps. When I reached the juncture of the two hollows, I decided to continue up the main creek and stepped across a fallen log.

I stopped, a-straddle the log, listening to a sound louder than my own. Somewhere up that other hollow was a deer, coming my way, as unmindful of its noise as the doe had been earlier. I was miserable, in a strain, and knew I had to move now, while the deer was too far away to see me through the leaves. I got my other leg over the log and stood beside it, ready. *Now where is that deer?*

The racket got louder and closer, echoing against the ridges, confusing me, rolling down the hollow from every direction. I tried to merge into that log as I wrapped my fingers around the shotgun; I cocked it, keeping my thumb over the hammer as a safety, and raised it slightly, ready to turn either direction, to raise the shotgun to a buck or lower it from a doe. I was facing the same knoll the doe had come down.

The buck materialized from nowhere.

He stopped broadside to me and looked at me eyeball to eyeball.

At twenty yards, I couldn't miss, but Betsy was still pointing to a cloud. For a moment, the buck and I were painted on a canvas, destined to never move again, hanging on a wall and captioned *Carelessness Is Costly.*

He did not move, but Betsy slowly came down, snuggled against my shoulder, and spoke once.

The buck leaped over the low bushes and vanished into the swamp. I flipped the gun open with one hand while digging out a shell with the other—a single-shot is light enough to carry all day but it has that one-shot disadvantage.

Before the shell slid home, silence fell. Smoke still drifted from the barrel; the running had stopped, not faded. He was close, either dead or playing a wait-and-see game. I didn't wait but reloaded Betsy and went to see, my steps loud in the quiet.

He stood in the bushes, his head turned to me, his tongue hanging out.

I snapped Betsy to my shoulder, ready to fire again. He didn't move. He was dead standing up, held onto his feet by the thickets.

There he was, my noontime buck. All I had to do was field dress him, get him back to camp, and time tomorrow's hunt with Mr. Knight's feeding tables. Maybe I'd catch up with this one's grandpa.

RECORD KEEPING

After three years of hunting, I decided since I couldn't be everywhere at once to observe the deer, their numbers, sex, behavior, and food choices, I would get the hunters in my group to help gather the information. So I printed up a record form. It had space for all matters related to each deer we sighted:

Date, weather (sun/rain/cloudy/windy/temperature), location, direction of movement, estimated age or size (i.e., adult/spring fawn), sex, antler configuration.

My group kept these records for about twenty years, long before computers were available to analyze the data. But we would file the data into our heads and often knew by weather conditions the best place to go that day to score a deer.

We also kept records of how many deer we killed, their sex and age (we had a tool to open the jaws and a chart showing age by tooth wear). Because the land lies beside a state highway and also a railroad, we often walked the railroad to determine what the train had killed, and we counted the carcasses along the road—those shot by poachers and those hit by vehicles.

I don't remember my first conversation with Joe Kurz, director of game management. Looking back, it seems that I knew him from the time I developed an interest in the health and preservation of the deer herds. At times, I would call to let him know the condition of the herds on our land, and eventually I began to provide written, detailed reports. We even counted embryos for several years to determine the fertility level of the does.

To provide Joe Kurtz with complete data on two square miles, I had another group tally their kills and include any bodies found later and any poacher kills.

By 1990, I had quit aging the deer and considered them either spring fawns (6-months old) or adults. My records for that season show:

For the doe days of October 27 and 28: Temperature October 27 registered 30ºF; clear sky; still. Deer that day: four 6-month does; two

6-month bucks (antlerless), one spike (one-inch), and two adult does (small, about 18 months).

October 28, no deer. BUT one 6-month shot from road, *and three poachers arrested.*

November 8: Adult doe found dead on property (poacher kill?)

November 14: Small spike killed.

November 16: One 8-point killed.

Doe Days:

November 21: 14 deer
    Three adult bucks
    Two button bucks
    Four adult does
    Four 6-month does
    One unknown (dead on road)
November 22:
    One 18-month old buck
November 23:
    One unknown dead on road
    One adult buck
    One 6-month buck
    Six adult does
    Five 6-month does
November 24:
    One adult doe shot, not found.
    One buttonless buck, no visible testicles
November 25:
    One small adult doe
    One doe, dead on railroad
December 1:
    Four adult does
    Two 6-month does
December 2:
    One adult doe
    One 6-month doe

Our records showed where each deer was killed, as well as the weather conditions and the deer's behavior. The hunters in our group numbered ten or more, plus as many as five guests.

For several years, I reported our tally to Joe Kurz and also to Dick Whittington, game and fish biologist for my area of the state. I felt that these reports helped the biologists in their decisions on bag limits, doe days, and season lengths.

I kept off-season records also. Every sighting of deer (and turkey) on the land was recorded. But the most important information about off-season activity was the location of after-season scrapes.

I found fresh scrapes after the season ended on January 1, and even as late as mid-March. From these scrapes, I knew where to hunt for the dominant buck the next fall.

THE SILVER FOX OF MILLEDGEVILLE

Culver Kidd, a politician who served as county commissioner, state representative and then state senator, was known in the legislature as the Silver Fox. Even journalists referred to him by that nickname in the newspapers.

In the late 1970s, one of Kidd's employees was charged with night hunting and the ranger confiscated his vehicle, as well as his firearms. If he were using a spotlight, it was also confiscated.

Kidd, the consummate politician, introduced Senate Bill 20 the next January. The bill would be retroactive, and anyone night hunting would NOT have to lose his vehicle, his firearms or his spotlight, or any other equipment that was used in the illegal hunting activity. By making the bill retroactive, Mr. Kidd apparently hoped to have his employee's property returned to him free rather than have that individual, and anyone else recently convicted of night hunting, have to purchase his equipment and vehicle from the state.

I wrote letters to the Chairman of the Senate Committee on Natural Resources, to the Chairman of the Senate Subcommittee on Natural Resources, to my representative in the State House, and to the Commissioner of the Department of Natural Resources.

This was in the days before computers, when each letter had to be typed separately, and so I gave the letters the same themes but wrote each individually.

I summed up my letters with:

The legal hunter wears a red vest in daylight hours; if Mr. Kidd's bill is allowed to pass, the night hunter will wear a laugh all the way through the State courts.

I stressed that the night hunters are mostly ego-driven and those who are financially driven are not starving, but are profit-mongers. They don't know what lies beyond that deer, and neighbors have bullet holes in their walls.

I had a lot of help from the editorial staffs of local and regional newspapers who wrote several columns about the dangers resulting if his bill passed. One stated, "The knowledge that they may lose their car or rifle is the major deterrent to the practice of hunting at night.

Relaxing the penalties will only encourage more hunters to break the law and thus complicate an already serious problem even further."

Joe Tanner, Commissioner of DNR, was quoted in the papers: "If that law were to pass, for all practical purposes you would have taken all the muscle out of the game laws of Georgia."

I knew how stern, immediate punishment prevents crime. I had been in Nigeria in the 1960s and learned that any crime committed with weapons was punished immediately by death. They had no violent crime.

But Kidd wanted even more in his bill: He wanted to make it legal in Baldwin and Wilkinson Counties to *dog deer*. That is, he would allow the use of hounds to chase deer to the hunter. Dogging deer is legal in the Southern sections of Georgia but is strongly opposed by most of the hunters I know in our county—how does a dog know where to drive the deer? One dog can run a deer to death. We wanted no part of that law.

My letters praised the efforts of the local rangers: "Thanks to their long-term efforts, those of us who own property in Baldwin County can walk and sleep without fear, with the secure knowledge that night hunters will face arrest and punishment. Night hunters know, too, of our rangers' dedication and efforts and are active less and less each year."

I also mentioned the challenge of facing down Mr. Kidd:

I have known of the power wielded by Mr. Kidd, both at home and in Atlanta. To face the unknown in the night to protect the wildlife of the State takes quite a lot of courage. To face political pressures that a man of Mr. Kidd's power can exert takes a courage that words cannot describe.

I wrote an open letter to Kidd that was published in the *Union-Recorder*. In it, I challenged him to wear dark clothing with reflective buttons and stand on my land near the road. If he did so at night, he'd be shot for a deer before dawn.

Kidd also introduced another bill—he wanted to limit an individual's right to carry a handgun. My letter to the editor about that bill ended with:

Won't we women who carry a handgun for protection look silly doing our evening shopping with a .12 gauge in the grocery cart?

Thankfully, these bills did not pass.

DOGGING DEER

Someone in my county sponsored a petition to allow the use of dogs to hunt deer in Baldwin County, and that petition probably led Culver Kidd to sponsor a bill for the same change in game regulations. I jumped in and put together my own petition for my hunters and neighbors to sign. I directed it to the Game and Fish personnel:

We the undersigned LANDOWNERS and HUNTERS of Baldwin County petition the Georgia Game and Fish Commission to CONTINUE TO PROHIBIT the use of dogs to hunt deer in Baldwin County, Georgia.

We understand that a petition to discontinue this restriction is being circulated in Baldwin County and (1) is sponsored by an individual who has been convicted of violating this very restriction and (2) is being supported by transients, nonhunters, and non-property-owners, who sign it in a general merchandise store.

Our reasons for our petition are:

1. The article by Jim Morrison, "Dogged to Death," in your magazine *Game and Fish*, January 1968.
2. Dogs attack fawns.
3. Dogs attack does.
4. Dogs do not recognize open and closed seasons.
5. Dogs pull down deer and leave carcasses to other predators.
6. Dogs frequently are not found by owners and go wild, breed wild dogs and prey on both wildlife and livestock.
7. Dogs drive deer from their normal range, to which the deer may not return.
8. Dogs do not recognize land lines.
9. Use of dogs is not sporting in a geographic region with the topography of the Piedmont.

I sent it on to the Game and Fish Division and don't know how much it helped. At least the legislature did not support Kidd's bill. I am grateful that Georgia does not allow dogging deer in my county. We have enough problems with thrown-away dogs and their feral offspring as well as a growing coyote population.

HALF A BUCK IS BETTER THAN NONE

I clicked the flashlight on for only a moment, just to look for the intersection of the Jeep trail with the small path leading to the cross fence and my stand. In the predawn light, I went down the path. The light pollution from town silhouetted trees and turned their winter-bare limbs into scrawny witches' fingers. Cold slithered down my back and I tried to tell myself I was just cold and no headless horseman or broom-riding witch lived in my version of Sleepy Hollow. Just as I shook the feeling off, the dawn was split with a loud blowing snort. I froze in mid-step.

Could that deer possibly be blowing at me? How could it see me? That snort had to be from the next ridge, behind that clump of scrub brush and honeysuckle, across the overgrown meadow, through the trees, across the creek, and up into the tall pines. No way a deer saw me from there. I hurried on. I was already late to my stand. My watch said 6:00 a.m.

I left the path before I reached the tree. I needed to approach it from the side away from the path to avoid stepping in scrapes on the path. Once I had my rope around my supplies and shotgun, I scampered up the tree. Our stands are unique. I designed them, copying ideas from others and changing first one item and then another until I had small swings that didn't move when we tied them down. Norman would even dance on some to ensure their safety. We didn't need much time to put them in place. All I needed were nails for steps, which I could drive in easily—the guys were all right-handed, but as a lefty, I could swing a sledge hammer from either side. So I usually drove in the nails while I swung from a lineman's belt. One of the boys would climb up, use the second belt to secure himself, and pull up the seat, chain it to the tree, and tie it down.

The board was only a few inches wider than my hips and the chains swinging it to the tree provided me with some security on each side. I had purchased a number of canvas belts at the Army-Navy store for safety belts and kept one at each stand.

I leaned down, pulled up my supplies, converted the pull-up rope into a foot rest, donned my extra jacket, and commenced to hide my face behind a black dickey. I turned its collar up over my nose; by snugging my cap down, I left only my eyes and nose exposed to the possible gaze of a buck.

The cold turned my breath into puffs, like small clouds of cotton. This small oak always boasted two or three scrapes under its limbs, and always provided one or two bucks a season. Today would be my day, I felt, but it would be a lonely hunt with the rest of the group still in the sack, avoiding the cold.

My long wait began and I wondered which way to face my .12-gauge. I had a short shot over my left shoulder, to the hedgerow by the cross fence, about twenty feet, a perfect shot for a right-handed hunter. But I had fired a gun right-handed only a half-dozen times; my aim was perfect with a Ruger .44 magnum at sixty yards, and I reckoned I could down a deer at this close range with my .12-gauge if I needed to shoot right-handed.

Most bucks seen or harvested from this stand, however, had been in front of the stand, partway up the ridge, and either feeding or walking toward the east (to my right). I decided to expect a left-handed shot and snuggled back against the tree, ready, with three mini-magnums waiting to put some meat into the freezer.

Everyone else had his buck, and after seven days of hunting hard, I was beginning to feel discouraged. A buck who had danced around a ridge with me one morning had only gotten me riled up enough to send someone else there, and a 250-pounder wore another hunter's tag to the freezer. Here I was, the only one in the club who had paid entry fees into a Big Buck contest.

Our youngest hunter, who carried his books to his stand to maintain his A average in college, had wrangled my heart until I sent him off to my special far-away stand in a tall sweetgum growing on a mostly pine hilltop. He saw only one deer that morning, caught a glimpse of it over the edge of his book. He laid down the textbook, lifted his shotgun, and fired at what he thought was a funny rack. It **was** different—ten points, perfectly balanced, with twelve-inch tines.

Ever our club clown, Norman often went to sleep in his stand. A couple of times, he woke up when he hit the ground. But clown or not, he had used both of his tags on opening day—one buck a five pointer but the other a fine buck, pushing over 200 pounds, with an outside-the-ears eight-point rack. Norman got each buck from a site I selected, and one from a portable stand I had swung up for him only four days before the season opened.

As I thought back over the week, it seemed I had limited my own hunting to advising the rest of the club and sending them to my stands for them to collect big bucks. Oh, I had seen bucks all right, six of them. And I had passed up each one, not intentionally, not because I wanted a big bruiser, but because they were either running or in thickets, and I did not have a clean shot. Always, I took the first buck that strolled—not ran—into range. Usually it was no problem; just harvest the first one, and then spend the rest of the season roaming the land, enjoying the fall woods and watching buck after buck pass by, some not ever knowing they were close to a freezer. Last season, one buck came close enough for me to pet, but none cooperated this year.

I was ready to settle for a small buck. Herbert had teased me that he had beat me this year, for the first time, since he had a spike and I had none, and it sure would be nice, he insisted, if he finished the season ahead of me. His teasing had somehow made my not having scored much easier to take. But I had no intention of letting my deer go—smaller or larger than Herbert's. I'd take any legal deer for my freezer in the long winter ahead.

Herbert was our oldest hunter, and our good humor man. Not the ice cream, but the man who teased and joked with us all. Even himself. He told us of crazy events in his life. Like the time he was wiring his house while sitting on the ground in the crawl space. He realized he was kinda bouncing off the ground, and only then recognized that he was being shocked because the wire he worked on was hot.

On the job, he rebuilt generators, and he had made himself a tool from a bent coat hanger to help snatch the wire inside the generator he was working on. When a man came to him for help to rewire his own generator and Herbert used his snagging tool, the man was so impressed he asked where he could buy one. Herbert said, "Oh, you can have this one. I have another." The customer tried to pay for it, but Herbert refused the offer—he had plenty of wire coat hangers at home. The customer left with his valuable, irreplaceable tool.

My favorite Herbert story involved Norman. Herbert was hunting from the porch of a former tenant house, where deer food was plentiful: Two white oaks in front, persimmon trees in the nearby woods, and a producing pear tree to his right. Norman was behind the house in a swinging stand, about 100 yards away. Norman shot.

Herbert figured he had a deer and would be strolling up any minute. But a half-hour passed. Herbert began to worry. Just as Herbert was fixing to leave his porch seat and go search, up strode Norman. Blood all over his arms and splashed on his clothes.

"My gawd, Son. Did you shoot yourself?"

Norman laughed. "No, I just field dressed the deer." A first for Norman, who tackled the job so as not to disturb Herbert's hunt.

When Herbert left the house for the first hunt each weekend, he always took only one cartridge—"I'm only going to shoot one deer," he said.

Herbert's spike he challenged me to beat.

The morning he downed this buck, he was in the stand we called *Herbert's Hilton,* a four-by-six foot stand in a three-foot diameter white oak in the front pasture. We constructed all of our permanent stands with 2X4 supports we treated with copper naphthenate to deter both insects and rot. We used the same treated plywood for our permanent stands as we used for the swinging ones. Almost rot-proof, the plywood lasted far longer than the treated pine supports.

When Herbert said it was too cold for him to sit in a tree, someone in the group (probably Herbert) came up with the idea of a portable heater. We removed the cardboard center from a roll of toilet paper, squeezed the toilet paper into a coffee can and soaked the paper with alcohol. The lid prevented evaporation. This heater would fit into a gear bag that could be carried to the stand over the shoulder. It weighed practically nothing. Once in the stand, Herbert removed the lid and lit the evaporating alcohol. Since any odor would rise in the air from the heat deer did not smell it.

I turned my mind away from Herbert as dawn threw sunlight over the world. Weeds whitened under a layer of frost. From somewhere a buck way bigger than Herbert's—well, at least a four-pointer—would come in sight and range. Total silence greeted the day as the cold crept into my very being, stiffened my hands, defied my toes to try to move away from the encroaching pain. Time was marked only by a lone leaf bumping its way down through its brothers, cold, crisp, crackling a greeting to all as it fell. Far from the nearest highway, I lived in that winter silence for two long hours, moving only my head ever so slightly, but my eyes constantly, looking for a speck of white that might be an ear or the edge of a tail or the inside of a leg. But no straight line of back, no curve of an ear anywhere. Only the silence and the frost.

I jumped from the explosion. Up on that same ridge, several hundred yards away, it continued to blow. Then the crashing began, the blowing continued, as the deer charged my way, unmindful of the underbrush, not trying to slip away but running headlong.

It was over my left shoulder and I turned the shotgun, raised it, eased my finger to the safety. I had once forgotten a safety and kept trying to fire at a deer, and when I remembered it, the deer was leaving. I got him, but barely, and I did not want to forget again. Closer the deer came, snorting every few leaps, and I knew I would not shoot unless it slowed from its charge.

Then I heard the grunting, a soft bellow, like a bull mooing quietly to himself. I knew then a big buck, somewhere in those pines, was charging toward me. The blowing continued, passed behind me and on down the hollow. That one had to be a doe saying "No!" to the buck whispering his determined "Oh, yes!" as he followed.

He loped behind the brush, his rack massive and black in the tall pines. Easy range, but moving too fast in the shadows. I lost sight of him in the brush, but the soft lowing continued as he moved behind me and toward the hollow to my right.

I turned around. There he was, his rack lifted high and bobbing a little as he nibbled at an overhead limb. All I saw was antlers. His head and body were hidden behind the hedgerow.

I had learned the hard way years before. Don't shoot the buck when all you see through the brush is his rack and head. I did not lift the shotgun but watched. Within seconds, he turned and loped after his lady.

The woods went silent. For about five minutes, and then a rifle blasted my ears. A poacher yelled and whooped his joy—he had killed the buck I had let go.

I cursed. Th*e buck wasn't even twenty yards away. I couldn't have missed.*

Mama always said if you gotta cuss, get a head start and do it right. Her version of doing it right was too tame: "Gee whiz, golly gosh, deuce, durn, damn, oh hell." I just muttered the "Oh, hell." And reminded myself then, however, and still today, that I had no business shooting at that buck with the view and angle I had.

As the last sounds of the poacher died way, I realized that I was shaking so much that I shook the tree. Buck fever racked me. The leaves around me rustled slightly and my heart thumped in my ears. I breathed deeply, trying to relax the tensions and recall the excitement from an objective viewpoint. Impossible. The size of the rack haunted me and still infected me with buck fever. I cursed the poacher again.

Leaves crackled. Footsteps to my left. I eased my head around. Antler, twenty yards and closing. I struggled to get the shotgun turned for a right-handed shot. I couldn't get the butt of that gun higher than my upper arm, but one shot dropped him.

Me with my half-buck and my dog Gretel, who loved fresh deer legs for chew-bones

Herbert helping me skin out my half-buck.

I had my deer for the season, and Herbert still had his dream—his spike beat my deer, because, as he said, all I got was a half-deer, with only one spike (half-spikes didn't count).

But I'd be back for his grandpa or uncle. Tomorrow. Next week. Next year.

THANK YOU, REWARDS AND BUCKY

Think of being at home when someone fires off a 30.06 in front of your house and the double boom echoes in the hallway and shakes the windows, and when you pick up the phone to call for help, it's useless. One of the other folks on the multi-party line has the phone off the hook.

You hear a crying baby, a squeaking rocker and the soothing sounds of the mother. You yell into the phone, over and over, "Please hang up! PLEASE HANG UP!"

You go unheard, and the culprit goes free.

When we finally got a private line, we could call the ranger. But we had a strange phone situation. We lived not far apart, both in the northwest part of the county, but his phone was with one company and mine with another. Every call was long distance.

After DNR transferred a ranger out of our county, another one would come into the community. In spite of the dedication of these men—they sometimes worked as much as thirty hours at a stretch and never complained—the poaching continued. I joined forces the only way I knew how—I wrote letters to the editor and I offered rewards.

I printed up notices and slapped them up on trees and fence posts on every tract of land my family owned. The bright red ink was highly visible from the road. I also ran this notice in the newspaper. I would pay the reward to anyone—except lawmen weren't allowed to accept the reward.

One evening just after dark, on my way to town I found a deputy stepping out of his car, flashlight in hand, and wondered what he was detecting.

"Hey, what's going on?" I asked. We introduced ourselves and he explained that he'd seen blood on the road and stopped to investigate. Together we studied the road and the shoulder and found deer hair. Only a few hairs. Whoever hit the deer had taken it home for butchering—I hadn't heard shots.

$ REWARD $

$50.00 for information leading to the arrest and conviction of ANYONE poaching on lands I own or manage in North West Baldwin County.

CALL:

(Home numbers of local rangers, my home number and the T.I.P. hotline)

SUSAN LINDSLEY

The phone numbers have been deleted here since the rangers have retired. The Turn In Poachers (T.I.P.) hotline is still the same:

1-800-241-4113

"Well," the deputy said, "I was hoping to find something and collect your reward. Guess I'll just have to keep trying."

"I can't give you the fifty dollars," I said, "since you're a deputy. But I sure can put it into your retirement fund."

That deputy, Howard Sills, was elected sheriff in a neighboring county and gained national attention when he spearheaded the arrest of the leader of the Nuwaubians, a local religious cult, for a variety of criminal activities, including sexually molesting children. He also handled the arrest without bloodshed.

It wasn't long before another deputy also pitched in and collared a night hunter. He got his deposit into the retirement fund and I wrote a letter to the editor, thanking him for going beyond his usual duties. I also felt that no thanks were complete without a letter to the officer's supervisor.

In 1990, Deputy Sheriff Robert (Bobby) Langford and State Trooper Randy Hartzell apprehended three poachers several miles away from my lands. They had stopped the vehicle because of headlight problems—and discovered a game violation. The officers separated the men to prevent their plotting a story, called the ranger, and even helped with the legal paperwork. Because the event was outside my self-set jurisdiction, I did not donate to their retirement fund, but I did donate $150.00 in each officer's name to the Bucky Fund, to be used to purchase a mounted buck for the wildlife rangers to use as a decoy.

Until then, the rangers had taken outdated car tags and fixed reflective buttons in the holes used to attach the tag to the car. They would hang these imitation *deer eyes in the headlights* on bushes so when a poacher swung his spotlight across the tag, the culprit would think he had a deer and would shoot. These fake deer didn't last long, but they did serve to catch a number of bad guys.

When I learned about these makeshift deer eyes, I started the Bucky Fund. I required each of my hunters to donate $10.00 to the fund; with some seventy-five hunters, we were able to purchase a mounted buck.

Unfortunately, Bucky The First managed to escape from a moving truck one night and was never recaptured by the rangers. Somewhere, a hunter has the original Bucky as a decoy to challenge a buck in to range. Bucky II performed well until he was semi-retired after Bucky III came along. My hunters all contributed to these purchases—after all, they wanted to catch the night shooters as much as I did!

Bucky III could *move!*

The first two didn't move, but they were still shot numerous times and the villain not only had to pay his night hunting fine but also had to buy back his vehicle and his weapons.

Setups for Bucky III were a bit different. Instead of rangers hiding at both ends of the road, one slipped onto the land far enough away from Bucky to be safe from any shooting, but close enough to use a hand unit to control the buck's movement. When a spotlight hit the deer, he'd make it flip its tail and turn its head. The villains shot, the second ranger drove up to apprehend them, and off to jail they went. Bucky III captured two sets of night shooters on his first posting, and never went out at night without doing his duty and sending the villains *directly to jail without passing GO.*

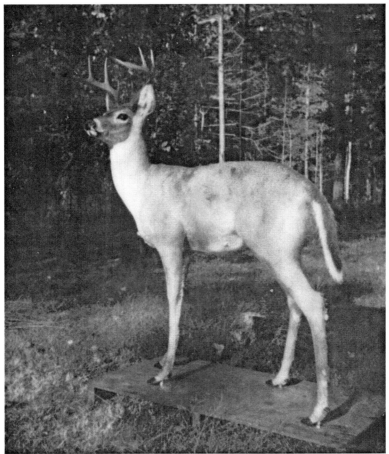

Bucky III looking for a poacher. (Photo by Marion Nelson)

The night shooting in Baldwin County took a deep dive to near oblivion when the word got around about the moving mounted deer that might be a buck, but also might be a doe since the antlers were removable.

Fines included $500.00 for night hunting, $500.00 for shooting from the road, the loss of both the vehicle and firearms, and the cost of repairs to Bucky and his electronic guts.

We have a long way to go once again, however. Fines have been reduced to about $100.00 in our area, the amount set by local judges although Georgia has a mandatory sentence of $500.00 for anyone caught night hunting, and at the discretion of the judge, jail time can be added. For a second offense, the *minimum* required fine is $1,500, and the judge can fine him up to $5,000 and include jail time up to a full year.

If the herds decrease, from coyotes or other causes, poaching may increase again.

ONE RANGER'S FIRST DAY

Home at last, John thought, as he stepped into his green Ranger's truck on opening day of deer season. *But now I may really have a problem, what with all the locals thinking I'm gonna give 'em a pass since I used to hunt with them.*

Day barely brightened the eastern horizon as he drove from his yard. He tried to shake off the cold. The truck heater hadn't warmed up yet. His headlights glistened on frost. Hunters would be coming in early today with this cold, but the deer would be moving too.

He headed for Bennie's Place, where yesterday, after getting a tip, he had found a deer stand with apples and corn only yards away. *If the hunter's there, he'll be my first arrest. And I hope to gawd he's not somebody I know.*

He wasn't. John ticketed not only that fellow but also his hunting buddy just down the path. He learned they did not have the landowner's permission to hunt and ticketed them for that offence also. And warned them not to return to hunt there.

Two cases made before 8 o'clock. But he needed something different. A case to upset the locals, to let them know he wouldn't favor anybody. He might have been a rascal in his teens but now he was *the man*, and he meant business.

He had driven only three miles, on his way to check a hunting camp, when he spotted a man in camouflage with a rifle over his shoulder, walking down the road. The man's boots had a high shine; certainly, John thought, a novice. *This hunter won't ever see a deer with those boots flashing in the sun. Probably getting blisters from the new boots, too.* John stopped, rolled down his window, and asked, "How you doing?"

"Oh, hello, Ranger. I'm good."

"Need a lift to your camp?"

"That sure would be nice. Thanks. It's down the road a mile or so." The hunter walked around and opened the passenger door.

"That rifle unloaded?" John asked

"Uh. No."

"Well, you can't have a loaded firearm in my vehicle. Unload it before you get in."

The hunter opened his mouth to speak and then closed it.

"What's the matter?"

"I. Uh. I don't know how."

"What do you mean, you don't know how?"

"I just bought it yesterday. The guy at the store loaded it for me."

John tilted his head back and stared at the roof of the truck. He took a deep breath and said, "Well, you walk on to your camp, and you learn how to load and unload that rifle. Until you do, you don't leave camp again. I'll check back with you about lunch time, and you be there. You understand?"

"Yessir." He closed the door and walked away, head hanging.

John shook his head and drove on. Not exactly the situation he was hoping for, but it was a start. He by-passed the novice's camp since he'd be there at midday, and continued to another one two miles up the highway and then down a dirt road.

He turned into the drive between two massive oaks that were draped in poison ivy and dust. The driveway went by a dilapidated barn and then turned into a field where one-room cabins, campers and trailers stood nestled beneath pecan and oak trees. A house dating to depression times stood near a magnolia. Trucks were scattered around, but most were parked off to the left, apparently to give room for everyone to turn around and move in and out at will. He noticed blood ran down between the bed and the tailgate of several.

Big changes since I was a boy. I remember Miss Nancy making ice cream on that porch when we came to visit. A long time ago.

He parked and stepped out of his truck. Men in various stages of cold-weather dress, from heavy jackets to camouflage jumpsuits, began to filter from the various structures, and two ladies walked onto the porch, waved and went back inside.

"Morning, Ranger," one man said. He was tall, slim, unshaven, and wore a holster with a .45 Colt. His pants were stained with fresh blood from field dressing a deer. "I'm Sheriff Mike Sanders, from north Georgia."

"I'm John Gibes, the new ranger here."

"I figured you were new. Hadn't seen you before. Welcome to our hunting grounds."

Other men began to circle around to listen.

John smiled. "Thanks. Actually, I could say the same. I used to squirrel hunt out here. Miss Nancy couldn't get a good pecan harvest because of the squirrels, so I'd come over the help her out."

"Then you're local? I thought rangers weren't allowed to serve in their home county."

"Only if you've worked another county first and done your job. I notice your Colt. You aren't wearing it into the woods, are you?"

The sheriff's blush showed through his whiskers. "I know better," he said. "We've had a problem with road shooters and I'm just ready to go after them is all."

John decided not to pursue the matter. The pistol was illegal while hunting, but he had no proof, the guy was a sheriff, and every dirt road had shooters, day and night. *But maybe I should come back here tomorrow and check them out while they're in their stands.*

"Good. I see you got a deer." He nodded toward the bloodied pants.

"Yep. Come take a look. We got some good ones today."

"Well, first, I need to check everybody's license."

"Sure," Mike said. "Come on, fellas, show him you're legal."

One by one, the men pulled out their wallets and displayed their licenses, smiled at John, welcomed him home, and shook his hand.

They all walked with him from campsite to campsite to view the seven bucks hanging from pecan tree limbs.

"You really have had a good day," John said. "Seven deer."

He turned to the trucks lined up near the old barn and counted the bloodied tailgates. *Eight.* Only seven bucks swung on the tree limbs. He walked over and looked into the beds.

"Uh-uh," he muttered. Four deer legs lay in one. He leaned over the bed, lifted one and used it to drag the others toward him. No tag anywhere. All seven deer hanging had four legs.

He looked up at the men. No one moved. No one spoke. As a group they looked like children caught with cookie crumbs all over their shirt fronts.

"Where's the rest of this deer?" he asked. "Is it tagged?"

Everybody kinda shrugged. The men looked back and forth at each other. Some muttered, "I dunno."

"Who killed this deer?"

"I dunno," again came from the men.

"Well, whose truck is this?"

Same response. No one knew anything.

"Okay. Who killed this deer?"

"I dunno."

"I guess I better go talk to Miss Susan about this," he said and turned away.

"Ah—" "Maybe—" "Wait—" "Do you have to—?" "No, don't."

Everyone stammered some plea for him to stay away from me. They knew I was a stickler about poaching.

One stepped forward. "I killed it. It's our camp meat. We're cooking stew for supper."

"Let me see your tags."

The hunter pulled out his license and handed over his tags. The ranger tore off one, did his paper work, and handed the ticket to the hunter. "You can pay the fine down at the sheriff's office. Since the deer wasn't tagged, I have to impound the meat."

"But it's in the stew. It's cooking."

Just what I've been looking for. Bet they'll never be trouble again.

"Sorry guys. It wasn't tagged and I have to impound it. You'll have to take it out of the stew. You can dump the tools out of the bucket in my truck bed and dump the meat into it."

This chapter was originally written as an entry in a literary class, about real events. It contains three actual events, but they did not occur on the same day or to the same ranger. I have collected them here for the convenience only, and the ranger's thoughts are my imagination. The story of the untagged deer happened on my land. The fellows hunting over apples were on a neighbor's property. The walker was near my family land.

BAMBI SENTENCED

I wrote this letter to the editor after I visited a local veterinarian who also rescued wild animals. Several fawns had been brought to her that spring.

Atlanta Journal
June 8, 1978

The Editors:

Bambi got a life sentence in prison last week. Some "do-gooder" found a baby buck and since Mama Doe was not there beside him, decided that little Bambi was abandoned and needed people parents and a lifetime in a pen to survive.

That little buck is being bottle-fed by people, but, born in the wild, he will spend his life looking through fences, unable to ever frolic across a meadow or nibble the leaves of honeysuckle or newly fallen acorns; he will never run from a hunter, true—but don't most of us prefer the day-to-day dangers of life to the relative safety of a state-supported institution where we would have to make no decisions, where food would be placed before us and we would be told what to do?

Little Bambi will spend his life eating the donations of some people—maybe salted peanuts or lettuce—whatever he is lucky enough to be fed.

Not for him space, wilderness or freedom.

A Mama Doe does not abandon her young; the day I saw the jailed Bambi, I saw another youngster, still wobbling as he tried to walk; Mama was nearby, darting from brush to brush, hiding. But the baby snuggled belly down in the grass and waited for us to leave because he is camouflaged to blend with the background and even trained hounds cannot scent him.

Fawns, apparently abandoned, are left by the mothers who must eat; but Mama Doe returns to feed her baby. Cattle do the same—hide the calf and return to feed it. Are birds in a nest abandoned because Mama Bird is not perched over the nest?

Please ask your readers not to sentence a newborn fawn to a life in prison.

Susan Lindsley
Decatur

THE FLAT TIRE

Blam-blump. The back of the car yelled at me in the darkness. I stopped, got out, and discovered I didn't have just a flat. I had only a few pieces of tire left hanging onto the rim.

The night was quiet at 9:30. The moon, nearing full, hung in the pines. Down near Ida Mae's spring, a whip-poor-will shattered the silence once. I tried my CB radio, but no one in the crowd had his ears on, so I put it down and considered my options. Bill, my mechanic, had been the last to put on the tire, and I knew his machine had the bolts too tight for me to juke them loose with my four-prong lug wrench. It'd take a fella to handle it.

I was only a few yards from a hunters' campsite, so I strapped on my pistol, shoved my wallet into my back pocket and dug the flashlight out of the glove compartment. I started off along the road to Campbell's Camp Gate.

Something crashed around in the woods, and my heart hit my feet, my hand reached for the pistol, and then the deer blew its nose at me and ran. I exhaled and tried to get my heart to stop galloping around and settle back in place.

The thumping finally softened and silence fell again, except for the whip-poor-will whose calls became continuous. Must be desperate for company, I thought in sympathy. I didn't like being out here after dark and alone.

I reached Campbell's gate and found it open. So somebody had to be at camp, and whoever it was would come up the hill and change the tire. Hated to admit to him that I couldn't manage it. How many times over the years had I changed a tire? But never after a machine had tightened the bolts.

I started down the hill through the shadows and splashes of moonlight that shifted as the breeze moved the pines. I whooped. Only the whip-poor-will answered. So close that his call almost hurt my ears.

Behind me, a car moved along the highway, but didn't slow down as it passed my wagon. I had more than 100,000 miles on that Buick and never had a problem with it. I'd hauled everything from dead deer (laid out on a plastic sheet) to a pick-up truck-load of concrete block. It had a hidey-hole under the floorboard in the back, where I often stored my hunting firearms with no one the wiser. But not tonight, midsummer, and no game in season.

I hollered again. And again. Only darkness. My voice echoed from the hollow and the bird's melancholy call answered.

Light showed down the trail. Someone was there. Maybe. I walked closer, reached the first cabin, and shined my flashlight around the meadow. The light was a lantern in the screened porch of the main cabin. No vehicle. No help.

Alone in the woods, I heard every twig that cracked in the faint breeze. Every mouse that scurried through the leaves sounded like an intruder slipping around me. I stopped at every sound. Oops. Was it a snake? I closed my eyes and concentrated—the sound slithered, there was no footfall. It was a snake. Where? I shined the flashlight around and caught a glimpse of it coming onto the Jeep trail. Only a black chicken snake, but I gave it the right of way.

I thought I'd never get back to the highway and was relieved when the pavement gleamed near-white in the moonlight. Anything would be better than sitting here doing nothing, and I began the walk to the house, where my hunters, who had come down for the weekend's work, probably wondered where I was. I'd told them I'd be late, but hadn't said how late. Now it was after 10:00 p.m. I hoped they hadn't sacked out for the night.

I stretched out my stride, stayed on the left-hand shoulder, and stepped off into the ditch whenever a car approached. Nobody even slowed down to see if I was in distress—and thankfully, not to kidnap me either.

When I reached the shortcut through the pasture, I debated—walk on down the road another 200 yards and then back the same distance on the side road, or cut through the woods here? This shortcut was the roadbed before the county paved the two roads and made a smoother bend than the 90-degree turn, so it was the short side of a triangle.

I decided on the shortcut.

As I walked it I remembered the night I sat stakeout there, with the ranger down the road a-piece, both of us listening for poachers that didn't show up until after we'd left. No coyotes tonight. Since it was summer, there'd be no steel leg-hold traps here either.

A car cranked up at the gate in front of me. Headlights glared into my eyes. The vehicle roared backwards onto the road, turned south and tore up the highway. Musta seen my flashlight.

The car set off a coyote nearby. Its yelps sent a chill running down my back. I pulled out the pistol.

At the gate, I discovered evidence of the courting couple I'd scared off. At least they weren't poachers. The boy who'd had a patch of marijuana in my woods was off in jail, so I was grateful it wasn't somebody else trying to farm the stuff on my land.

I holstered the pistol as I stepped onto the paved road.

I had gone less than a hundred yards down the road when a truck came along, passed me a few feet, backed up, and a familiar voice said, "What you doing out here walking around in the dark?"

"I need help. I've got a flat tire. And you got muscle. How about some help?"

Rangers are out and about all year long.

The night was no longer spooky.

WHEN TURKEYS CAME TO MY COUNTY

Merle Campbell, an avid deer and turkey hunter, held a hunting lease on my family's land for many years. We had no wild turkeys in Baldwin County until Merle brought thirteen pen-raised wild birds to his leased property and began stocking the county.

I photographed the turkeys flying from the men's hands, but I gave all the photos to Merle. Just imagine, thirteen men, each holding a turkey by gripping it around the body and wings. They all bend down and open their hands—and birds flee, some into the air and some along the ground. In seconds, all are gone. As Merle said, you can have your shotgun on your shoulder ready to fire, but before you can turn 30-degrees, the bird is out of range.

Although the birds were pen-raised they were at least partially wild. Some survived, but within a week a neighbor had killed one to eat. Game and Fish Division, Department of Natural Resources, followed up and also released trapped wild birds on my family's land. Here they would be protected and would find acorns, persimmons and numerous food plots to satisfy their appetites. Chufas and clover were already growing in anticipation of the birds' arrival and to keep them from wandering.

Chufas are a tuber, and like peanuts grow underground, but they have no shell. The word is Spanish and means *ground almond* (not ground up but in the ground). It is a nutsedge plant. I tasted a few seeds and wasn't surprised that the birds liked them. I did, and had to stop myself from nibbling instead of broadcasting them when we planted.

The state's second wild flock also came to my family's land. Another wild flock went to a ranger's farmland, again because there they would be protected. His lands are bordered by timber company property leased to hunters who had established a reputation for protecting wildlife. Game and Fish released another batch on the farmlands of John West, a strong wildlife protector. He was not only a farmer but he also supervised the Georgia Power program for food plots beneath transmission lines.

I was excited to have the birds around and longed to see them in the open. Wild turkeys don't wander around in the open, I soon learned. But they did love crimson clover. One patch not much bigger than a large den stayed spotted with droppings all summer long.

I learned that the tom's dropping has a tail and the hen's dropping is sort of a blob. I learned that the tom gobbles for the hen to come to him, and that when I started hunting, I would see how the gobbler hesitated about coming to a call.

On wet ground in the spring, I learned to read the signs of a strutting gobbler, the scratches his wings left as he lunged forward, the double tracks he left when he turned in place.

It was like learning deer signs, habits, habitats and courting behaviors.

I bought mouth calls and practiced, although I knew a season was far into the future. Didn't take me long to give up on the mouth calls. Didn't matter how much I bent them to fit my mouth, they didn't fit. They gagged me. So I resorted to buying a cedar box and learned how to chalk it and to scrape the lid over the edge of the box to *yelp* and *purr*. Just in case the box didn't work for me, Merle suggested I also invest in a slate call.

I figured surely by the time we had a season, I'd be ready.

A flock took up roosting near a food plot and water hole, and when I discovered them, I'd go out in the evening and watch them fly up. What fun to hear the wings flap and the birds call back and forth. I was sure I knew what they said to each other.

I'm up here. Where are you? Limb sways.

Over here, this tree is better. Wings flapping and limbs swaying.

I'm going to a higher limb. Flap, flap. Higher.

Did you see that human down there? We better get to another tree. Lots of flapping as they fly to a more distant tree.

When the first season opened, I didn't do anything right. The next year, I invited Dave Waller, at that time Assistant Chief of Game Management in Game and Fish, to come down from the towers of Atlanta to turkey hunt. Before light, I turned him loose on land he'd never seen before.

He made his own luck and bagged a fine gobbler, the first one to come off the land I hunted.

Dave Waller and his bird.

I was a long time getting my first turkey, and it took an expert to help me.

MY FIRST TURKEY

At fifty, I'd gotten so deer hunting was about as exciting as shooting cows in the pasture. For more than twenty years, I'd studied deer in hunting magazines and in veterinarian research journals, in books, and in the field.

But turkeys were new, recently released on my family's lands. Would they restore the excitement I'd felt with my first deer? Perhaps, but I'd spent a couple of summers with a telephoto lens (600 mm), and gotten some interesting photographs.

Rachel Campbell assured me that seeing a gobbler strutting in to a call would be by far more exciting than watching a flock of birds stroll by. Calling in a tom was surely the most heart-beating experience of all.

Could I call in a tom, however? Had my hours of practice with a cedar box and two types of slates been enough? By the first season I hoped my *yonks* or *yelps* or *purrs* would sound enticing to a tom.

So off I went, armed with an ancient, long-barreled 12-gauge and 3-inch shot, a couple of turkey calls, and almost no knowledge, to try to collect a turkey on opening weekend of the first season in my home county.

Two toms gobbled around me for an hour, and all I managed to do was run them off without ever seeing them. By the end of the season, I was discouraged.

When Dave Waller collected a long-bearded tom he got my interest up again, so by year three, I was anxious and eager for a turkey.

Rachel's husband Merle volunteered to guide me—on my own land, no less, where I had run barefoot as a child, where I rode horses as a teenager, and where for twenty years I had hunted deer as an adult. Merle had been on the land twice, but he would guide me to a turkey. That is, find the right place, and call the bird to me.

A good half-hour before he drove into the yard, I was ready, dressed in camouflage, soaked with tick spray, 12-gauge loads in my pocket and Old Reliable in my hands. As I walked out to his Bronco, I knew I'd have my first turkey in the next two hours. There was not a shadow of doubt in my mind, for although he did not know the land, Merle surely knew turkeys.

I'd already bragged to my friends that he was taking me out, and I'd get myself a wild tom for fall feasting.

The day was cool—down to 45° although it was already after Easter. I'd layered my clothes as if I were going deer hunting in spite of the conflicting stories I'd been told: *You can't move* and *You have to walk and hurry a lot.*

At least, if we did have to walk a lot, I could remove a layer or two. If we didn't move, I'd be glad for that Roebuck vest snug against my back.

We parked just inside the pasture gate, loaded up, and walked swiftly to the ridge top. Merle was fifteen years my senior, but he stepped out, and I had to lengthen my stride to keep pace.

We passed the house where buzzards nested underneath the floor and deer knee-walked under the old kitchen to eat the salt-laden dirt. Behind it, under the white oak at the edge of the ten-acre hay field, Merle hooted what he called a sick-owl call. Not a gobbler answered. Dawn brightened the east, gave shape to bushes and threw color to patterns on the ground. We waited five minutes and he hooted again. And another five minutes for another hoot.

Still no answer. We decided to just pick a spot along Persimmon Ridge, where I'd seen some scratching and droppings a few days before. Not a short walk, but we hurried. I had to really push to keep up. Daylight was upon us. As a deer hunter, I would have been settled in somewhere long before daylight.

Swoosh. A deer blew at us once, again, and again and bounced off into the hollow.

As we walked the ridge, I pointed to a tree I'd leaned against a couple of days before. He perched where I'd kicked straw and leaves around, but after he checked the view he shook his head.

Another twenty yards down the trail, he found the right spot, a large pine with honeysuckle growing up a nearby bush to provide cover on one side but far enough away that it wouldn't block the swing of my shotgun.

He quickly kicked out a seat at the base of the tree, about thirty inches square and three-to-four inches deep, down below the mound of mulch built up a the base of the pine. The tree itself was large enough to block his shoulders.

Merle backed into the tree, his legs spread out flat against the ground, and he quickly mounded a pad of pine straw between his knees. "Can you sit here?" he asked.

"Sure," I said, not sure at all. No back rest? How was I to put my legs out flat when I could barely sit that way with a back rest?

I perched, pulled my knees up, dug my feet into the straw and leaned forward, elbows on my knees. Realizing I had no control over my shotgun in that position, I shifted until my right hand rested on my knee and held the front stock of the .12 gauge. I wrapped my left hand around the trigger guard.

Merle leaned around and threw straw over my feet, questioned my bent knees but accepted my whispered response that I couldn't straighten them out.

"We'll wait a few minutes and just listen," he said.

Small voices filled the woods as birds greeted the dawn, and from downtown a siren wailed. An 18-wheeler on the highway blared as it hurried to town.

No gobbler. We waited.

"Hear the cardinal? When a cardinal sings you can be sure the turkeys have left the roost. Be still," he said, and began to talk turkey.

He *yelped* and *clucked* a few times, but all I thought about was the violent cramp in my back. Starting at my spine, just below my shoulder blades, the cramp ran across my back to the middle of my right side.

Maybe if I can relax instead of sitting so tense, it'll relax too, I thought. But how? To relax, I had to move.

With that pair of woods-penetrating eyes only three feet behind me, I felt my every thought had to be visible. Surely he knew—*I want to move.*

Something made a noise to the left. I did not look. Time stood suspended in one big mass of back cramp and spasmodic calls of a love-sick turkey hen behind me.

Only silence answered.

"It's late in the season," he whispered to me. "Sometimes they'll come in without gobbling, especially this late."

Nothing to give me an excuse to *move.* After *eons*, he whispered again, "We should have had a response by now. One should be here or have gobbled by now, or he's not in hearing distance."

His words were slurred, and I realized he was talking around his mouth call. But his words did give me an excuse to ask, "Should we move?"

"No. Don't move. We'll give it a bit longer."

The sun winked across the pine straw in front of us. And two big black shapes moved in the logging road off to my left.

I had not moved since the beginning of eternity, and now I knew I'd never be able to move again. Merle would have to shoot the turkey.

He was silent behind me. Didn't he see them? I cut my eyes down quickly to the shotgun and then back to the turkeys.

The one on the left, in back, was a tom. A red waddle, a beard, yelled *gobbler* at me. The other wore a blue bonnet that politely spoke *hen*.

At least I don't have to worry about shooting a hen for a gobbler.

"Merle, here they come, and I can't move." I whispered. "Shoot him."

Only silence behind me.

The turkeys continued to move slowly toward us, pecking at something in the road.

Then he whispered, "Here they come."

Two heads went up, and both birds shuffled around, talking softly to each other, asking one another, *Do you see that funny thing by the tree?* And getting a response something like, *Yes. That's what mama told us about. That's a boogey man.* And perhaps saying, *Should we run off?*

No. Let's go over and see what it is.

One moved toward my right, stepping high and fast. Merle, with the authority of God, spoke. "Don't move."

I didn't move. How could I? My whole body was frozen into one massive muscle cramp.

The tom stopped for a few seconds and then moved forward again; the sun filtered through the leaves enough to dapple his feathers from black to gold, bronze, purples, reds and greens.

"When his head goes behind that tree, pull up your shotgun."

The head vanished, and somehow I managed to pull the stock to my cheek. Left-handed, I leaned slightly to the left, snugged my cheek tight against the stock, propped my right hand on my knee, and waited.

The tom peeked around a tree. "Shoot," came the order from behind me.

I didn't. I barely saw his beak and one eye, certainly not enough to shoot. Not even enough to get a bead on.

Turkey didn't move, and neither did I. But perhaps I leaned to my right, perhaps he poked his head forward. The bead settled on his neck, and I squeezed down on the trigger.

That extra-long ancient shotgun with the squeezed-down barrel blasted the morning. And me.

My face felt as if I'd gotten the wrong end of a baseball bat. Only starry blackness was visible. But I *did not move*.

"Hurry. Go put your foot on his head so he can't run off. Hurry."

Hurry I tried, but my joints were stiff and my head reeling. It took me at least five seconds from pulling the trigger to reach that bird and stomp my boot down on his neck.

Merle was beside me, laughing. "Relax. He's not going anywhere. He's cemetery dead. You've got your first turkey."

I managed to bag another bird once in a while, but I stumbled all over myself trying.

dEAr HUNTERS

No, that's not a misspelling or a messed-up title.

It all started when I pulled up to the gate to go hunting one morning, and the gate wasn't there. I never opened it. I always crawled through the wires to walk to my stand, to keep the smell of exhaust away from the field I hunted. But now a regular road had been etched by constant vehicle traffic.

Somebody had to be spotlighting deer while I was up in Atlanta during the week. I stepped out of the station wagon, took my Remington 30.06 from the back seat, loaded it, cranked a shot into the chamber, ensured that the safety was on and propped it against the passenger seat.

I drove down a smashed-grass roadway the culprits had created—in places they had worn the trail down to the dirt. Last Monday's rain had puddled in places that now showed ruts. We never, but never, rutted these fields. Tracks showed frequent traffic to the apple tree meadow where a multi-trunked sweetgum held my favorite deer stand.

I gritted my teeth at the thought that poachers were spotlighting deer on my land that far from the road. The neighbors would not have considered the night-time shots to be coming from here.

As my headlights poured into the darkness of the first opening, deer rose from their beds and flashed white tails at me, as if to say, "Bye-bye, I'm gone."

So, nobody in here now. At least they hadn't run everything off and hadn't killed them all.

I swung into a U-turn and headed back to the gate. I pulled it to and wired it shut. I'd go to my stand up on the hill this morning and set a trap for the poachers tonight. We would not even turn on the lights in the front rooms of the house, so no one would think we were down this weekend.

I came in early from my hunt, and as the others returned (like me, without a deer), I told them what I'd found. When everyone was home and breakfast of pancakes, bacon and scrambled eggs was on the table, we planned on how to catch the spotlighters.

Norman and I would hide in the underbrush inside the open gate and wait for them to come in. We'd let them go by and then call on the CB for backup from the house when they passed us. Lois would stay at the house by the radio until we called and would then telephone the ranger and drive the truck down to block the gate. We'd have them trapped.

Rain came by noon, and we wondered if we'd be able to stake out the gate, but it stopped a little after 5:00 p.m. and sundown would come at 5:30 p.m.

As soon as the rain ended, Lois dropped me and Norman off, and we set up folding chairs about twenty feet inside the gate, behind brush. We waited. And waited. We never were at a loss for topics—so many deer tales, our own and others we'd read about, Norman's time in Vietnam that had left him hobbling but had not slowed him down.

When he wanted to light a cigarette, I had to fuss at him. The poachers would smell it and know something was wrong, and besides, he'd smell like burning tobacco in the morning and no deer in its right mind would come near.

"Every deer I've killed I got when I was smoking," he said.

"Un-huh. That's 'cause you're always smoking."

"Here comes a rattle-trap truck."

It shook and banged its way south, down the hill and slowed as it neared us.

"That's them. Don't move," I said.

But it only slowed for the curve; probably that truck from up the road that rattled its way toward town many mornings when I was in my sweetgum stand. It picked up speed around the bend. Most locals slowed for the curve because deer crossed there—and it was a poacher's favorite spot to shoot.

The wind came up, driving into our faces, bringing the bite of Alaska and the Arctic with it. We'd left the house with the temperature in the upper 40s, and were not prepared for the chill factor's dropping below freezing.

We got cold.

"Let's get Lois to bring our jackets," I said.

"I'm about to freeze," he said. "Wish I had a cigarette."

"Well, you can't. They'd see it in the dark and smell it too, and not pull in."

I raised Lois on the CB and she said she'd be there in a couple of minutes. We heard the truck starter turn over in the quiet night and followed its sound as it approached around the curve. But from the other direction came headlights. Lois came around the bend, saw the headlights, and drove on up to the neighbor's to turn around.

The car came by, slowing as it approached the curve, and then it was gone. We watched Lois's headlights as she came down the hill from the Lowe's, slowed near the gate, and turned into the pasture. As she entered the gate, I stepped out of the bushes and around her headlights. I had the shotgun in my hand.

It wasn't Lois.

A young fellow was behind the wheel and a younger girl in the passenger seat.

Lois pulled in behind the car and blocked it.

Norman stepped out behind me.

"What're you doing here?" I asked.

They fidgeted, looked at each other, and the girl begin to cry.

"Give me your car keys," I said.

The boy shook his head. Careful not to point it anywhere near the car, I moved the .12 gauge up and held it parallel to my waist. "Give me your car keys. The law is on the way."

The youth pulled the keys from the ignition and held them to the window. I reached over and took them.

"Lois, call the ranger. If he's not home, call the sheriff."

She drove toward the house.

"Where's your rifle?" I asked. "Or your shotgun?"

"We're not night hunting," he said.

"Yeah? Then howcome you got a spotlight in the back seat?"

"I—I don't know. It's my daddy's car," the boy said. "I don't have any gun."

By then I realized they were a courting couple, but I felt no sympathy for them. "Okay, we'll just wait for the law," I said. "Let the officer decide what's going on."

Lois drove back, stepped out and said, "I couldn't reach the ranger, but the sheriff is sending out a State Patrolman."

The girl wailed as if someone were cutting off her arm. Her body shook with her sobs. The boy tried to comfort her, but she cringed away from him as if he had leprosy.

"Don't you ever touch me again," she said.

Sirens on the state highway drew closer and the girl seemed to wail louder. Snot ran from her nose and covered her hands. She didn't bother to try to wipe her face.

Red lights flashed against the trees as the patrolman came around the bend. He left them flashing when he got out of the car.

"What's going on, Miss Lindsley?"

"These folks have been going in my pasture off and on for a long time. I think they've been night hunting. They said they don't have a gun, but they've got a spotlight. And the gate chain has been cut."

He bent down to look in the driver's window. "Oh, my God," he whispered. "Nancy?"

He stood and turned to look at me. "The boy's the night hunter," he said. "Only he's hunting dear with an **a** and not a double **e**. Her father works with me. She's lucky he didn't get the call. If you don't mind, I'll handle this."

I almost snickered as I handed him the boy's keys.

"They're all yours," I said. "We'll fix the gate in the morning."

What's her daddy gonna do to the boy? He'll be lucky if all he gets is a traffic ticket every time he starts up his car.

* * *

Another night, I got a call from a neighbor some four miles up the road, beside land that belonged to my several-greats-grandpapa in the early 1800s. She reported that someone was shining deer on my place next to her. I called the ranger, who met me at that gate. It stood wide open and the locking-chain was cut.

I rode in with him. It took only a glance to spot the tire tracks and we followed them down that roadway to a food plot of clover, rye and wheat.

The tracks smashed down the plants and showed that someone had driven frequently across the meadow.

When our headlights reflected from the back of a sedan instead of a truck, the ranger told me to wait. He took a flashlight and walked up to the car, bent down, flashed the light inside and kept it in their faces while he talked through the window to the driver. I saw a male driver and a female passenger clearly in the beam of his light.

The courting couple left ahead of us, and the ranger couldn't help but laugh as we drove out.

"I know the guy," he said. "He pleaded with me not to tell his wife or her husband."

"You gonna tell on 'em?"

"No. It's their business. Mine is poachers."

* * *

That incident reminded me of the time back in the late 1960s when I came down from Atlanta and found another gate wide open, with fresh tracks going in. I had two passengers with me, so I didn't hesitate to drive in.

A polished sedan, parked in the middle of the driveway, reflected sunlight. The other vehicle, an older car, had been pulled nose first off the driveway, almost into some bushes. I parked so I blocked both vehicles.

When I stepped out of the car, Mr. Simpson asked, "What you gonna do?"

"I'm gonna find out what's going on as soon as I get my gun loaded," I said and walked to the trunk, popped it open, and pulled out my Ruger .44 magnum.

"We've leaving," a man called.

I looked up the trail. Two heads rose up from the bushes. Man and woman.

"Yes, you are leaving. You're leaving now and you are not coming back."

It took 'em a few minutes to get their clothes on. While they did so, I wrote down their tag numbers. The woman got in the shiny car.

That night my group went out to supper, to Sonny's restaurant. His brother Jimmy, the GBI agent, was at the bar. Sonny came over to wait on us personally, and I couldn't resist. I told him about the courting couple—he would be interested if for no other reason than he deer hunted there.

"Tell Jimmy," he said. "He'll be sure they don't come back."

So I did, and Jimmy took the note with the tag numbers and the note about which of them drove off in which car.

We'd just started eating when Jimmy came over to the table. His hands shook and his face had gone white.

"What's the matter?" I asked.

"The woman—I can't believe—she's my best friend's wife."

"Oh, no, Jimmy. Are you sure?"

"Well, both vehicles are registered to men. The husbands. I didn't know her car is in her husband's name."

"What does your friend's wife look like?" I asked.

"She's tall, redheaded. She—"

Mr. Simpson interrupted. "She wasn't redheaded. She was blond."

Relief spread over Jimmy's face. "Well, thank God! It was him, not his wife. That's good. That's okay."

With a smile, he headed back to the bar and called, "Hey, Sonny. It's okay! Buy you a Johnny Walker?"

TURKEY PICTURES

I was fortunate that the first wild turkeys released in my county were turned loose on my family land, where we had a variety of food plots. I added some feeders to keep the birds close and safe.

As the population grew, flocks came into the hay fields for grasshoppers. I put up two feeders, and when the feeders went off, the rattle of corn against the metal spinner pulled the flocks in for the treats. Oaks surrounded the fields and stood among the pines. Winter overplanting of the hayfields for silage also kept them close during the cold months.

In the 1980s I often saw a mottled brown-and-white hen. I figured a wild hen must have mated with a white domestic tom, and the mixed-color bird was their offspring. We saw her at sites more than two miles apart. If she raised any poults (young turkeys), they didn't bear her coloring. One of my regrets is that I never saw her when I had a camera handy.

In the early years, although they were truly wild, the birds were not as spooky as they became after the turkey hunting seasons opened. I was able to set up a Pop Top tent and use it as a photography blind.

I had four or five of these overlooking food plots for picture taking and later for hunting. The Pop Top, designed by Tony Chapman, was the first portable blind I found and used. I had to fight the wind to take the picture of the newer tent. Note the sunken-in area on the right. The bottom of the skirt has loops the user can push a stick through to hold the skirt in place when the breezes rise.

**Wayne and his bird with an original Pop Top on left.
On right is the newer one, with a different camouflage pattern.**

I needed a dolly to haul my 600-mm f 2.4 Nikon lens and camera to the tent where I sat away the mornings as birds worked their way across the food plots and strutted. Here are a few of those pictures.

He checked out the clicking camera.

Susan Lindsley

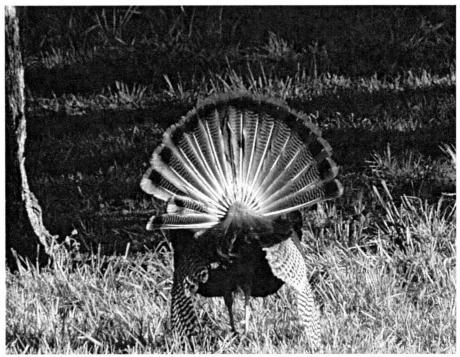

The view no hunter wants when he calls in the gobbler. As Wayne has said, "No shot there."

There is always one who discovers something amiss and moves on.

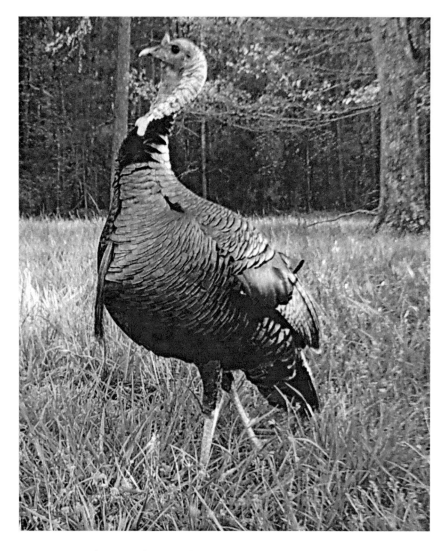

One morning, I witnessed the beginning of a mating and the fight between two toms for the hen. The big boys only threatened and ran around. After they finished their pretend fight, they both lost. The hen was long gone.

Susan Lindsley

Of my thousand or so turkey pictures, this is my favorite.

Today, in spite of the number of turkeys in our section of the county, I no longer see these large flocks passing through the fields. I don't hear them gobble from the nearby ridge in the early spring. It's as if there is a better food plot, a better feeder, a better crop of bugs elsewhere. Some of my neighbors enjoy seeing the wildlife and therefore provide a variety of food in their back yards, and the birds (and deer) may feel safer in these smaller patches, where the red-tail hawks can't easily turn poults into a meal and coyotes are less likely to visit. Or perhaps coyotes and raccoons have taken such a liking to fresh eggs that the reproduction has fallen off.

ACTION NEEDED, HUNTER BIDS

Union-Recorder
October 17, 1979

To the Editor:

Last winter, the *Recorder* printed several letters about hunting, trapping and the rights of dog owners, hunters and trappers. Now is the time for those who complained last year to begin to act.

Dogs do not recognize land lines; those persons who fox hunt or coon hunt should learn their hunting lands well enough to be able to call their dogs back when the dogs reach the land line. (Of course, this suggestion is based on the assumption that the hunter had released the dogs only on land he owns or has permission to hunt.) No dog owner can complain about harm befalling his dog if he lets it roam onto a neighbor's land, especially now that rabies has hit Baldwin County and dogs have been seen killing domestic animals.

On the other hand, those of us who are landowners should not lease conflicting hunting rights—that is, not rent deer hunting rights to one group and fox hunting rights to another. Each would conflict with the other.

Each hunter, trapper and landowner has an obligation to us all. If we saw someone crawling into a neighbor's window while the neighbor was on vacation, we would call law enforcement officers. We have the same obligation if we discover someone stealing game with illegal traps, with spotlights at night, with dogs if dogging is not legal, or by hunting without permission—since all game animals belong to the government.

Our understaffed Game and Fish Law Enforcement staff cannot stake out every illegal trap or every field the night hunters attack. But with our help, the wildlife rangers can continue to improve the quality of our game animals and our protected species.

I have made citizen's arrests; I've staked out fields where

night hunters often shoot; I prosecute poachers; I will remove any illegal traps I find on my land.

And if I find a hunting dog in my woods or in my yard, I'll call the owner (once) if his telephone number is on the dog's collar. But I'll also let the dog owner know that he is not to allow that dog on my land again.

I have encouraged each of my 150 or so hunters to follow suit, and they do.

In the United States, we are free to do most anything—we can swing our fist all we want to so long as we don't hit anyone else. The poacher steals from us all—from himself, his hungry neighbor, you and me.

Susan Lindsley
Milledgeville

A PERFECT ENDING

It was cold and wet that last day of deer season, with rain slashing down steadily as day tried to hold off darkness. Norman was ahead somewhere and to my right. I was trying to walk a very wide circle around him in hopes of pushing a deer to him. Of our hunt club, only Norman did not have a deer, and he was sitting alone this afternoon, swaddled in a poncho and probably trying to smoke away these last three hours of light.

The rain slacked up, but too late to help me. My boots squished with each step no matter how careful I tried to be. When I looked up at the heavy gray clouds, a cap-brimful of water dribbled cold down my back and soaked my clothes. I shivered.

I turned my gaze toward the woods on my left and spotted a jagged white line bordering a tail—a deer's hind end. *Good. It's between me and Norman and facing his general direction. Maybe, if it spooks, it might travel toward him.*

Waiting, I squinted into the rain and tried to outline the deer's gray body in the gray-brown pines. No good. I saw only a blend of winter color. The tail switched and showed white that instantly returned to gray again.

I took one step, totally silent in the pine straw except for the faint squish of water. The deer took a step. I took another, and met head on with a snort so close I jumped involuntarily and turned toward it.

A small doe eyeballed me, her ears forward, head up, and for a moment she looked like a stunted pine with limbs flaring on either side. She blew again, spun, and loped away, her white tail waving goodbye.

The other deer was gone when I looked back toward her. Not even a white tail in sight.

I sighed and sat down against a pine to wait a quarter-hour for the two deer to calm down and reunite. I hoped they would rejoin farther down the ridge, toward Norman. And maybe, just maybe, they'd go along to him.

The fifteen minutes crept by and my patience seemed to go faster.

I pushed myself up and took a few steps along the trail, then stopped. Was a touch of white anywhere in the grayness?

How can a deer, a reddish-brown body so unlike a pine tree, become totally invisible in a pine thicket? How can it blend into the colors of the pine trunks, wet or dry? How can the gray-bodied deer be invisible against the brown pine straw? Deer hunting sure isn't anything like what some people think. It sure isn't like a shooting gallery, with deer lined up to go to the freezer.

All summer long, however, no matter where we walked, deer seemed to wait for us to see them before they'd boogie off.

Norman, more than anyone in the group, should have filled his tags before now. But in one morning, two bucks in easy range were off to his right side. Wrong side for him to shoot, however. Perched in one of the small swinging stands, he couldn't turn around enough to fire from his right shoulder. He just sat and watched.

This morning, his hunting buddy Larry, about 400 yards across the field behind Norman, shot just as Norman raised his rifle to collect a big doe coming up the trail to his left. A perfect shot for him.

But Larry whooped and rattled his gear as he scampered down from his tree stand.

Norman's doe fled the terrors of the morning.

Now, Norman was in the rain and Larry was at the house, feet up before the fire, watching a football game while his doe chilled in the cooler.

Something moved. A flash of white. I waited. It had to be a deer. But the white disappeared and left only the late afternoon gray winter rain.

I circled a thicket, taking a good five minutes to move the ten feet. Down into the hollow a tail switched.

If I backed up and scurried out of their sight, I might head them off before they reached the land line and maybe push them back toward Norman. I backed up two steps, turned around, reached a hand from under my poncho and pulled my face mask up to cover the glare of my face. I might have already spooked them with my naked face shining in the evening light, but I hoped not.

I stood for a moment, running the lay of the land through my mind. They'd probably cross the land line on the other side of the next ridge, down at the break in the fence where the wet-weather creek spread out for twenty yards as it worked its way around and over and under the roots. I mentally pictured them topping this first ridge, meandering along the Jeep trail to the path that angled down to the creek. I'd have to move fast to get ahead of them.

I strode along the edge of the field until I thought I was well beyond the deer. I crab-stepped downhill without a path, crossed the small gully that now gurgled with runoff, circled the fallen pine top, entered the swampy growth in the hollow, and crossed it.

The ridge bottomed out just ahead of me, where the land flattened on the O'Connor's place (known as Andalusia). I slipped over to view the area where I thought the deer might cross the fence.

Too late. I'd first seen them almost an hour ago, and now they were just to my left about to cross my path, and close enough for me to hit the fawn with a rock. It stopped, scratched its ear with its hind toe, and scampered around as if it were out for afternoon recess. Mama looked at him and turned her head to look back to the other ridge as if she waited for me to show up. Her jaws worked as she watched, so I knew she had not walked steady but had fed some along the way. She stepped back uphill a few feet, snagging a leaf here, a twig there, a mushroom yonder.

All their forward progress gave way to browsing; mine, to trying to remain unseen.

If they passed me, they'd reach the edge of our land, but they had managed to turn completely around as they searched for tidbits. I sidestepped to get behind some brush while they had their rear ends toward me. The frisky fawn stuck its head under Mama for a drink, fortunately on the off side, so I stepped even farther back.

The wind gusted and swirled, picking up my scent and theirs, so we smelled each other. But with the wind turning on itself, the doe was not sure where I was. She may have remembered my being on the other ridge, and perhaps thought my smell came from that direction. I needed to hustle to get around them. They angled out of sight into a thicket of shoulder-high pine saplings. They couldn't see me, but I couldn't see them either, and had no idea if they were still feeding or moving along in the same direction again.

I cut straight away to the bottom of the ridge and the fence line.

Three deer burst from the thicket into the tall pines and plunged downhill, away from Norman.

Nothing I could do. Only stand and watch as they disappeared into the gathering dimness of twilight. The last white tail disappeared into the silence of my neighbor's land.

Someone shot, the double *ka-boom* of a 30.06.

Where? Across the fence I was facing? With the hood of the poncho over my capped head, I had no idea where the shot came from. All I knew at the moment was the gathering darkness and the almost mile walk to the Jeep.

I struck out. Larry had dropped me off hours ago, and I planned to catch a ride home with Norman. I needed to be at the Jeep when he reached it, but at least he was almost as far away as I was. I hurried.

In another half-hour, the season would end. And for the first time in more years than I could remember, one of my group would end the season without a deer. Our Cherokee descendant always showed so much excitement when he scored, always petted the deer and thanked it for its sacrifice, that I wished it were me and not him who had no deer this season. He wouldn't pout, but he'd be ever so disappointed.

As I neared the old abandoned tenant house, the Jeep cranked. Norman had beat me there. Yelling, I ran the few yards across the field.

He didn't hear me, but as he turned the Jeep, he faced me. He cut the engine, leaped out, ran to meet me, his face erupting into a smile, the rain dragging his blond curls into his eyes.

"I got one," he shouted.

I whooped, and together we acted like a pitcher and his catcher who'd won the final game of the World Series, hugging each other and jumping up and down and yelling and ignoring the suddenly heavier rain.

Norman was too excited to make sense as he stammered out his afternoon, about getting lonesome in the woods without knowing if another hunter were somewhere out there too, about coming back to the Jeep and not finding my car, so deciding that I was not out with him.

He figured it was so late he might as well go back to the house and dry out. As he had walked up to the edge of Dave's Field three deer had run into it. Almost across, almost in his lap, he said, they stopped, turned broadside to him, and looked over their shoulders.

He had a perfect shot at the deer of his choice. He took the largest one, and we ended a perfect season.

MEMORABLE ENCOUNTERS

July 30, 1986. Drove up to the neighbor's to count deer: Twenty-four in Mrs. Lowe's yard, and fourteen in my pasture. Need to talk to Joe Kurz about more doe days.

* * *

From my kitchen window early one morning—a first, and only: A doe came toward the feeder, with a buck a few steps behind. She paused, a sharp silhouette against the pines and rising mist. He poked his nose to her rump, rose, mounted her, thrust once, and the mating was over. They both ambled over to the feeder. I had no camera handy.

* * *

Dusk, late September in 1998, when the bucks had shed velvet, dropped testicles, and gone into full rut. Who'd-a thought we have gay bucks, but we do.

As twilight approached, I sneaked up to the edge of a clover patch already deep green from fertilizer. I leaned against a pine and peeked through the honeysuckle vines that crawled around the adjacent bush and on up the tree.

I waited. This food plot seemed to be a favorite for deer over the years—on a ridge top with wetlands on either side. A light breeze drifted from the meadow, so I hoped to see something.

I didn't have a long wait. A nine-point buck ambled into the field from the Jeep trail across from me, about thirty yards away. I was downwind.

If only it were firearms season, I'd have my trophy.

A spike strolled into the meadow from the far eastern end, lifted his head, and trotted toward the trophy. The large buck paid him no mind.

But the spike certainly noticed the larger fella. Head high, ears forward he almost pranced his way to the larger buck. The spike approached from behind the larger buck, mounted, and thrust.

The big guy stepped forward from under the spike, turned and swung his head at the smaller buck.

They splayed their front legs as if to fight, but stood still for a long moment as if each were trying to stare down the other.

The big guy went back to feeding on the clover, and so did the spike.

When darkness began to thicken, I left them to their supper and began planning to return in October.

* * *

One October a couple of days after deer season opened, I spotted an eight-point buck as he went into a thicket but did not go through. *Ah-ha, I'll sneak up on him.*

I tried, but he was off before I got into range. His gait didn't look right.

Off and on, I'd see him when I'd be out and about, on farm business or hunting, but never so that I had a clean shot to put him in the freezer.

He made it though the season, but became a resident of my yard. I had a small pool and a feeder in the yard, and plenty of bushy cover. Ole Crip, as I named him, came to depend on my charity—he had taken a load of buckshot on opening weekend. His left antler had a visible hole where one pellet had gone through it. Some pellets had messed up his hind leg just above the knee. The leg injury was a long time healing, and even the next fall the scars remained vivid. From the spread of the pellets (left haunch and left antler), I figured he had been shot from behind.

**The scarring on his left haunch is still visible two months later.
His left antler broke shortly after I took this picture.**

His holey antler broke off at the damaged spot before he shed them, but I never found either the broken tip or the sheds. He did return to my yard the next year. Easy to recognize from the scar on his leg. And his antlers were unbalanced—one side a full four points and heavy beam; the other, a spike. I did not see him after that season was underway.

ON HUNTING DEER OVER BAIT

In 1980, some folks pushed to make it legal to hunt deer over bait. Real hunters wouldn't have any truck with such, but the lazy ones would. The same lazy ones who were willing to ride the roads at night, I figured.

Hunting is not a guarantee, but a challenge, a contest between the hunter and his supper. The supper often wins.

When the prey is feasting on bait, he has little if any chance to evade the predator. I have a corn feeder in sight of my kitchen window and front porch, and from either location I can sit and watch deer, wild turkeys, coyotes, raccoons and other animals come to feed. Some in turn watch me rock on my porch.

All animals in these pictures were baited into camera range. None fled at the sound of the camera shutter.

When a law was proposed to allow deer hunting over bait, I wrote strong letters to state officials and legislators and somehow managed to summon enough courage to speak at a public hearing. A small public hearing. (See my notes in Appendix I.)

Game management personnel of Game and Fish were able to get the proposal squashed before it became law. I also fired letters off to the governor to ask him to veto such a law. Some years later, however, it became legal to hunt over bait in the southern half of Georgia, and attempts are underway now to legalize baiting in the rest of Georgia.

With the camouflage patterns, the scents, the variety of stands and the food plots available, there is no reason to allow such.

Hope that never happens. There is a certain, unexplainable thrill in learning deer behaviors, their food sources, and the woods. The activity is called *hunting*, not *shooting*.

TEENAGE POACHERS

His daddy didn't know what the boy was up to. The sixteen-year-old son asked if he might drive the truck to go visit his cousin.

Daddy handed him the keys. The son left in the truck.

But he didn't go see the cousin. Instead he picked up a high school buddy and they set out on the backroads to see what they could see. Hanging on the gun rack behind them was his daddy's .12 gauge shotgun.

It was soon in the passenger's hands.

Unfortunately for them, they came along the road by my place just as a deer stepped onto the shoulder. The buddy poked the barrel of that .12 gauge out the window and shot.

Good way to go deaf.

I was home and heard it. How could I not? They were only a few yards from the entrance to my yard, and the sound rattled the windows. Barefooted and without a coat, I grabbed my own shotgun, ran out the door as I pulled my car keys from my pocket. Before the boys even thought about fleeing the scene, I drove onto the paved road.

They skedaddled. But too late. I wrote down the tag number and let 'em go. Then I went back to the house, called the ranger and gave him the tag number. While I waited to hear from him I put on my shoes and gathered up my house keys, wallet and coat.

He traced the tag and was at the truck owner's home before the boy had dropped off his friend and arrived home.

At the ranger's call, I went to the local jail, where he had the father and the son, as well as the son's buddy. When I entered the waiting room, an older black man was the only occupant. I nodded to him and asked him how he was. His hands trembled.

"I dunno what I'm gonna do," he said. "My boy's cost me my truck. He went out and shot at a deer and it's costing me my truck and my coon-hunting shotgun. I can't work without my truck. I jest don't know what I kin do."

Oh, my. What am I gonna do?

The ranger walked into the waiting room from somewhere in the back, nodded toward me and signaled I should follow him.

Once alone in a deputy's office, he repeated what the older man had said.

"What do you want me to do?" he asked. "I picked up the other boy on the way here, and I think they're both scared to death. I hate to take the old man's truck. I know the family, and there's no way he can afford the costs."

This was a ranger with the reputation of being willing to arrest his own mother or brother if either should violate the game laws. And he wanted to go easy on the two boys? But not for their sake, for the father's.

"You seem to think they've learned better."

He nodded. "I don't think it'll make any difference if we fine them. The father would be the one to suffer. It's a hard choice, I know."

But I had no choice. I could not ask the ranger to punish a working man for something his son did without his knowledge or permission. I had to let them go because of the father.

Besides, this was not the first time I had to decide the fate of teenage boys who decided to go deer hunting. Another ranger handled that pair of youngsters.

A car parked along the road told me I had a poacher or two, and I parked kinda crossways in front to block it. If they reversed, they'd back into the ditch. Norman was with me, and we walked up onto the railroad. The woods were noisy, too noisy for the slight breeze. Too noisy for a deer or even a pair of squirrels to be chasing around.

There came two boys. In white tennis shoes, blue jeans and white tee shirts, shuffling along in the dry leaves like children kicking their way to make as much noise as possible. Obviously they knew nothing about deer hunting, but when I asked them what they were doing, one said, "Deer hunting."

Well, I had never seen a deer hunter decked out like these two, nor I had seen one carrying a .22 rifle.

"Le'me see that rifle," I said. "I've not seen one like it before."

The boy looked over at Norman, shrugged, unaware of my usual method of disarming the culprits, and he just handed me his rifle. I immediately jacked out the bullets and told them to sit down and wait, I was sending for the game warden. I turned to Norman and asked him to go to the house and make the call; the ranger's number was by the phone.

Norman left, and I waited with the boys. He hadn't been back but minutes when Possum Cop Dennis arrived. I handed him the rifle and explained that I'd seen the boys walk up onto the railroad from my land. I waited in my car while he talked to the boys. A few minutes later, he asked, "What do you want me to do? They're just children."

"Yeah. And hunting without permission. They don't even know where they are, and certainly don't know anything about property rights or about deer hunting. Take them to jail."

"You sure?"

"Yeah. I want their daddy to have to come to jail to pick them up. I want their parents to know what they've done. Take 'em on to jail. Scare the hell out of 'em, call their parents and make 'em sit there for an hour or so and then let 'em go."

So, remembering that event, I said, "Fair is fair. I let another two boys go a few years back, and those two didn't endanger their parents' livelihood. Keep 'em awhile. Scare 'em good. Can you make them think they're gonna have to spend the night in jail if they ever pull that kinda stunt again?"

He did. That youngster didn't get the truck keys again for a long time.

BLAZE ORANGE BECAME THE LAW
But I Called the Vests "Red"

The day was still crisp in spite of the brilliant sun since dawn. For early Georgia November, the day was ideal for hunting. But, I thought, the new law prohibited my ever slipping through the woods to look for a buck.

I headed to the platform stand in the pecan tree on Persimmon Ridge. Movement to my right caught my attention, and I froze, my leg in midair. I almost tumbled over and fought to keep my balance.

Shadows danced over the gray-brown forms; sunlight filtered through the trees enough to flash over antlers. Deer closer than twenty yards, and me with my .12 gauge unloaded. I could only stand and watch and grin at the buck's victory—his harem of three does and four fawns, a belly full of persimmons, and a helpless hunter. An old doe looked at me, blew, stomped a hoof. The others picked up their heads and looked around. And saw me. We looked at each other for a long minute.

"Bang, bang, you're dead," I whispered.

The mama doe snorted and bounded off four leaps. She stopped, turned, studied me again and walked toward safer territory in the hollow. The fellow simply shook his head, turned and trotted off behind her. The others decided I must be a threat and threw their tails up as they cantered away.

As the flashing white tails bobbed out of sight downhill, I looked down at myself, my blaze orange flashing in thc sunlight. A beacon warning all wildlife of danger. I complied with this new law only because I respected the rangers whose job it was to enforce it. I didn't want my friends to have to give me a ticket.

My hunters were not trigger-happy fools. Not one of them had shot carelessly in all our years of hunting together. Only I had erred that rainy morning when I shot at the buck in the bushes—my aim right where his chest was, only his chest was behind that of a doe. True, we'd had a few arrows stab trees, as had a couple of bullets, but why did we, a small private group on private land, have to wear red vests? Surely we would be considered exempt; but, no, our rangers said that law included anyone hunting deer anywhere in Georgia. So we complied.

I had hunted since the mid-1960s and learned to hide myself in brush on the ground or on a stool, my camouflage blending me in with whatever was around me. I didn't want to wear a beacon that announced, *Look deer! I'm here! See my red flag!*

But what surprised me that day was the flash of red aroused their curiosity and held them spellbound for long moments. If I'd been ready, I had plenty of time to put down that buck.

As the season passed, my group had more and more experience with the hypnotic effect of the orange vest. Norman's wildman's dance was perhaps the most unbelievable. Rain had poured for three days of doe season. Cold and wet, Norman left his stand and headed for his truck. Rather than crawl in to escape the rain, he passed it to take a last look into the next field.

Several deer fed in the edge, and when Norman slopped through the rain, they looked up at the apparition clad in olive green slicker and orange vest glued to it by the water. And went back to browsing.

He brought up his rifle, only to realize he had it under his slicker and vest to keep it dry. Down he crouched, uncovered the weapon, and stood up again. Two deer looked up and watched him as he tried to sight through the scope. It had sweated and fogged beyond use. Down he went again, to wipe the scope with his now soggy shirt tail. And up again. All five deer watched this bouncing man dance around in the storm. When he finally shot the closest one and dropped it in its tracks, the others only trotted off a few yards, still spellbound by the orange vest.

Even up a tree, my orange vest has attracted almost no attention. I was perched some twenty-five feet up an oak which a buck browsed almost on eye level with me. He fed along in the mixed pines and hardwoods and kinda drifted my way with each nibble. Then up came his head and he strode purposefully downhill, headed for the honeysuckle in the hollow. I watched, my shotgun still in my lap, and considered the steaks ambling by. I made no move, not my hands, my head or my feet; my eyeballs moved a little to follow his movement, but nothing else. Then he was almost directly below me—I could have killed him by dropping my gutting knife onto his backbone. Suddenly he jerked his head back to stare up at me. I stared back, but he didn't seem to be eyeballing me. Maybe it was that orange beacon that held him frozen to the ground. I spoke, finally. "Go along, fellow. I'll consider you when you're bigger and can fill up the entire freezer."

He only wobbled an ear, shook his head and ambled off, not concerned abut his future.

The orange vest only aroused curiosity. With our poaching problems, I've been glad to have it many times, especially that day I got shot at.

_____

This segment about the blaze-orange ("red") safety vests was originally written to submit to *Deerhunters United*, but the magazine went under before the article was published. It is given here because it relates to the next item, about the day I got shot at.

THE DAY I GOT SHOT AT

I know, don't end with a preposition. But I did get shot at, and there's no better way to say it.

The joker didn't know I was on the other side of the deer when he shot (or he didn't care), but he learned in a hurry.

Three of us had gone out that afternoon, and we parked on the ridge top. Lois and Norman dropped off downhill and I strode along the ridge road to the back line.

I slipped down the hill to the bottom, where I planned to *still-hunt* the afternoon away. And if I spooked a deer perhaps it'd mosey to Lois or Norman. And if it didn't spook, maybe I'd have a chance at it. I'd already filled one tag and didn't want to shoot a small buck—I'd be *macho* and wait for a big one for my second tag.

Not wanting to stand out like a wart on a nose, I eased into the thickets beside the soggy bottom. If I kept my boots out of the muck, I wouldn't *squish* when I picked up my feet. Take a step, stop, look, listen for any sound in the leaves on the hillside to my left. Each step meant *still* for anywhere from one minute to as long as ten minutes, so in an hour, I hadn't gone far.

The only sounds were a few songbirds and one squirrel that announced danger, much to my annoyance. Its barking and tail-flipping were bound to warn any deer in sight or hearing. And it did. A deer, not far behind the alarm-maker, rustled leaves and then went still. No sounds except the fluffy-tailed rat and a jay who joined him.

The explosion came from beyond the deer, and shotgun pellets hit the bushes in front of me.

I yelled and ran in that direction.

The culprit clattered down the wooden steps from the stand, his shotgun slamming on each step, his sounds drowning out my own noise.

I reached my hilltop stand, barely able to catch my breath, my legs burning from the hard run uphill. The stand was empty, of course, but I found a shotgun shell on the ground.

I clicked my CB radio on, called Lois, and she answered, "What'd you get?"

"Shot at. Meet me at the Jeep."

Norman also had his CB on and said he'd be there too.

I trotted until my legs and breath gave out. When I reached the Jeep, Lois and Norman waited for me. I sent Norman in his truck back to the house to call the ranger, and Lois and I went off in Nellybelle.

The shooter would exit the woods onto a short street in a residential area on the edge of town, and I didn't even bother with the gate as I pushed the old Jeep to its limit. I had to drive four miles after that long run, and the poacher had only a half-mile to get to his vehicle.

I desperately wanted to get to his car first.

Two cars, a half-block apart, sat on the embankment. No truck, so which car? I took the tag number of the first one and then drove up behind the other and wrote down its tag number. It was farther from houses, and I figured the driver of the other one might be visiting the house across the street. In about five minutes, a youngster walked out of the woods toward the car. I reached it before he did.

He did not have on a safety vest as required by law, but he did carry a .12 gauge shotgun, which matched the shell I had found.

I stood between him and the driver's door. "Hi, there," I said. "You have any luck?"

He shook his head and stepped sideways as if trying to figure out how to get by me. He didn't look even sixteen, the legal age to hunt without an adult.

"I hunt with a .12 gauge, too," I said. "What's yours?"

"It's a Winchester."

He kept looking around as if for help. His hands trembled and he nibbled at his lower lip. I was sure I had my culprit.

"May I see it?" I held out my hand.

He extended the firearm toward me and I took it. "Loaded?"

He nodded. I ejected the shells.

"Hate to tell you, young fella, but somebody just about shot me back in the woods there. We've called the ranger, and he's on his way."

The boy turned pale; his hands shook so hard he stuffed them into his pants pockets. "My daddy's gonna kill me."

A car stopped behind me and a voice said, "You need any help?"

A young man stuck his head out the window. Camouflage clothes lay heaped in the back seat.

"No. Thanks. The ranger's on his way. I just about got shot back in the woods there."

"Glad you're safe," he said and drove on.

The car looked familiar and I looked back. Yep, it was the other one. At least if this boy wasn't the shooter, I had the tag number. And that driver had been hunting.

The ranger arrived. I waited in the Jeep while he talked to the youngster and gave the boy a ticket. The boy drove off.

The ranger said, "Well, he's not the shooter. His shotgun hadn't been fired since it was last cleaned."

"Crud!" I handed him the paper with the tag numbers. "This one. He was parked about fifty yards back yonder. He stopped to find out what was going on. He had hunting gear in his car."

The next day, I got a report on the follow-up activities. The second boy was the son of a powerful local politician who refused to allow the ranger to even see his son's shotgun without a warrant. We didn't have the evidence to get a warrant—the evidence was the shotgun.

I do hope the boy learned a lesson about poaching. Education is more important in the long run than having the culprit fork over a little cash to the county, unless he learned that Politician Daddy can get him out of trouble, no matter what he does.

My letter to the editor about the incident came out a few days later and the *Union-Recorder* also ran a news article about the event. See Appendix II.

OTHER KINDS OF HUNTING ACCIDENTS

After this shooting event, I said there is no such thing as a hunting accident. Was I ever wrong! I managed to provide myself with two accidents without help from anybody else.

The most common accident among hunters is falling out of the tree stand. My buddy Norman fell twice while asleep, but was not injured because asleep he was totally relaxed.

If the stand fails, the hunter can be severely injured or killed. Portable climbing stands fail when the hunter does not tighten down the bolts that hold the parts together. I learned to take small hand tools with me to attach my climbing stand to the tree.

Failure to use a safety belt (or rope) can result in hunters hitting the ground. Some hunters, especially archery hunters, stand up on their elevated platforms and can lose their balance when they turn to hold their aim on a deer.

But standing on a four-square-foot platform, turning while you keep all your attention on a moving buck and suffering an attack of buck fever can lead to disaster.

One alternative to the climbing stand is a leaning ladder. It is not any safer unless the hunter uses a safety belt.

And the biggest mistake a hunter can make is to climb into his stand with a loaded firearm over his shoulder. Sure, the strap is not supposed to break. Sure, the shotgun or rifle is not supposed to fire if the safety is on. Sure, the hunter remembered to put the safety on. Sure, the hunter knows to keep the weapon pointed down, not up, when it is on his shoulder. *But* the strap can break, the rifle could be pointed up, and when the butt hits the ground and the rifle fires upward, the hunter takes the bullet. It has happened.

Fortunately, my hunting neighbors taught me how to safely climb into a tree stand and the necessity for a pull-up rope, with the firearm chamber empty and the clip in my pocket.

But my accidents were different.

I heard about a laser spotting scope for shotguns, and decided I just had to have one. It did not magnify. It just put a red dot on the spot the buckshot would hit. (Or the bird shot if the target were a tom turkey.)

I mounted it on my .12 gauge, and on opening day went to one of my favorite stands (where I got the picture of the buck Lois killed—see chapter on Quality Hunting).

I climbed the ladder to the stand before light, slid under the camouflage hood and tied myself into my rotating chair. I pulled up the long-barreled .12 gauge, shoved in two # 2 buckshot shells, pumped a shell into the chamber and added the third shell.

And waited.

Along came a set of antlers. Not a big buck, but young and tender. He had not been chasing does. He had not been running. The meat would not be tainted with testosterone or adrenaline. I put the red dot on his chest, made sure I saw the entire circle of the scope, braced myself for the kickback, and pulled the trigger.

I reeled from the impact. Blood ran down my face. I couldn't focus.

Fortunately, the stand was about 3X5 feet. I remembered to push the safety on, laid down the shotgun and tried to wipe my face and to focus on what happened to the deer.

He lay where he had been standing.

I opened my gut kit and pulled out the paper towels. I had only two, but they could sop up the blood and maybe stop the bleeding.

My head wanted to fall off. I was twenty feet in the air. I had to get some help. But my other hunters were too far away to hear my whistled signal for help.

After a few minutes, my head stopped ringing. I could hear again. And see. Now, could I get to the ground? With greater care than a tight-rope walker, I crept down my ladder and went over to the fallen deer. Yes, his eyes were open and his tongue was out. He was dead.

I pulled my tags from a pocket, tore one off, and stuffed it into the buck's mouth. I'd worry about tying it later. I was gonna get to the Jeep and honk the other hunters in.

As I neared the top of the hill where Nellybelle waited for me, I heard commotion out on the highway. What the heck was going on?

I looked down the driveway and saw an ambulance and heard voices. The bleeding from my forehead had about stopped, and I kept the cleaner towel pressed against my forehead as I walked toward the road.

Had there been a wreck? Was a neighbor injured? Or one of my hunters?

I was at least twenty yards from the highway when one of the men who had been standing by the parked ambulance began running toward me. Behind him, people trotted along the highway, headed toward town.

The man reached me, grabbed my arm and said, "Are you all right? What happened? We'll get you to the ER right away."

I jerked my arm free. "What the heck is going on here?"

"It's the annual run for (*whatever, I forget*). Come on, you have to get to the hospital."

"I'm okay," I said. "All I did was hit myself in the face with the scope. I'm not going anywhere."

But all I did was start an argument. The other EMT joined the first one, and on and on the discussions went. They were about to manhandle me into the ambulance before I managed to stop them.

"I have three hunters in those woods. What do you think they are going to do when they discover I have vanished and that there's blood in my deer stand and my shotgun is there?"

I finally agreed to let them "patch me up," and promised to go to the ER for stitches when I got my hunters in from the woods.

So here (next page) I am, with the buck that sent me to the ER:

**That bandage hides five stitches. The scar is still there,
an arc showing a portion of the backside of the scope.**

I took that scope off, never used it again and don't even know where it is.

I apparently had installed it too far back on the shotgun, and had also put my own face too far forward on the stock.

But that was not the only hunting accident of my own making. One afternoon I headed for the Osage orange tree. The stand overlooked the hollow where I collected my first buck over a scrape and where I got the poacher's buck. I knew I'd see something there. If not a deer, then probably the flock of turkeys that wandered through and sometimes roosted a few yards down the hollow. Maybe the brown and white hen would come by.

I climbed into the stand—a permanent plywood platform about 4X6 feet, with a built-in stool. One of the several trunks of the tree provided a backrest. I pulled up my gear and firearm and sat on the stool. Picked up the rifle, pushed in the clip and cranked a cartridge into the chamber. Shifted my weight a little on the stool so I would have a good view down the hollow.

Stool, platform, gear bag, rifle and I tumbled to the ground.

The rifle landed point-first into the ground and then flopped over. I just flopped over. Pain seemed everywhere. I made no attempt to move, just to breathe.

Nothing broken. I just lay there for awhile, and was able to walk out with my gear. But for several days, I was the prime example of the Southern term *stove up.*

The rifle also survived thanks to my Marine hunting buddies who field stripped it, cleaned out the barrel and gave it survivor treatment.

I never again climbed into a stand that had not been checked for safety.

Carelessness, not thinking, ignoring what you know you should do, doing what you don't know how to do or being just plain stupid are only a few of the reasons anyone gets hurt—at home, in the car or in the woods. Often, in the woods, the hunter is alone and not missed until hours later—sometimes after dark when the possum cops, local deputies and the K-9 crew must come to the rescue.

Neither time did I have any way to communicate with the outside world. I was lucky to be able to walk out.

THE CRIME OF POACHING CANNOT GO UNPUNISHED

The *Union-Recorder*, my local paper, published this editorial about poaching that I saved because of the truth and the humor it carried. And because it recognized my group of hunters—the Poacher Patrol:

It's an all-too-common occurrence: A hunter has gone out several times before dawn, sat crouched in a cold deer stand, only to come home empty-handed. Discouraged—and with the season's end approaching—the hunter resorts to illegal tactics to bag a deer.

Such poaching, unfortunately, often goes unpunished. The odds of a poacher getting caught are slim, game officials admit.

But despite the long odds, law-enforcement officials are watching for poachers and don't hesitate to prosecute. Illegal hunters can face a fine of up to $1,000 and 12 months behind bars.

True hunters look down on poachers and their technique. There's even a citizens' "Poacher Patrol" which stays on the lookout for the law-breakers and evidence of their crimes.

Some hunters might say there are too many deer around, and poaching is one way to keep the deer population down. Nonsense. A hunter who can't bag game legally should not be allowed in the woods.

Maybe deer should take a page from a recent movie and arm themselves with rifles. Then they could go about bagging poachers as a way to keep their number down. Turn around is fair play, right?

KEEPING RECORDS ON POACHERS
or Heading Them off at the Pass

Along with records on the deer sighted and killed, I kept details about poachers and possible poachers. My files contain a lengthy list of suspects. Some were charged with hunting violations, and some we didn't have enough proof against to charge.

When I spotted a vehicle circling my neighborhood several times, I jotted down descriptions and tag numbers, which I provided to the rangers. More than once, this information led the ranger to the culprit's home, where he found a freshly killed deer in a pickup bed or hanging and dripping in a carport.

After my letter to the editor about being shot at hit the papers, I received numerous phone calls about who might have been the shooter. The list of potential poachers includes a local banker, a finance manager, a judge, two brothers who lived nearby, a collection agent, an insurance agent, a sales manager, and an attorney's son.

All poachers are not *rednecks*—many wear fancy suits.

I sent each of these potential poachers a strong, curt letter:

Dear Mr. __
I understand that you have hunted or now hunt on lands near or adjacent to some I own or manage in NW Baldwin County.

My purpose is to notify you that my lands are posted to you. You may not cross my land line for ANY reason or at any time.

If you injure a deer, do not follow it onto my lands. You may report the wounding to a wildlife ranger, who may follow it up without you.

One of these gentlemen was later charged and convicted of illegal hunting in my neighborhood. I think the rest got the message.

My old files include many tag numbers as well as descriptions of trucks and the dates and locations of suspicious activity.

The list of vehicles includes red pickup, blue Datsun pickup, Dodge Adventurer 150 with high mufflers, dealer's car from Hall county, Coors beer van (they got caught!), black '86 Chevy pickup with Forsyth County tags, vehicle with Ft. Valley real estate sign on doors, green pickup, Buick Regal, red Toyota pickup, blue Chevy pickup, white long-bed pickup with tandem wheels, yellow-green Ford pickup. I also had each tag number, to track the owner if need be.

One October Saturday night the weekend before deer season opened, at 2:00 a.m. I jumped straight up in bed at the *ka-boom* of a 30.06 so close it sounded in the yard. I called the ranger and then ran to my station wagon to ride the roads myself. In minutes, I found the ranger with a truck pulled over and three men standing beside it. The ranger impounded the truck and all the firearms, and gave the men a personal tour of our jail. Unfortunately for them, the bond was $300 per charge—for night hunting and for hunting on a road. Cost them $600.00 each. None of the three had enough cash, so they sat in a cell until a friend showed up **late** the next afternoon to bail them out.

For most, we obtained tag numbers, but unless there was a reason (turned sideways in road, using a spotlight, shots fired, etc.) to legally stop the vehicle the ranger only watched for the trucks. My hunters and I did the same—checked the make and color of every truck on the roads after dark. If it matched one we had seen before, I would turn around and follow it at a distance. With my lights off.

If it kept up a steady speed, I followed only a short ways. But if it dilly-dallied and stopped often, especially beside open fields, I concluded they were up to mischief. In the days of the CB radio, I would call a friend to telephone the ranger; later I purchased a two-way radio for my truck—my dispatcher would patch me through to the sheriff or to the rangers.

Some men crept by my open, deer-populated fields; some parked at my gates or along the roadside, and some just drove up and down the roads after dark, and when my headlights approached, they would flee at high speed.

One night after gunfire lured me onto the roads, one white van kept driving around. Easy to spot, it was a Coors delivery van. It didn't take our possum cop long to arrive in the middle of the night. With blood running from the tailgate, he had reason to pull it over. Three men inside said they had unloaded the beer that was to be delivered the next day and gone night hunting. They admitted to having already killed one deer, carried it to a house and gone back to look for another. All three were prosecuted.

On October 18, 1986, at 7:45 a.m., I drove up on a vehicle parked at my gate near the railroad. One of my hunters helped me measure the distance from the road to the vehicle to be sure it was on my land. The hood felt warm to the touch and the motor was still ticking as it cooled. I parked my truck behind the poacher's to block him in.

Someone coughed in the hollow, and two deer ran up, crossed the train tracks and loped across the road.

I wasn't about to tromp down the hill and into the woods to face some unknown poacher, armed and probably dangerous when I had his vehicle. I honked and waited for him to come out. He appeared from around the bend on the railroad and climbed the bank from the railroad back onto my land. A few minutes later, he returned to the tracks.

He wore camouflage and carried a bow.

I introduced myself, told him I was the landowner, and that he did not have permission to hunt there. He actually appeared to be surprised—visiting from out of town, he was directed to the site by his host, a local government official. His host knew my family well, and because of his government work also knew the location of our land. I had caught that local resident on my land nearby during deer season and let him know to skedaddle and not to come back.

This visitor, from Woodstock, Georgia, insisted that he had been along the railroad all the time. I shook my head. "I don't think so."

I pointed out his boot tracks. The heavy fog and dew still damped the crossties and his tracks were easy to see, coming back to the truck. The only footprints leaving his truck went to the edge of the drop-off, where autumn-dead weeds had been mashed and broken.

"Besides," I told him. "You have a bad cold and we heard you coughing up a storm right down yonder."

This was one of the few times I felt sorry for a poacher and did not prosecute. His host was known state-wide, probably across the south, for his craft fairs. Since I had caught the host himself on my land, I felt sure the youth was telling the truth and did not have any idea who owned the property, only that his host had sent him there. But he got a good talking to.

With the deer population exploding and thousands of acres of public land open to hunting, as well as many landowners leasing to deer hunters, men don't have to drive the roads to shoot deer, or slip uninvited onto private property to kill a deer to prove their manhood, which suits me just fine.

THE WONDER OF WALKING

A two-mile walk began my day. When in town, I had nothing to look at except houses, and maybe a few birds and squirrels and chipmunks, and once in a while a dog or cat that had slipped away from its *slave*.

But walking in the woods is different. It's a chance to listen, to hear a leaf as it walks its way down a tree; to hear wind dancing and rattling the dry oak leaves; to hear last night's rain dribble, splatter and whisper like an animal slipping along.

Walking the woods demands looking as well as listening. Labor Day is the beginning of buck activity. Maybe that's why we have the holiday, so we who labor can escape to the woods.

Time to look for scrapes and rubs. Time to *look*. One day I strolled right by two rubs on my walk, but noticed them the next day. No buck made them overnight; the sap had run down the trunk and almost dried; the shredded bark had darkened. One tree was a five-inch diameter cedar, so I figured the buck was sizeable. The other was a hardwood sapling. Maybe the same buck, but probably a smaller one trying to show out to boost his own ego.

I had been careless the day before. How many deer had I walked by and not seen, and not heard when I spooked them and they fled?

I thought of the study I'd heard about so often. Researchers put tracking collars on several bucks, and similar devices on some hunters. The researchers were able to watch the movements of both men and deer on a screen—had something like an X and O to represent them. Sometimes a hunter came within a few yards of a deer, but at day's end no hunter had seen one.

I might not be spotting deer, but I was watching where I put my feet and had not stepped in a scrape. I almost did step in one that was *so* obvious! The rain had ended about 4:00 a.m. and the scrape had been pawed out after the rain. He'd scattered wet dirt from under an oak limb all the way across the path. I seldom scouted that path because the underbrush was too thick for me to hunt. I couldn't see pea-turkey from an elevated deer stand and sitting on the ground was no longer a comfortable option for my arthritic backbones.

I had to keep watching where I stepped. I didn't last spring and almost stepped on a mama quail. I was walking a road with scattered grass and covered with leaves from an Osage orange tree and some elms. Mama Quail rose up like the devil from hell and scared the willies out of me. Hate to admit it, but I almost screamed at the suddenness. Off she went, one wing down, the other flapping as she told me, *I'm hurt. Come on. Chase me. I can't get away.*

I knew better. Under my feet, under the leaves and grasses, were her children. I bent down and moved a few leaves. Her golden babies, eyes wide in fear, stared at me. I took a step to the side, eased my toe down until I knew there was no baby there, and I was soon out of the danger zone for the babies.

Another mama bird scared me a lot worse. In the middle of a large field and approaching a massive white oak about fifty yards from the woods, I spotted a dead turkey, sprawled flat on its belly with its wings spread.

Who, I wondered, had shot a turkey and left it in the field? It was turkey season. Maybe it had flown after being shot and died in the field and the hunter, from a neighbor's land, decided it was best to stay off my property and not get arrested for trespass or such. I approached the dead turkey.

Only it wasn't dead.

A fifteen-pound kamikaze lifted at 100 miles per hour straight at my head. I made like an infantryman and hit the dirt.

The turkey hen landed on a fence post some thirty feet away. Like a pterodactyl about to launch an attack, she kept her wings outspread. She *yonked* at me with fury, daring me to bother her babies.

Like the baby quail they had gone under leaves and grasses, but I found a few before I fled her anger. I regretted not having my camera, but those babies remain a memory picture.

Another day, I walked up the path to the edge of the ridge-top meadow we call Larry's Field, where I expected to see deer in the food plot. A pine at the end of the road, to the left, grew its own camouflage—honeysuckle draping over a sapling. I eased up behind the pine to scan the field. No deer, but the wheat and rye were almost waist high. Maybe something was bedded down, hidden in the tall growth.

I rolled around the open side of the pine, like a running back rolling around a tackle, and inched up the ladder to the stand, about eight feet up, to see over the food growth. No deer.

Might as well walk the length of the ridge and see what I would see besides the other end of the ridge. I almost took a left at the first trail, to head back to the house, but figured why not keep going? Who knows what lies ahead? Besides, when I started across the field, I'd promised myself to walk that far. And am I glad I did.

I came up on the big pine where I once had a deer stand. Only a ten-foot stump remains. I had quite a morning there one year. Billy had come down to hunt with us (*us* included his younger brother Larry and his father Herbert). I guided Billy to a stand near the land line, on a ridge top, where he overlooked a path dug out with fresh deer tracks. I was sure he'd have a good chance at a deer.

I had gone to this big pine and crawled up into a built-in stand, four feet by three feet. Then pulled up my 30.06.

It was one of my early years hunting, and my only firearm at the time was that Remington 30.06, with a scope. It never crossed my mind that I needed a shotgun—my only view was along the Jeep road in front of the stand. At most, I had a forty-yard shot; closest, fifteen feet, almost straight down.

At a half-hour before light, what better place to curl up and have a quick nap and let the sunrise wake me up.

Only the sunrise didn't wake me up.

Billy's rifle *ka-boomed* and I sat straight up.

Fortunately, I had my rifle snuggly wrapped in both arms. I looked to the west, toward the shot, as Billy's rifle sounded off again and then again.

"Missed," I said.

That was my first day in that stand, and I was discovering it was a lot more comfortable when I was lying down than when I tried to sit up. The stand was too wide to hang my legs down, and too miserable to keep my knees bent up.

I was still squirming when the buck appeared, galloping headlong down the road. Ten points, heavy body, and me with the wrong firearm.

Try as I would, there was no way to see him in my telescopic sight. It was mounted against the iron sights (the aiming sights made onto a firearm), so I couldn't use them. I never expected to see a legal, shootable deer within ten feet.

The buck of my dreams kept going.

I decided to go see about Billy, see if we needed to trail his deer or if his extra shots put it down.

I met him before I got back to the field.

"You get 'im?"

"I think I missed, but he ran kinda this direction. He's big. At least ten points."

"Maybe he's the one that ran by me."

We began to search the roadway for tracks.

My previous tracking experiences had been sad failures. Maybe this would be successful. We walked steadily behind the tracks—the soft earth was torn up and the trail easy to follow. For a distance. Until he left the path and plunged into the woods. Thick woods. Search we did, but our inexperience led us to failure. After well over an hour, I gave up.

Two weeks later, I found what I thought was the buck. It cut downhill to a creek with banks deeper than I am tall. Nothing remained but bones and hair, and signs of feral dogs.

Now I passed the massive stump and continued along the ridge road. Not fifty yards farther along the road, a doe stood broadside to me. I stopped. She stared for five seconds and leaped into the woods.

A small figure fell to the ground.

I stepped as slowly as if I were *still-hunting* toward the fallen figure. A newborn fawn, flat on its belly, nose extended, front feet tucked under its belly. It didn't move except for its eyes rolling back and up to look at me, and when I spoke it didn't flinch.

Mama deer charged back and forth in the undergrowth.

When I knelt down, the fawn jumped to his feet, leaped once, fell, rolled, leaped up again, fell again, scrambled up again, jumped a log, and, steady at last, joined Mama Deer and fled.

About two months after seeing the newborn fawn, I made the same walk. No sneaking around, just a heart-healthy stride. When I stood by the honeysuckle pine at the edge of the food plot, I didn't see a deer, but as soon as I stepped into the field, a buck leaped up. He was so small he disappeared in the grass between jumps. But he had a spread of maybe twelve inches from tip to tip, and one tine sprouted off each side. Not bad for an eighteen-month-old in midsummer. I hoped to see him come November.

Yep, I've never had a dull walk in the country.

MORE PUNISHMENT FOR POACHERS

Fall 1982 seemed to be a poacher-repeat of previous seasons. Hear the shooting, call for help, and cheer on the posse! Fortunately, with the night hunters becoming more numerous, the other local lawmen joined with the rangers to help us out.

I complained so often and so vigorously the state court judge asked me to meet with him, the superior court judge, the local head ranger, and the sheriff to discuss what I thought was proper punishment.

I suggested: Always take all firearms, spotlight and vehicles from the culprits. Set the bail at a minimum of $500.00 for each charge. All fines should be at least $500.00 per charge, plus an additional $100.00 to be paid to the T.I.P. Project. Each culprit should lose hunting rights for at least three years.

The judges and law officers agreed that such punishment would deter most poachers. The new system went into effect shortly thereafter.

If the accused did not show up for his day in court, he forfeited his cash bond. Many of the out-of-town defendants would not show up— by the time they would take off from work and drive the distance, then sit in court until the case was called, they often decided the loss of the bail money was the lesser evil. They knew if they came to court they might get jail time as well as the hefty fine.

THE SKY-HIGH STAND

Two days into the season, and I had not seen a deer, much less put one in the freezer. One club member had scored and left for his job on Sunday evening. Two hunters stayed at the camp with me.

After the Monday morning hunt produced not even the sight of a white tail fleeing, I decided to take Ole Betsy and walk somewhere. To wherever, I wasn't sure. I would decide as I meandered over the land just where to sit away the afternoon.

I told the others I would go only as far onto the land as the sky-high hollow. They could hunt all the other 300-plus acres, and who knows, I might push something to them if they got into their stands before I got into the woods.

They boarded Nellybelle and left.

I snugged up my boot laces and set off on foot.

The day had warmed up to a comfortable 68° F when I left the house, but at sundown cold would slip in ahead of the night. I took a jacket with me, its sleeves tied around my waist. I set a brisk pace down into the first hollow and up onto the ridge, and then slowed to a *still-hunting* pace.

Sunlight flared off my blaze-orange vest as I crossed the hilltop meadow. Oops, I thought, I shoulda stayed in the woods.

I avoided the Jeep trail and drifted through the food plot to an old cow path that the deer had taken to using. Maybe one would meet me on the trail.

It took me almost two hours to work my way down the hill, across the soggy bottom, up a twisting path, to another small field, half-grown up with brush and broomstraw. Shadows darkened the field.

What the heck. I might as well slip across it—no sun to flash a warning off my vest to the deer. But I treaded slowly, a step and wait, another step and wait. I had managed to reach a leafless persimmon, about my height, and was searching the brush in front of me, when I spotted the curve of an ear.

Yes! A deer!

Too far away for the shotgun. I had to wait and see—buck or doe?

Would it come across the meadow?

It pulled on some leaves, stepped a bit closer, and I saw her head. No antlers. She was safe. Not a doe day.

Behind her, another bush shook. Must be the buck. They were supposed to always follow a doe, some said, because they were skittish and wanted the doe to take the bullet or be tackled by the wolves or other predators.

My heart beat increased. My hands began to sweat.

Then her spring fawn moved into sight, his buttons only humps under the skin of his forehead.

I took a deep breath and tried to relax. And not scare them away.

It's said that the future does not exist, only the present. Well, that *present* lasted until the nonexistent future had become a lengthy past before the deer came out of the brush and fed along the edge. Then the doe realized something was wrong.

Head up, she stared at me. I almost read her thoughts—*Is that a stump? A new bush? Or one of those two-legged killers?*

She stomped one foot. Waited. Stomped again. Snorted. Stomped.

And ran, snorting with each leap. The yearling didn't waste time following.

Noon had turned to after 2 p.m. Time to decide where to sit out the rest of the day.

I topped the ridge and decided. Ahead, to the Sky High Stand. When the boys swung it into that sweetgum, it was so far up the tree I was afraid to get into it. I avoided it that first year, but last season had taken the advice of Lady Macbeth and managed to "screw my courage to the sticking place" and crawled into the stand. It provided a great view down the creek and up the ridges that flanked the bottom.

Might as well try it out. I slipped down the southern side of the ridge to the creek flowing at the base of the tree.

Our pull-up rope was still there, the lower end wrapped around the bottom step. A nylon, it would probably be there another ten years. I tied on all my gear and went up.

After I tied off my safety belt, pulled up my gear, and got settled, I checked my watch—a bit after 4 p.m. Two hours till dark.

Honeysuckle grew everywhere in that bottom. It was once so plentiful it helped carry our cattle through the winter cold, but now is a rare sight. The deer have devoured it down to nothing.

But then and there, it ran across the ground and up bushes and wound its way along the dilapidated fence line that crossed the creek just in front of me. It turned fence posts into miniature Christmas trees. A Jeep trail angled eastward from the ridge to my right, crossed the creek below the stand, and continued east as it went up the other hill. I kinda expected the deer, if one came, to slip down the ridge on my right. It would be perfect for a left-handed shot. Plus, the deer would have to come through a patch of oaks, and its movement in the dry afternoon leaves would alert me.

But only a squirrel rustled the leaves, and it was on my other side. Time dragged. The sun went down. Only a half-hour left of hunting time.

A honeysuckle-covered bush up front shook, as if a squirrel hopped on it. No. Not a squirrel. A deer nose stuck up in the air. Buck or doe? Hafta wait. It wasn't close enough to shoot anyhow.

The nose came down, and antlers showed above the brush. Big antlers. *Big antlers.*

The fever hit. I began to shake and sweat.

Would he see me? Which way was the wind? Would he smell me? Would he come closer? Was my pine scent gonna hide my people odor?

Get ready. Just in case.

He browsed, ambled a few steps closer, and lowered his head to reach more honeysuckle. I put my forefinger on one side of the slide-through safety and my thumb on the other. Pushing the safety off while pressing the other side silenced the *click* that would spook him away.

Two more shuffling steps my way. Broadside. Head down again.

I raised the shotgun, clinched my teeth, pulled in a deep breath, eyed down the barrel to his neck, let out my breath, and squeezed off.

The tree rocked.

He dropped.

I sat. Let the fever subside.

My hunting buddies arrived a little after dark.

Herbert took one look at the deer and said, "My lord, that's no deer. It's a bull with antlers. How we gonna get that thing in the Jeep?"

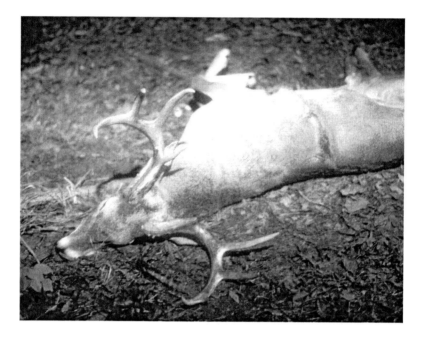

All three of us struggled mightily to get that skeester loaded. We had to haul him up with a rope through a ring on the Jeep roof, which we turned into a makeshift pulley. Note the rope marks on his middle.

This is best picture to show the spread.

The main beams stayed wide and the antlers would slide over the waist line of a 300-pound man. It was ever so much fun to ride up and down the road with the antlers visible on the dashboard. Until one time, on the expressway, a man nearly wrecked when he spotted the size of the rack.

Me with the big boy.

This deer I killed back in the 1970s must have sired a number of others and passed his genes for a balanced, wide rack to his offspring. About forty years later, only two ridges and less than a half-mile away, a similar deer was killed. It could have been a twin to mine: Both had short ear guards. Both had the short extra tine on the left beam. Both sets of antlers stayed wide open.

LETTERS ABOUT POACHING

In the early 1980s, poaching increased dramatically, and I began to write more and more letters to the editor of the local paper, in hopes that somewhere a poacher's wife would take note of her husband's night-time adventures and manage to keep him home and off the roads.

Besides, I didn't want to get shot at again.

SHE WRITES A LETTER TO HUNTER SHE CALLS "LOUSE"

Union-Recorder
September 7, 1982

To the Editor:

I don't know what you call yourself—man, laborer, professional, hunter, worker—but you, Mister, would be honored by the name "louse." You are a killer, not a hunter who kills for food, not a soldier who kills for his country, not even a mercenary who kills for money.

You kill to satisfy a blood lust, because you thrill to the sound of your shotgun, because you revel in the power of life or death you hold in your hands.

If you could see the orphaned fawn, bleating, lost, seeking its mother whose carcass lies rotting in the September sun, would you care?

Do you even care that you violated several laws: Shooting from a public road and from a vehicle, shooting at night, killing out of season, hunting without a license? Do you even care that PEOPLE were only yards away from your victim?

Never call yourself a hunter, Mister, you who ride the roads to kill. You're not as honorable as a louse.

Susan Lindsley
Milledgeville

* * *

REPLY TO MY LETTER: HUNTING SPORT REAL VICTIM

Union-Recorder
September 16, 1982

To the Editor: RE: Letter from Susan Lindsley

You wrote it beautifully, Susan! Your description Tuesday was perfect, of one who is above the law, who cares little for the safety of others, and who obviously lacks the essential ingredients which make a hunter—ethics and morality.

As a hunter, my greatest and most genuine concerns for the sport come when I read a letter like yours. You see, I know that "louse" you so aptly described! He is but one of thousands who call himself a "hunter," a sportsman. What he had forgotten though, or probably never knew, is that the hunting tradition, which is particularly rich in America and in the South, does not bestow hero status on killers.

Outdoor writers fill volumes in their attempts to describe the rewards of the hunting experience. The kill, for a true hunter, is likely the least important of those elusive values. Sadly, though, the single most obvious reward, and the one most attacked by non-hunters, is the kill.

The real victim in your scenarios is not the "rotting carcass," nor the "orphaned fawn." Neither is the victim the louse which you so deservedly blasted in your letter, nor is it "you" who was so hurt by what you apparently witnessed. "I'm" not the victim either, just because I was concerned by your letter, although I may become a victim down the road.

The real victim here is the sport, the tradition, the heritage of hunting. I only hope that she can stand up to what the "louse" is doing to her.

Jim Thompson
Lake Sinclair

* * *

COOPERATION BETWEEN LOCAL
AND STATE LAW ENFORCEMENT

Union-Recorder
September 15, 1984

Dear Editor:

We are lucky in rural Baldwin County to have a sheriff's department that cooperates and works with the Game and Fish Rangers.

And we are fortunate that our political leaders have gotten us 911 emergency service.

All were a big help Thursday night—4:00 a.m.—when the early shooting started on the roads. Deputies and rangers responded and my feelings of security shot up.

Unless you live out of town and have been awakened by gunfire, you probably cannot comprehend the anger such behavior arouses.

These night shooters deserve the loss of hunting rights and very stiff fines on even the first offense—fear of strong punishment would decrease the number of men shooting on the road for fun.

Publicity would help, too. Men, how would you feel if your name was listed as a night shooter?

Ladies, how would you feel about your husband or son if you read in the paper that he had stolen from your neighbor (which he does when he shoots a deer on the road)?

Let's all support our deputies and our wildlife rangers.

And I personally want to thank the lawmen who worked extra hard Thursday night along Highway 212 and Meriwether Road area. You and your efforts are appreciated by a large group of hunters and animal lovers.

Susan Lindsley
Milledgeville

* * *

The sheriff and the prosecutor had agreed to enforce a bail bond of $500.00 for each offence of night hunting, hunting from a road or a vehicle, or hunting without permission when I met with them, two judges and the ranger back in 1982. When they released culprits for less, I wrote this letter:

LEGAL SYSTEM NOT EARNING SUPPORT

Union-Recorder
December 20, 1984

To the Editor:

When I get up to gunfire at 5 a.m. and personally help apprehend criminals—putting my life on the line—I expect some support from our local legal system.

The County judge and two Superior Court judges established bond for various offenses: $500 per charge of hunting on the road, for hunting at night, for hunting from a motorized vehicle or hunting without permission.

But, in spite of admissions of guilt, in spite of knowing I was coming from Decatur for the trial on December 27, in spite of my personal pleas for help, our legal system (Mr. Jimmy Watts and Sheriff Arrington) released these men on a $250 cash bond (per offense) for a total of $750 rather than $1500, I guess so they would not have to miss a day's work.

How can people in the legal system expect support from the public if they do not support us?

Jimmy Watts does not awaken to gunfire in the night, he said. He also assured me in person that he'd follow up on those two cases and prosecute.

Had these night hunters killed Mr. Watts' collie, I'll wager he'd prosecute! (Some of these nighttime Robin Hoods killed a ranger in Florida last year when she pulled them over in the middle of the night.)

Without help from these men in our legal system, why bother to apprehend a criminal and gather evidence to convict?

I've no problem with the cash bail in lieu of court or our bond schedules, but I do object to being promised one thing by politicians who then do something else—like ignore the bond schedule set by judges, or, after setting bail at $1,500, cut it in half on the Saturday before the trial.

Susan Lindsley
Milledgeville

SHEDDING VELVET

Antlers are the world's fastest growing animal tissue. As they grow, they are essentially a form of flesh, with blood vessels feeding them. Bucks usually won't battle until the antlers are grown and the velvet has fallen off. This outer layer gets its name from its appearance: It does indeed look like velvet.

In my neighborhood, bucks shed their velvet around Labor Day. I seldom see them with the velvet hanging, but the two bucks pictured below sashayed in front of me when I had a camera handy. They look as if they're toting dead vines on their heads.

This buck is indeed toting vines on his head. He probably got them tangled onto his antlers when he thrashed a bush, typical buck behavior in the fall when they go into rut and shed their velvet.

This young buck did not seem annoyed by the velvet dangling near his eyes.

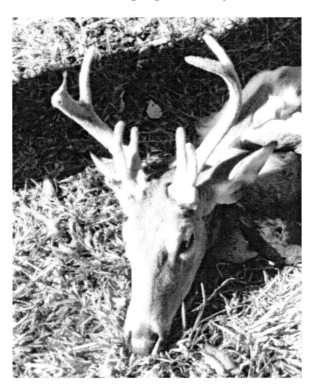

One hunter who leased land several miles away from the house came by with his buck, still in velvet in mid-November. The buck had been gelded (neutered), perhaps by getting himself snagged on a fence. He had been running with a herd of does. That day the 5:00 a.m. temperature was 32° F and it fell to 26° by 7:00 a.m.

I talked to Dick Whittington in Ft. Valley (biologist with Game and Fish), who said he'd heard of others killed in Georgia. A timber man who spent a lot of time in the woods told Dick he castrated all buck fawns he could catch. Once a buck is castrated, he never grows more antlers; if he has antlers in velvet at the time, they stay in velvet. If he's without antlers, he'll never grow any.

When the rut (courting time) starts, a buck goes crazy over all the does. He goes through puberty every year: His antlers harden, his testosterone levels rise, his neck swells, and his testicles drop.

A dominant buck loses weight in his annual pursuit of the ladies. All he has on his mind is loving a receptive doe, and to achieve that goal he often must chase her—sometimes for long distances. He will usually ignore danger. Thus, successful hunters take advantage of the new teenager, whether he be an eighteen-month-old youngster or a dominate old fella.

If you are gonna drive your car into a deer, wait until late winter when weight is down from all the running around and courting.

* * *

Just as some bucks stay in velvet, some does are killed for bucks almost every year. In 2014, the *New York Times* reported four antlered does killed for bucks—in Montana, Maine, Kansas and Arkansas. The Kansas doe carried an eight-point rack with heavy beams and a spread beyond her ears, a trophy for any hunter

* * *

Just as some does have antlers, some bucks grow a hodge-podge of antlers, far more weird than those of the stag shown above. One such set of weird antlers is given on the next page.

A TURKEY HUNTING WEEKEND
WITH A LITTLE FISHING

As I aged, I found it more and more difficult to follow the call of the gobbler. The ankle I broke years before began to wobble and hinder my long walks. Sitting hunched against a tree trunk and in a small swale I'd kicked out of the mulch generated another set of aches and pains. I reached the point I hurt too much to hustle after the gobblers or even to enjoy propping against a tree trunk.

I figured if I no longer had the feet and legs to chase after the dawn gobbling, maybe the birds would chase after me while I violated all the standards of turkey hunting, sat in comfort and talked eager, love-sick hen talk.

So when I discovered the Pop Top hunting blinds, I invested. The design was simple and easy to use: A camouflaged umbrella on a support rod that stuck into the ground. Velcro around the top rim held up the skirt that completely circled the unit. Sections of the skirt could be opened for viewing and shooting. The blind was large enough for two people to share while sitting on folding chairs. Numerous imitations have been produced since I first purchased my supply for picture taking.

No more hobbling up and down the hills for the gobblers on the roost. I'd figure where they roosted night after night, pop the tent top, get comfortable on a cushion in my chair and call them to me. I hoped. (Didn't always work, of course!)

In 1995, I set up a blind in a thicket near a creek where I'd seen numerous turkeys during the previous deer season. I'd heard them on the roost in pines as they scrabbled their toes on bark and listened to them *yelp* on cold mornings in November and December.

Twice in the fall, I had been in my deer stand long before light, and had the terror of the devil himself grab me as the birds hit the ground around me—from limbs over my head. These two trees were often used as roosts into spring. I'd found roosting trees by scouting constantly from the end of deer season into early March.

Now I found the perfect spot—a clover patch not far from roosting trees. Turkeys had speckled it almost white with their droppings, as they had the chufa patch a couple of hundred yards up the trail. I'd greet them here tomorrow.

What more could I ask for? Only a blind with a chair inside and an enticing decoy standing in the clover. I set up a Pop Top tent and supplied it with chair and a decoy.

I arrived at the blind well before light, pulled the Redi-Hen from the blind and stuck her in the middle of the food plot.

After I crawled into the blind, I spread the camouflage cloth over the aluminum folding chair, and perched myself in it. I adjusted the net camouflage over the windows for a shooting opening in the front and both side windows. The window behind me was totally blocked with camouflage so that I would not silhouette against it.

I pushed two shells into the magazine, cranked one into the chamber and loaded the third into that extra-long old Remington shotgun. Off to my left, toward the creek, a jake (a yearling tom) woke and yelped once. Then silence. I double-checked the safety. I was ready. I waited for daylight to rouse the birds.

A jay was the first to awake, not to my surprise. It squawked, and a gobbler answered to my left. A few turkey feet shifted on limbs. Dawn spread over the food plot and brightened treetops. Dew glistened on the clover.

A crow cawed, and another answered. The gobblers woke up and hollered back at the crows.

Excitement filled me as the *swoosh* of wings announced the flock's alighting for the day.

I *yelped* my box call, softly, once.

A hen *yelped* back, her call so soft she sounded as if she were inside a pillow case. Close. Where? Behind me? Over my head in the pine? As she shifted on her limb and clawed the bark, I realized she was behind me to my right. But not long. She flapped once and sailed overhead with a whispered *whoosh* and landed on another limb with lots of clawing and *yelps*.

The gobblers called, and she flew to them.

Drat. They'll never come to the food plot. Won't even come close enough to see the decoy.

The Redi-Hen is supposed to have the *come-hither* posture that says *I'm ready* to the toms. She must have, cause she said *come-hither* to several toms that I invited to dinner.

The morning was too young to leave. I waited. And was glad I did, for less than an hour after good light here came the toms. A flock of two-year olds.

They spotted the decoy and grouped toward it. One, the imbecile, tried to mount it, his toes making a racket like fingernails on a blackboard. Blue-red heads bobbed and ducked, and I slipped the end of the shotgun through the front window.

Pain cramped my back and shoulder and caused me to flap the skirt on the blind.

Drat.

One squawked. All flew.

I listened to the woods. Far off a lone gobbler called. And gobbled again. Then silent. *Probably on Benny's Place. Too far for me to run.*

Down to my left, near the roost site, a couple of toms flapped and carried on. *Maybe those youngsters are getting their come-uppance from the old man. He won't come down here after they spooked. But I'll wait it out.*

No way could I follow those spooked toms to the older one. The woods were open. Understory had fallen to the winter cold and had not revived enough to give me any cover. Jays and squirrels would sound alarms before I made any distance. Besides, my bad ankle wasn't happy.

Time passed. I called, soft *yelps*, off and on, with about a half-hour between. A passel of crows harassed the turkeys down the way and the gobbler hollered back. Birds sang to the morning. I propped my chin on my hand and dozed.

When the hand I leaned on let my chin fall, I woke up. The woods had gone quiet. Even the wind was still. Nothing stirred the leaves on the ground. I used the silence to rearrange the position of the chair and prepare myself for a better shot without flapping the blind. Maybe tomorrow.

While I was squirming around, a shotgun fired over the hill behind me. I hadn't heard a gobbler in that direction, but my ears, like my bones, were losing some skills.

It must be Norman.

In spite of his knee injury from his service in Vietnam, he could sit on the ground and be still. I left my blind and went to meet him. He laughed that he was swatting mosquitoes when two hens wandered across the unplanted food plot where he leaned against an oak. A tom ambled behind them, showing half-interest in romance by swelling into a half-strut then dropping it for a few steps.

"It was an easy shot," Norman said. "None of them ever saw me."

After I hugged him and pounded him on the back, we returned to the house, dressed out his three-year old tom and got it into the freezer. He was one happy fellow.

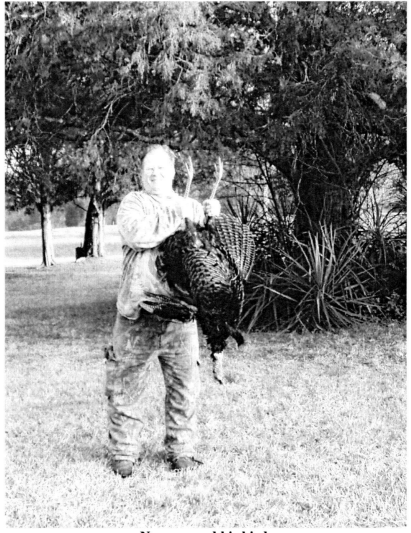

Norman and his bird

We spent that afternoon fishing, got lucky and caught enough bream for supper. We ate well before dark and went to the woods to listen to the turkeys hit the roost. Since I can't make like an owl worth a hoot or ask "who cooks for you" well enough to even bother a crow, I could only listen. An expert turkey hunter went with me one evening and asked "who cooks for you" so well that twenty or more crows flocked in to attack the barred owl. No gobbler answered him, however. If a tom turkey hears a barred owl hooting, the tom usually gobbles back.

For several years turkeys had scrabbled on the pine limbs next door to my place, on a neighbor's ridge, and they were back again that evening and just as noisy. Up into the same pines they had fertilized with piles of droppings. I had already prepared for tomorrow—I had a pile of brush in front of a wide-based oak, and a camouflaged umbrella tied to the oak over my head.

I'd be there before they left the roost at sunup.

NEXT DAY

With only a penlight to guide me, I reached my blind as silent as an Indian in moccasins. Silent walking lessons from a childhood game benefited me in both turkey and deer hunting. I stuck my hen decoy about twenty yards in front of the blind, off to my right.

I had settled on my cushion by the oak before light spread in the eastern skyline. Gloves covered my hands; a camouflage net held in place with a matching skull cap covered my head and face. My box call lay to my right side. I rested my shotgun on my right hand on my knee. I was ready.

No sound of a turkey overhead. No sound of anything except my breathing and the *swoosh-swoosh* of blood in my ears.

Seemed forever before the morning's first voice, a blue jay, called for the world to wake up. A crow answered in the distance. Overhead and to my right, a turkey clawed a limb. *Close. Now just see the decoy and come pay her a visit.*

A hen whispered the first *yelp* of the morning—sounded like through her nose and a sack. A gobbler answered. I shook with excitement. He was almost overhead.

Sound erupted. Wings flapped. Birds *yelped*. Gobblers exploded the morning.

Some fifteen birds dropped around me and changed the ground from pine straw and grasses to clucking, blackish shadows coming to check out the new rude lady who did not talk to them.

One tom fluffed up and did the strutting two-step toward the decoy. Surprise. He fell in love with my decoy and ignored the real hens. Maybe his eyesight was bad. He kept closing his eyes while he strutted toward her.

How the heck was I gonna get that shotgun around to him? I'd had it propped on my knee and shoulder, just in case, but he was to my left and the barrel pointed to my right, toward the decoy.

Com'on, fella. Keep coming. Just a little more.

Maybe I talked him into it, for he thrust himself forward, toward her, toward my right.

Slower than leap year, I lowered my cheek to the stock and eyed the bead.

Com'on. Two more steps. One more.

He was in full strut, his head buried in a mass of feathers.

Did I dare whistle, as I did to stop a running deer? No. Everyone would fly.

I hissed.

Up came his head. Right in line with the barrel—and the bead. I squeezed. The .12 gauge roared. Birds flew. He flopped. I ran to him, but he was *cemetery dead* before I had charged over those fifteen steps.

A nice bird, but one heck of a long walk to my truck to tote that load.

TALKING TO THE ANIMALS

I *bleated* on the deer call for the third time in an hour and sat still. Downhill, to my right, the leaves rustled. Something moved. Squirrel? No, they *hippy-de-hop* or *scrabble*. Then another sound. Feet moving, so not a snake. Maybe a chipmunk? No, not enough constant rustling. Maybe a deer? Silence. I waited. And waited. The afternoon stillness seemed to become even more silent. No songbirds. No distant crows— just a normal late afternoon in my woods during deer season.

A leaf made enough noise to scare off even courageous squirrels as it dropped from the poplar tree on my left. Movement from the corner of my eye, and I turned my head slightly to the right. A buck stepped into sight but remained in the shadows of the hardwoods, at the edge of the broomstraw of the small field. His thin forked antlers gleamed white against the gray of the trees.

Nose up, ears cocked, he sniffed, listened and stared in my direction. Did he see me? Smell me? Surely I had enough pine scent to cover any human odor—clothes and body washed in soda water, clothes stored in the pine scent I had developed years ago. No, I was hidden with only my eyes uncovered, and I didn't spread human odor, only pine scent.

He stepped into the broomstraw, almost as tall as he was. He glanced around the meadow once, strode across it toward the path into the oaks, and disappeared into the growing darkness of the timbers.

Three minutes later, I *bleated* again. And waited. Hooves thumped on the hillside. He trotted back down the path and into the meadow. He looked back and forth eagerly, ears alert, sure that the doe was waiting for him. Twice more he started uphill into the hardwoods, and twice more I called him back. The third time, I left him in peace.

I made no effort to lift my rifle and take the young buck to the cooler. Instead I thought about going to my favorite hunting site in the morning, to the patch of chestnut oaks that lured the big bucks up from the swamps, oaks I had protected from the timber cutters because these trees fed a variety of wildlife.

Maybe if I sweet-talked just right, a buck would sashay into range and be on his way to my freezer.

Before dawn, I walked my climbing stand twenty feet up a sweetgum tree that I had already de-limbed. Once above the understory, I fastened my safety belt, eased my rifle up with one rope (butt first, of course), and my rattling antlers up by another. First light broke. The alarm clocks of the woods—the jays—welcomed dawn.

I waited until the sun was about to reach the horizon and grunted the call of a buck in rut and on the prowl for a receptive doe. Holding the call between my teeth to be ready to use again, I tickled the antler tines against each other for a few seconds and then slammed them together twice, grunted, and raked the tree with one of the antlers.

And nearly fell from the tree trying to see everything.

An eight-point buck charged up the hill from the creek bottom; a four-pointer ran to me from the north, and a doe led a ten-point buck, grunting, along the ridge behind me. I had no chance to shoot I was so busy laughing at the bucks running around each other and the doe snorting her dismay that the superior buck who called had disappeared. I stood (actually, sat) convinced that Jerry Peterson's WoodsWise deer call—both the bleat and the grunt—would work and would call up deer. *Nothing* to equal it.

But an event only a few months later, as spring peaked down at my farm, made me wonder.

With spring came daffodils and azaleas and dogwoods snowing across the lawns. And fawns.

Memorial Day weekend found me back in the country, at my garden of deer, squirrels, bluebirds, chipmunks, foxes, raccoons, and the wild turkeys that entertained me while they strutted and courted and led their fluffy babies across the hay field.

Sunday morning I glanced out the kitchen window and saw three does, heads up, ears cocked forward, their attention on my front porch, on something out of my sight. A tail switched; one doe turned away, looked back, snorted.

They charged away, their raised tails waving goodbye. I shrugged and opened the front door, coffee cup in hand, and stepped onto the porch to watch the morning mist ghost its way into oblivion as the sun rose behind the elm tree.

A calico cat quit chasing a bug on the porch; she mewed and wove herself around my ankles. "Oh, kitty," I said, "looks like you got dumped out, little one."

I gave her some cat food I keep just for the kitties people throw away in the yard. I didn't invite her inside—I figured she had fleas and ticks. Late that afternoon, she sat on my front porch, ready for another meal, which I was happy to provide.

The next morning, I checked for deer before I opened the door. Mist lay over the fields and the long shadows of spring reached for the west. Sunlight kissed the dew to glitter. A pair of geese honked their way to my pond.

A bowl of cat food in my hand, I stepped onto the front porch and called. When the calico did not respond, I went to the back porch where I again called, "Kitty, kitty, kitty, kitty, kitty."

Still no cat. Only the last shadows of mist and the stillness before the breeze got up. A jay squawked at me.

Brush crackled to my right. A doe charged from the trees toward the house, stopped mid-meadow, and looked around, ears twitching forward and back to catch sounds.

What flushed her from the woods? No barking dogs. No train going by. She stomped a hoof, once, twice, and kept turning her head to study the area. Lifting her feet high enough to touch her chin, she marched to the end of the house to my left. When she went around the corner to the front yard, I stepped inside and left the back door ajar, not wanting the click of the closing door to scare her into running.

Tippy-toeing from window to window, I watched her stomp her way around the house. She paused about every ten or fifteen feet, studied the area, and then moved on. She disappeared into the woods.

What was that all about? What scared her? Why hadn't she run the other direction, away from my yelling? Unable to answer my own questions, I shrugged, returned to the back porch, and called the kitty again.

Before I said "kitty" the third time, the doe charged from the thickets to the porch steps and stopped, so close I could count the ticks on her face. She looked up at me—her mouth wide open, her breath heaving. Our eyes met. She spun and fled.

Did she think my calling was a fawn in distress? She was heavy with her own young, so would not have thought the cries were from her own fawn, but hunters have told me a deer will defend any fawn.

I've tried the "kitty, kitty, kitty, kitty" call several times, but no deer answered again.

Not even this spring, when again I was calling another thrown-away kitty. But something else did answer. With the first series of "kitty-kitty-kitty" a long-bearded gobbler sounded off. I saw him in the distance, at the edge of the woods, and couldn't resist the temptation to call that kitty again. The old gobbler answered again, and then again.

The kitty did show up later, and as I do with all the pets thrown into my yard, I managed to get it a new home so it didn't have to eat fluffy poults. Maybe I should edit that statement because the local coyotes and passing vehicles manage to do in some of those pets.

I've given up calling the game with a man-made caller and also surrendered my firearm for a .35 mm digital Nikon. Now I can shoot the same bucks and gobblers all year long and record their growth and family life.

This chapter received Honorable Mention in the Josephine Mellichamp literary competition at the Southeastern Writers Workshop in 2008.

SPEAKING OF TICKS

Ticks were only an itchy pest for us—we weren't afraid of Rocky Mountain spotted fever. But when Lyme disease spread into Georgia, I began to worry a bit. More than once I walked into a bed of newly hatched ticks and came out covered with about a square foot of black dots that I literally shaved off my shirt.

If the offspring of an infected mama, a newly hatched tick can carry the spirochete. But it usually does not feast on humans until it reaches at least the second stage of its life cycle.

Just as we check each other for ticks, so do the deer. Many times, especially in the summer, I watched deer grooming each other. When evenings were still and the deer nearby, I heard the ticks *pop* as a deer pulled them from a buddy.

Deer, like mammals such as gorillas, often groom each other to remove parasites.

Susan Lindsley

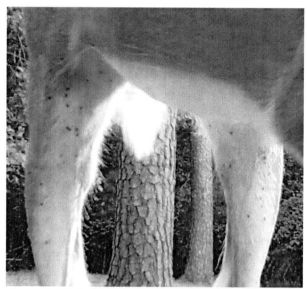

In cold weather, the ticks seem to migrate to the belly and the long hair of the upper legs, where they become a real nuisance for the hunter when he field dresses the deer.

PROJECT T.I.P.

When I learned about Project T.I.P. in 1984, I gave it all the support I could. I talked to my representative in the State House, who was a hunter. I approached the editor of my local newspaper and asked for his editorial support. Bobby Parham introduced the resolution I drafted for the House, and it passed in January 1985.

H. R. No. 253
By:
Representative Parham of the 105th

    A RESOLUTION
    Commending Project T.I.P., Inc.: and for other purposes.

    WHEREAS, Project T.I.P., Inc., (Turn In Poachers), is a nonprofit organization that helps protect wildlife in the state and helps to educate the public concerning wildlife and conservation laws: and
    WHEREAS, Project T.I.P., Inc., provides a reward of $100.00 to private citizens for tips given to wildlife rangers and other law enforcement officers that result in the arrest and conviction of persons violating any of 14 wildlife laws; and
    WHEREAS, Project T.I.P., Inc., is funded solely from private donations; and
    WHEREAS, the activities of Project T.I.P., Inc., significantly encourage greater public support of local jurisdictions in the more stringent enforcement of game and fish laws,
    NOW, THEREFORE, BE IT RESOLVED BY THE HOUSE OF REPRESENTATIVES that this body commends Project T.I.P., Inc., for its many important contributions in protecting the wildlife in the state.
    BE IT FURTHER RESOLVED that the Clerk of the House of Representatives is authorized and directed to transmit an appropriate copy of this resolution to Project T.I.P., Inc.

Shortly after this resolution was passed and the copy transmitted to Rex Baker, Chairman of Project T.I.P., I received a thank you letter from Rex. The letter is given in Appendix III.

I have no idea how Rex learned I had drafted the resolution, unless he had gone to Bobby Parham for information. Bobby had begun hunting with a group of Milledgeville men in the 1960s, before he became involved in politics.

When Rex stayed to hear me speak at the house Chamber hearings, I was honored.

My local newspaper ran this column:

Opinion

Saturday
February 9, 1985
The Union-Recorder
Page 4

TIP offers help
to stop poachers

Susan Lindsley, of Milledgeville, has written us on several occasions to comment about problems she has encountered with people shooting or mistreating animals. A few weeks ago she wrote about a concern she had with the prosecution of a person who had violated game and fish laws.

We hope other Baldwin County citizens share Lindsley's concern for animals, as well as her belief that hunting laws should be enforced and people who violate those laws should be prosecuted. People who hold these beliefs may find it of interest that the Georgia Department of Natural Resources has a service which makes it easy for people to report suspected violations of the state's fish and game laws.

It's a service called Project TIP (Turn In Poachers). It offers Georgians the opportunity to report suspected fish and game hunting violations. TIP pays $100 (the money comes from a fund supported by private donations) to anyone who provides information which leads to the arrest and conviction of someone involved in one of 14 law violations.

TIP pays rewards for information on the following offenses: illegal killing of a turkey, bear or Canada goose; hunting deer at night with aid of a light; taking more than the limit of deer; hunting on a closed management area; illegal killing of an antlerless deer; buying and selling wildlife; hunting ducks over bait; possession of a Canada goose.

Also, taking or killing endangered species; illegal netting of fish; fishing baskets in closed waters; shocking fish; illegal selling of game fish; illegal trapping of quail.

We are encouraged that sportsmen's groups like the Georgia Trophy Hunters Association, the Georgia Wildlife Association and the Georgia Trappers Association support Project TIP. And we are encouraged because people are reporting poachers, DNR agents and local law enforcement officers are apprehending the violators and the courts are handing out stiff sentences.

The DNR has established a toll-free telephone number (1-800-241-4113) which is available to anyone, anytime, day or night. People who call the Project TIP number will talk to a DNR enforcement officer who has been trained to respond quickly.

People like Susan Lindsley are helping to raise public concern for enforcement of fish and game laws. Other people can do the same by participating in a good program that works — Project TIP.

POACHING IS VERY SERIOUS OFFENCE

Union-Recorder
September 11, 1984

To the Editor:

THANK you for the publicity you have given to Project T. I. P.

Poachers do more than hunt without permission. They destroy game out of season—stealing from all of us. Unlike Robin Hood, they are not heroes. They are just common crooks.

A bank robber who kills someone while robbing faces first-degree murder charges, but our system calls a poacher-killed person an accident victim.

Usually the poacher shoots without regard to where the shot can go. He shoots from the road, both in daylight and at night. He crosses land lines (fences) with full knowledge that he is wrong.

Many of these men and boys equate themselves with Robin Hood, who poached the king's deer because the king was usurping the throne. They must somehow find delight in their behavior—but are they not like the drunk who barrels his car down the street unmindful of the damage his lethal weapon can inflict?

Please remind your readers that the state will reward anyone for turning in poachers (T. I. P.) to the tune of $100, and if the culprit is on my lands or along the highway bordering me, I'll add another $50 to the pot on conviction.

Poachers face a strong bail bond in Baldwin County now—as much as $500 per offense for hunting without permission or night hunting.

Let's stamp out poaching with the same determination that we've exerted to stop the drunks in our community.

Susan Lindsley
Milledgeville

My local paper continued over the years to provide publicity against poaching. A feature article it ran in 1986 is given in Appendix IV.

Some folks give all hunters a bad name

Photo by Tom Ervin

This deer was found along Highway 22 with a bullet wound through its neck. Apparently the animal was shot by someone as it was grazing in a field near the road. The season for hunting deer hasn't begun and the only legal way to take a deer now is with a bow and arrow, said Sgt. Marion Nelson, law enforcement officer for the Game and Fish Division of the Department of Natural Resources. Killing a deer out of season or from a public road is a misdemenor, punishable by a maximum fine of $1,000 and one year in prison, Nelson said. In addition, anyone caught hunting from a public road faces confiscation of their vehicle and firearms, he said.

WILDLIFE RANGER DESERVES COMMENDATION

Union-Recorder
February 5, 1985

To the Editor:

THREE cheers for Ranger Calvin Stewart!

He saved three lives on January 19—his own and those of two game violators. Two other rangers, one in Florida and one in Alabama, did not respond quickly enough to a life-threatening situation and they both were shot to death on the road by wildlife violators.

Policemen usually ride in pairs and have a close-by backup when facing an armed violator. Our rangers usually ride alone since wildlife violations are misdemeanors. But all game violators are armed—sometimes with half a dozen weapons—and events of the past two months indicate that some of them are willing to take chances on felony murder charges rather than submit to misdemeanor charges.

Have our courts turned murder into a misdemeanor? Is human life now valued less than an auto or a $500 fine? What's wrong with our system that we have made the game violator into a hero, cloaked with the mantle of glory and adventure? Why do so many people consider the game warden to be the villain?

I personally don't like criminals, and the game violator is a criminal like the armed bank robber or the armed house-breaker.

Since legal hunters provide so much income for so many people, especially rural counties like Jones, Putnam and Baldwin, we should each one protect our source of this income: Our wildlife.

Would you become an accessory by hiding information about a bank robbery? So why protect the poachers? They steal from your bank account—and no FDIC will replenish the loss.

We are indeed lucky that we did not lose Ranger Calvin

Stewart on January 19, and the violators are fortunate that we have rangers like Calvin: Men and women who can keep their heads in a crisis.

Someone with less self-control might have emptied his revolver at both violators rather than simply incapacitate the one who offered the threat.

Thank you, Calvin, for a job well done, for keeping yourself and the two violators alive and for protecting our wildlife in a manner that makes us all proud to have you as one of our lawmen.

Susan Lindsley
Milledgeville

* * *

Not satisfied with the newspaper item, when I heard that a lawsuit was being prepared against Officer Stewart, I wrote Governor Joe Frank Harris and carbon-copied the *Macon Telegraph*, which published the letter on February 9, 1985, under the title "Stronger Laws Needed to Protect Rangers."

Dear Governor Harris:

Wildlife rangers in the South have become targets for game violators recently; a lady ranger was shot to death in Florida in December 1984, and a male ranger was murdered in Alabama in January 1985.

When Ranger Calvin Stewart looked down the business end of a loaded, cocked 30-30 in Jones County on January 19, the violator was fortunate that Ranger Stewart kept his cool and shot to injure rather than to kill.

When a man breaks our game and fish laws in Georgia, he commits a misdemeanor, NOT a felony. Why would even a night hunter want to face a murder charge rather than a misdemeanor?

Are our laws and court system so weak and so favorable to criminals that murder is now considered to be nothing more than killing a deer at night with the aid of a spotlight on our roads? Has ranger hunting become the acceptable norm amongst the men who violate our game and fish laws? Can we allow such incidents to continue? Shouldn't the State rise up and support our rangers?

A cop killer was once so terrified of the punishment that awaited him that he'd even abandon the United States to avoid arrest. We need to strengthen our laws, and punishment should be—must be—just, swift and harsh.

When I went to Africa in 1966, local political leaders told me I need not fear if I toured alone—ANY crime committed with any weapon was punishable by death, even if the victim was not injured, and, therefore, violent crime did not exist in that country.

I'm proud to say that I know Ranger Calvin Stewart, and I'm mighty grateful to the Lord that Calvin handled the crisis so well; the last time a Georgia Ranger faced a life-death situation, he, too, shot in self-defense. The violator then tried to kill him with a vehicle rather than a firearm.

No wonder so many people don't like hunters. To most nonhunters, the night hunter is simply a hunter rather than a killer looking for any target under any circumstances. He is a robber because he steals from us all; he's a rapist because he ravages our wildlife; and now, in Georgia and the South, the poacher is turning into a murderer.

The night hunter is not trying to feed his family. He's not starving or out of work, and he certainly is not a hero.

If that same man were robbing a bank, any citizen who walked by and saw the robbery in progress would report it immediately to the law. We each have the same responsibility to report wildlife violations.

No, I don't expect wives and mothers to report their husbands and sons who they know are deer hunting out of season and at night, but I DO expect the co-workers and neighbors of these men to report their thievery.

He who steals the king's deer does not steal from the government; we, each of us, are the government, and that night hunter steals from each of us.

The deer herd, stocked over Georgia at taxpayer cost, brings money into the State, into the rural communities, as hundreds of men and women swarm over Georgia from October to early January to bag a deer LEGALLY, spending money on licenses, food, clothing, land leases, gasoline, firearms. These hunters spend hundreds of thousands of dollars in Georgia and thereby provide jobs for employees of various businesses.

If poachers kill the deer, the legal hunters will go elsewhere. We as citizens, as taxpayers, owe the same support to Wildlife Rangers that we give our local policemen and sheriff's deputies, and even to that Highway Patrol whose presence makes us slow down.

These Rangers daily put their lives on the line for us all, doubly so now that ranger-shooting is becoming common in the South.

Let's give our support to our local rangers, and three cheers for Calvin Stewart who kept his head when those about him lost theirs. After all, he did SAVE three lives: His own, and those of the two violators.

Note: Fortunately, the powers that be found that Calvin's actions were justified and he was completely exonerated.

THE 1985 FLAP OVER DEER SEASON

The arguments over when the deer season should run became a political-wildlife war. It consisted of numerous skirmishes and lasted for almost two years—the most important time in my involvement in deer management.

The Flap Begins

The arguments between a hunters' organization and Georgia Game and Fish began in January 1985 over a proposed change in deer season. It took a while for me to get all the characters straight in my mind. The Georgia Wildlife Federation's leadership was on one side, and the state biologists on the other. Individual hunters were divided. I jumped into the middle of the fray, on the side of the biologists.

At the time, our regular firearms season opened in October and ended the first weekend in December. We had what was called a "bonus hunt" Christmas week, December 26-January 1. The proposed change would delete the first two weeks and replace them with three in December.

The Atlanta paper ran several columns in the sports section and quoted hunters' varied reasons for wanting the change. The most prominent reason: It was too hot to hunt in October when the snakes still crawled and ticks remained a threat. For me, the warmth of October was an excuse, not a reason—too many mornings in October, I had kicked frost off the winter-brown grass onto the toes of my boots on my way to my deer stand, and even when the sun fell on the boots, the frost only glistened. It did not melt. I certainly did not want to swap these two cold weeks in October for the even colder three weeks in December. The cold of the bonus week was almost unbearable at times.

A search of the Weather Bureau records proved no significant difference in temperatures for the proposed November date and October start date. October 20: 61° F and November 7: 59.4° F. Not enough difference to change the seasons.

I personally didn't like the idea of hunting after most does had been bred because the bucks stay in rut—sometimes into the early spring. Dominant bucks become mindless in their search for does. With most does already bred the bucks would have a harder time finding a receptive doe and therefore they would be easier targets in December than in October. Conditions good for the hunter seeking a trophy, true, but bad for the older, not-so-wise-at-the-time bucks.

On February 13, the *Atlanta Constitution* ran a lengthy article by Kent Mitchell, headlined **DNR seeks input on deer season** and subheaded **State tries to lessen hunting pressure in North Georgia.** Mitchell stated the Georgia Wildlife Federation and the DNR were "working with each other again instead of working against each other." Mitchell also stated that a committee was to be formed, to be headed by Jack Crockford, formerly head of Game and Fish Division, to study the conflict.

I knew and greatly respected Jack Crockford. Not only had he restored Georgia's deer herds, but he also had developed the tranquilizer gun (Cap-Chur Gun) used worldwide to tranquilize wild animals for close-up study, medical care and transport. That weapon is one of the best developments ever for wildlife research, and it earned Jack an international reputation. One of the good guys, Jack would fight for what was best for the deer.

Another member would be Guy Stancil, president of the Georgia Wildlife Federation (GWF). I knew nothing about Stancil until I learned he had started the ruckus. With him on the committee, I hoped the *good guys* outnumbered the other Guy.

I knew the proposed change would not *decrease* hunting pressure but *increase* both pressure and the number of bucks killed because the bucks would be searching far and wide, even outside their home range, to find a doe in heat. So thinking I was entering a brief battle, I entered the war. My first volley was a letter to the editor that was directed to store owners in Georgia's northern hunting zone. I summarized the economic losses facing the shop owners if 180,000 hunters were to stay home for two weeks.

I asked shop owners to express their opinion to their local representatives and gave the names and addresses of the political leaders in Atlanta for them to write.

A few days later, I sent letters to the state political leaders— Howard H. Rainey, chair of the Game and Fish Committee, and

Thomas Murphy, Speaker of the House. With copy machines available, I sent copies of Murphy's letter to Rainey and to the state's DNR leaders: Leonard Ledbetter, Leon Kirkland, Terry Kile and Jack Crockford. I included information on kill rates for my hunters for October and November (higher in October) as well as data on temperatures (no significant difference between mid October and early November). (See Appendix V for copies of two of the letters.)

Meanwhile, a large portion of the GWF membership filed suit to oust Stancil from the presidency and to oust the executive director Jim Morrison. I heard also that Mr. Kent Mitchell, who wrote for the Atlanta paper, was Stancil's close friend. As a columnist he was able to slant his articles any way he wished—a column is an opinion piece, not a news article, which is supposed to be nonbiased.

I could also use the newspapers. Letters to the editor were opinion pieces, and I had opinions to share. I launched my first public shots in the Middle Georgia paper, in a letter to the editor of the *Macon Telegraph* on March 1, 1985.

Don't trim that deer season

Editors: The butcher, the baker and the candlestick maker have a possible economic loss facing them in the fall of 1985—and for years down the line. So do the owners of sporting goods stores, quick stops, sandwich shops and restaurants.

If a small vocal group of hunters—who don't want to hunt in October—have their way, *no one* will hunt deer in October, and a lot of pockets will miss a lot of money that has come in routinely over the past few years.

The move is to cut the first two weeks of deer season. Not only will hunters stay home then, but some who hunt in the warm days of October *will not* be there in December to share their wealth. Their health will keep them home in the colder, wetter days of December.

So, businessmen, speak. Your profit will fall if you do not. Drop a letter to your local state representative, state senator, and the two other men who are watching over Game and Fish: Howard H. Rainey, Game and Fish Committee, and Thomas B. Murphy, Speaker of the House.

A couple of weeks later, I wrote to the *Union-Recorder*, which published my message on March 21. I had more fun writing that letter than any other one I wrote about game laws.

Special interests can't change hunting rules

Fishing time is here but, instead of getting out the tackle, some deer hunters have stirred up a political flap over when to allow our Game Biologists to open deer season.

Some hunters want it warm, some cold; some want it short, some long; some want it archery, some firearms; some want it handgun, some muzzle loaders.

The loudest just seem to want it what it's not.

Some of the special interest groups have exerted lots of political pressure on Game and Fish officials and on our politicians to change opening day to some time in November; some want no break for early December. If these pressures keep on and Natural Resources is forced to submit to these differing pressures, we could wind up with regulations that satisfy no one while attempting to satisfy everyone—a sort of Catch 22 set of rules.

For example:

1. Because of the danger of ticks and snakes, no one will be allowed to hunt deer until the first killing frost each fall (whenever that may be), but hunting will be prohibited on any day the temperature drops below 55 degrees Fahrenheit to prevent any danger of flu-like illnesses from the cold.

2. Since some hunters object to a season when leaves are still on the trees, all trees will be required to drop their leaves the day before deer season begins.

3. Since tree stands can damage timber, all hunters must remain on the ground at all times; but as a safety factor, everyone hunting deer must hunt from an elevated platform.

4. Since archery hunters always spook the deer too much for gun hunters to be able to enjoy hunting, the gun hunters will always be allowed to have their season first. But for reasons of tradition, archery season will always precede firearms season.

5. Because so many hunters are also football fans, no hunting will be allowed on weekends so they may watch football on TV (and no one else can get their deer), and no hunting will be allowed on weekdays to prevent anyone from killing a deer that a

workingman might kill.

6. Members of special groups and clubs will have their deer seasons as listed:

--The "Below 10 Degrees Club" will hunt only October 1-10.

-The "Sunshine Club" will hunt only on Doe Days (guaranteed rain).

-The "Pistol Club" will hunt only on days the .357 magnum is deadly at 250 yards.

-The "Muzzle Loaders Club" will hunt only on days the wind is 25 mph so smoke won't get in their eyes.

7. Every hunter will be required to spend every night, holiday and weekend with his family to prevent any family disruption.

8. Since special interest groups want the season changed to suit them and the total hunter population of 360,000 is only one-half the deer population, the interests of the deer outweigh those of the hunters; at the request of the "Bucks-Only-Membership Club" (which of course hunt only does) only deer will be allowed to hunt in future years.

Ridiculous? Yes!

Any time special interest groups demand that the rest of the world cater to their whims, the rest of the world gets problems.

The Game and Fish Division of the Department of Natural Resources has problems now that several groups are exerting such pressure to get the season changed to suit them without regard for the rest of the hunters—and, unfortunately, most of the rest of the hunters do not even know what's going on behind the scenes.

It's time to keep politics and special interests out of game management or we can get distortions that read like Catch 22.

* * *

Going on the front lines: The Atlanta hearings

I called Joe Kurz, Game Management chief, about the proposed changes and the rising deer population. We agreed we had a good population, but opening the season two weeks later and closer to the end of the rut could result in a high kill rate of the older, dominant bucks. As a result, in a few years the breeding bucks would be younger and perhaps even in a weaker gene pool.

I told him about my letters to the editor and he said the usual spring public hearings would be held around the state. Everyone was welcome to voice an opinion. He did not invite me to speak, however.

No way was I going to give a speech, especially when he told me the first hearing would be held in the House Chamber in the capitol. Yikes! Home of Tom Murphy. Hallowed chambers where our laws were born.

I really didn't want any part of that event.

But did I have a choice? Not if I wanted my opinions heard.

I hunkered down and began to prepare a talk aimed at hunters statewide. I charted success rates for the 100-plus men and women who hunted my lands. I had a beautiful talk, and planned to hide in the dark, put my support tables and charts on an overhead projector, and *read* my speech.

I called Joe to tell him I wanted to speak at the Atlanta hearings and would need an overhead projector.

"Oh, no," he said. "You can't do that. We've had so many people call to speak that everybody will be limited to three minutes. No projectors. No charts."

"But I need fifteen minutes."

"No way," he said. "Everybody has to have an equal chance to speak."

"I'm scared to death to get up in front of a crowd. Can you put me first?"

"Can't do that either," he explained. "There'll be a sign-up sheet. Get there early and sign up first."

I had no choice. I would have to get there early, but how the heck was I gonna cut my speech by eighty percent?

I resorted to the first two mandates in the speech preparation guidebook I wrote some years before. First, keep it simple. Second, have no more than three ideas and support each one.

I cut the speech here and there, tightened it up to what seemed like three minutes, and walked around the house practicing aloud until I had it down to two minutes and forty seconds. Time to spare if I were to get nervous.

Would these men, from all over the state, who did not know me, accept the words of a woman? Few men thought women knew anything about the outdoors or wildlife or hunting. How could I convince them I knew what I was talking about?

Antlers! I'd take some antlers as references so they'd see I was a successful hunter.

On April 25, toting a box loaded with antlers, I arrived at the House Chamber well before the meeting was to begin. I set the box down and went directly to Joe to sign up. With my hands already shaking, I scribbled my name on the top line.

While people entered, I placed the antlers along the front of the House Speaker's podium. I would refer to them when I got up to speak.

My stomach had butterflies and a nest of wasps, and my hands had even gotten the trembles the day before the meeting. To say I was nervous was an understatement. I was terrified. The shakes were worse that evening than any case of buck fever.

I was more scared than when I faced a poacher—then I was mostly too mad to be scared. My gut twisted and burned. I never wanted to become a public speaker. But the situation described by Joe Kurtz called for action.

Fewer than ten other women were there, but it seemed like a thousand men had come to sit in judgment of my arguments.

Joe went over the rules and the time allotted for each of us to speak. He said Rex Baker had another appointment and was allowed to jump to the front of the line.

Rex explained the details of the new Turn In Poachers program—how to report violators and to collect the reward. When he finished and started up the aisle to leave the chamber, Joe called my name. Rex stopped, turned, and stood in the middle of the aisle. *Oh Lord, now I've got another somebody to talk to. There're already too many men here.*

My legs felt as if they would buckle under me as I walked down the aisle. I made it to the podium and my first words surprised the men.

I'm Susan Lindsley.
I'm a deer hunter. I know you're not used to ladies who hunt, so I brought my references with me.

I pointed to the antlers in a row on the front of the Speakers podium. Of course, I included the rack of my big skeester from the Sky High Stand.

The men applauded.

The clock ticked away precious seconds.

I stood silent until they quieted.

I handed Joe a handful of petitions, took a breath and began my arguments. (See Appendix VI for my speaking notes.)

At the end, I hit the hunters where it would hurt the most: The excuse for wanting the changes was that it's too hot to hunt in October because ticks and snakes are still out. I suggested we **eliminate the statewide turkey season** because snakes and ticks are crawling in March.

Two interruptions by applause and several hunters saying they couldn't add to my talk filled me with the spirit of success.

On April 26, 1985, the *Atlanta Journal* ran an article titled "Hunters oppose change in deer season" about the hearings at the Capitol and mentioned me by name. Not even Stancil was named in the article. It stated that I represented the 1,000 member Deerhunters United of Georgia and quoted me as saying that ticks, snakes and wasps were not enough reason to delay the opening of the deer season.

It also quoted my comment "Little old ladies like me don't like that cold weather." (And stated that I gave the attendees a chuckle!)

My comment about cold weather apparently was considered by some to mean that little old ladies aged fifty-five didn't hunt and knew nothing about hunting. It came back to haunt me after the Macon hearings.

The Macon hearings

I knew I had to attend the May hearings in Macon, only thirty miles from my farm. I gritted my teeth when I told Joe Kurz I wanted to speak, but I knew some of my local hunters would make the trip from Milledgeville to Macon and I would have a friendly audience.

I would also have a chance to turn in more petitions. My references this time were enlarged photographs of deer, which I stood on a table in the front of the room. Because the proposed change would have two opening days, one in the northern part of the state and one in southern zone, I stressed the effects of two opening days and ended with this challenge:

When your grandson asks you, "Grandpa, why don't we have deer in Georgia?" will you have the guts to tell him the truth, that in 1985 it was you who put personal preference ahead of game management?

That talk is outlined in Appendix VII.

After all the hassle and tons of effort by many people about what to do, the committee gave its decision in late May: The deer season should not be changed. DNR agreed.

A major victory for my side. As Prissy said when Melanie's baby was born, "I brung de baby and Miss Scarlett, she holp a little."

I felt that I had won a major war and that the DNR "helped a little."

* * *

Stancil and Me

The decision was handed down, but the squabble wasn't over. Stancil made the Atlanta papers again. He stated Game and Fish packed the hearings with women who didn't hunt and didn't know the muzzle of a firearm from the butt.

Slander. I responded publicly:

'Gals' unfair game at hearings read the headline over my letter to the editor in the *Macon Telegraph* on June 9 1985:

Editors:

"When you've got women up there (at the hearings) *talking about hunting and fishing who don't hunt or fish and don't know the muzzle of a rifle from the butt, you know they've been briefed."*

So said Guy Stancil of the Georgia Wildlife Federation (GWF), as reported by the Associated Press. And the Federation's Jim Morrison said Game and Fish had "packed the hearings" about proposed hunting regulations.

I take offense at Stancil's words. He slandered me and the two other women who spoke at the hearings about Georgia's deer season. He told untruths about me in three ways: (1) He said we cannot or don't hunt. (2) He indicated we were involved in some plot with the Game and Fish Division against him and the Wildlife Federation. (3) He said we had to be "briefed" to be able to express ourselves!

Game and Fish did not ask me to attend. They would not have considered it, as many times as I've hassled them about decisions I didn't like, although I've supported their position in this matter because their decisions are best for the deer herds. I opposed part of their regulations this year, but I felt my opposition was minor in light of what GWF was trying to do: Change the deer season to suit the personal preference of some hunters and thereby cause detrimental effects on individual deer size and overall herd health. I reacted *on my own* to stop that!

Stancil, as president of the GWF, belittled his own membership by those words; one of the two ladies who spoke in the northern zone hearing is a member of one of the hunt clubs affiliated with GWF.

He put down us gals, but how many men does he know who have personally spent several hundred dollars annually to feed wildlife (plow and plant food plots, not put out bait)? Who ride "poacher patrol" night after night in their local areas to protect deer from night hunters? Who have turned down reward money from Project "Turn In Poachers" so the reward could to go others who "tipped" a ranger? Who got their deer opening day on four of the past five years? Who photograph their deer live before putting it in the freezer? Who spend at least 150 days afield annually? Who can track a deer for two miles in Middle Georgia without benefit of ice, snow or blood trail? Who can unload a weapon, climb down from a tree stand, reload, stalk and kill a buck spotted from the tree but out of range from it? Who can field dress a deer without spilling colon or bladder contents, and with blood no higher than the wrists? Who have killed one deer (or more) every year for 18 years and have by-passed anywhere from one to ten bucks a year?

Well, the men from GWF met a lady hunter in Macon and

Atlanta, at the hearings, who qualifies on all counts. Would *they* qualify? Someone may question whether they know the "muzzle" from the "butt."

Susan Lindsley
Milledgeville

* * *

Control of deer season

Stancil lost one battle. But he started another: Take control of deer season away from the biologists and give it to the state legislature. Unlike biologists, politicians could be influenced.

I entered that battle, and Stancil continued with his not-so-subtle attacks on me.

On June 16, I shot a letter off to the newly formed Hunting Seasons Study Committee of the House of Representatives. And with it, a lot of support material: A statement from Bobby Parham, my State Representative, that I was a hunter and a landowner; copies of my letters to Commissioner Ledbetter and House Speaker Murphy; tables showing hunter success and the temperature averages for October and November; and a copy of each of my talks (Atlanta and Macon). (See Appendix VII for copies of two of these letters.)

I also fired a letter off to Governor Joe Frank Harris to be sure he would veto any bill designed to give control of game regulations to the legislature.

Deerhunters United, a national magazine, ran my editorial a few weeks later:

BIOLOGISTS SHOULD SET GAME REGULATIONS

Thanks to legislative action across our country in years past, every State now has a Game Division or Commission or Department staffed with highly educated and trained biologists whose primary duties are to ensure the continued proliferation of game species and to protect the endangered species.

But Georgia is facing a dilemma that could spread into other states and decimate the merit systems that have led to successful game management. Only a sound merit system, immune from angry, powerful, selfish dissidents, can ensure protection for our game.

In Georgia this year—the second year in a row—a small group of hunters and dissidents has pressured legislative leaders to take the authority and responsibility for hunting/game management from the biologists and to place control into the hands of the legislators.

The dissidents include a small group of individuals who have influence with some legislators and who are willing to wield this influence to gain their own personal desires in spite of the long-term effects on the deer herds.

This combination has made a loud, squeaking wheel on the wagon of game management, and the wheel is demanding a lot of oil—but it could cause serious problems for game management in the future.

Game biologists are flexible, able to adjust seasons and bag limits from year to year as the populations shift and the hunting pressures change. But most legislatures act more slowly—sometimes a year or two TOO LATE to prevent the destruction of a species.

By taking responsibility from biologists and re-assuming it, the legislature is stating to the world that the merit system it developed does not work.

Can you image the legislature of any state taking control of a ball team from the coach? Can you believe a coach would let the FANS (the hunters) dictate the "rules of the game"? Imagine fans telling the coach that the Refrigerator has to be quarterback during the first quarter of the next game, or demanding that Doctor J not be allowed to shoot at all except for 3-point shots?

Our game biologists have given us a quality hunting experience in every state of our Nation; any legislature that takes from the biologists their responsibilities and their authority will eventually see a reduction in game, a lower quality in habitat, more unhappy hunters than they expect at the polls, and an end to quality hunting in their state, not because they don't care but because legislatures cannot act fast enough and because when they do act, they are under emotional pressure from those special interest groups who cannot influence the merit-system biologists.

I prepared a petition, directed to the Georgia legislators, which stated:

We would like to see all fishing and hunting regulations left in the hands of our fish and game biologists. We may not always personally like their decisions, but we believe their decisions are best for the game and fish of our state.

I then printed the petition on one side of a sheet of paper and the editorial on the other, and mailed copies to all the hunting groups I could find, and handcarried some to stores that sold hunting and fishing equipment.

I attended the August 22-24, 1986 Buckarama. The largest hunting exposition in the Southeast, the Buckarama is sponsored annually by the Georgia Wildlife Federation as its major fundraiser. I helped man a booth and distribute copies of the petition. I asked everybody who came by the booth to sign it. I collected about 1,000 signatures at that hunting event.

Guy Stancil, still president of the Georgia Wildlife Federation, telephoned me on August 28 as a result of the article and my soliciting signatures at the Buckarama. He sounded a bit angry, and we had quite an adversarial discussion. I asked him what he wanted from Game and Fish, and he said he wanted:

—The State Legislature to pressure the Game and Fish biologists into doing what he (as president of GWF) says for it to do, but not for the legislature to actually set the deer season;

—More time to hunt management areas and more time for muzzleloader hunts;

—Deer season in the Northern Zone to run from November 1 to January 1.

He informed me that because of that article I would never be allowed to man a booth at any future Buckarama.

His threats held little water. The next Buckarama was a year away, and the next months were filled with activity than negated his threats.

Once again, I flooded members of the House of Representatives with letters to try to halt any law to make the changes Stancil wanted. I also wrote Governor Joe Frank Harris about the proposal and informed him of the 4200-plus signatures I had collected on my petition to keep control with the biologists. (See Appendix VIII.)

Seldom have I received a letter from a government official that was not in direct response to something I had written to him. But in February as this war began to wind down, I was thrilled to receive this personal letter from Terry Kile of Game Management, on DNR letterhead, February 2, 1987:

Dear Susan:

It is so easy to get tied up in busy work that we forget to tell our friends how much we appreciate them and the supportive efforts they make. Your intuition of when and how to help is a valuable asset.

Thanks for being concerned enough about professional management of Georgia's wildlife to spend your time and money supporting conservation.

Sincerely
Terry Kile

The war was over. Stancil was unable to control the House Committee, and after two long years of battles, the Hunting Seasons Study Committee of the House of Representatives announced that game regulations should be set by those who knew best: The game biologists.

A court case brought by members of the Wildlife Federation against Stancil and his colleague Jim Morrison was settled, with both men ousted from their positions of power and from the GWF.

The new president, Doug Rithmire, was a long-term member who had fought desperately in the courts to save the organization. For some thirty years he has managed the Buckarama.

The new executive director of the GWF, Jerry McCollum, had worked for Game and Fish for a number of years as a biologist and when moved from the field to the Atlanta office had dealt with the public and the legislature on behalf of Game and Fish Division.

When I saw my local ranger later, he asked me why in the world a man as respected as Jerry McCollum would join that terrible organization. I told him about the lawsuit and the change of leadership. He didn't take long to support the new Federation.

I attended the Buckarama for many years, and manned my own

booth on several occasions. In 1994, I stopped by the GWF office one day, and Jerry McCollum presented me with Honorary Lifetime Membership No. 066 in the Georgia Wildlife Federation. The letter is given in Appendix IX.

My membership plaque hangs over the wall above my computer, so I am daily reminded of these tense years.

And the long, hard battle to victory.

THE NEW WILDLIFE FEDERATION

When the dust settled after both the big flap over deer seasons and the conflict within the Georgia Wildlife Federation, I felt that the *Deerhunters United* magazine should offer support to the newly reorganized Federation. Thus, my editorial, which was originally published in that magazine in the Sept/Oct 1987 issue, page 23, with my by-line:

Personal View of GWF

Georgia's deer have faced several crises in recent years, but the one with the greatest potential for damage is over and the deer have won.

Leadership has changed in the Georgia Wildlife Federation. Disintegrating from the top down, torn apart by interpersonal conflicts and misdirected goals, and by a major court action, the organization for about three years has tottered on the brink of self-destruction.

I took a personal stand on a local hunting issue in 1985 and was immediately—and frequently—asked if I were part of the GWF. When I said *No* the individuals offered support for my position.

Today, I hope to see public support return to the Georgia Wildlife Federation. Its internal problems are rapidly being solved; the court case is over, being resolved out of court by judicial instruction. Elections were held in March with the 1984 membership reinstated.

The newly elected leaders are setting high standards for the Federation. They will ensure that Federation efforts are directed toward providing quality outdoor experiences for both this generation and for generations to come.

No more will good wildlife management be secondary to the personal goals of individual members.

Today, seeing the new direction the Federation leaders are

moving, I see increased cooperation among the leaders in the State's conservation organizations: Deerhunters United, the Georgia Wildlife Federation, the Wildlife Conservation League of Georgia, the Georgia Conservancy and all the various professional and amateur conservation groups.

But best of all, each of us who enjoys the outdoors—whether hiking, fishing, camping, hunting, bird watching, photography—will benefit from their efforts, as separate groups and as a cohesive unit cooperating with our Department of Natural Resources and our legislature to generate the regulations and laws needed to perpetuate the high quality of our outdoor experiences.

SUGGESTIONS TO
STATE SENATOR CULVER KIDD

In 1987, when Culver Kidd asked for comments about the deer problems, I was quick to reply. I considered these suggestions to be a means for Game and Fish to track deer populations and the deer hunters. And perhaps to be able to better control poaching.

Dear Mr. Kidd:

I'm writing in response to your letter in the *Union-Recorder* asking for ideas on how to improve the deer situation. I'm a landowner who deer hunts, who leases to deer hunters, and who is an activist in matters relating to deer herd management and to deer hunters. Your concern over the crisis we face with the deer herd of Central Georgia is appreciated.

The deer problem is complex but stems basically from four factors which reflect attitudes stemming from ignorance of the facts and from the attitudes from the Depression era and from stories of Robin Hood that poaching is honorable to feed the family.

1. Underreporting of legal kill.
2. Poaching
3. Hunters seeking only trophies.
4. Landowners' attitudes/hunters' lack of respect

The complete letter is given in Appendix X.

MY NONFIGHTS WITH GAME MANAGEMENT

The same time I battled with the Georgia Wildlife Federation and supported Joe Kurz and the Game Biologists, I started up a fracas with both Joe and the rest of Game and Fish. The good part of it all, however, was that these disagreements were friendly discussions that reflected our mutual respect.

The deer population exploded in the years hunters were allowed only one doe tag. The hunters I called "Macho Men" did not believe in killing does, but wanted a massive trophy to hang over the fireplace. I met several hunters who waited years to kill a deer—all they wanted was a trophy buck.

We needed some sort of change in deer regulations to reduce the overall herd in some areas where crops were being destroyed.

Some battles were by letters to the editor, some through letters to Joe and others in Game Management, and many by phone.

One of our discussions began during deer season in 1989, when I told Joe we needed more doe days. He told me I needed more hunters to kill more does on our either-sex days.

"You gotta be kidding. They're the end of the season. There's no cover for the hunter. The deer can see you across the hollows and up the hills. They're spooked to heck and gone. You come show me how it's done."

So he and his two sons came down. I gave them a sketch of the 200-acre area, which showed creeks, fields and deer stands. They hunted all day, but did not see a deer.

Ergo, no does killed, although three hunters added.

He would see about more doe days.

But more doe days were not the answer. I continued to bug him about the increasing population and in 1989, I sent a report of all deer killed on about two square miles of our land to Joe Kurz. The report, which covered the years 1986-1989 inclusive, was one of my many ways to urge an increase in the bag limits.

The kill rate averaged 100 deer per year, and ranged from 86 to 113. With a carrying capacity of thirty-five per square mile, that kill rate showed we had far too many deer. (See Appendix XI for the entire report.)

In 1991, the last weekend in February Joe came to my rural neighborhood to survey the deer population. I had an old 1946 Jeep, CJ-2, Nellybelle.

We called her Nellybelle after the Jeep in the Roy Rogers movies, but she was far different from most Jeeps. Someone before me had built a hard metal body, with a flat roof strong enough to hold several people. The area behind the driver had seats on both sides to hold another four people. The original tailgate was still attached, and when let down flat on its chains, it served as a standing platform for two people.

Another hunter drove. Joe and I sat inside the Jeep on the highway, but when we reached fields, we stood on the tailgate, with him holding a spotlight. A mile north of home, we counted about a hundred deer scattered in the various fields. In my front pasture we spotted about thirty as we drove down the adjacent road. At my southern neighbor's, Joe gave up trying to count—his rough estimate was again more than 100 in one field. Total? Double or triple the carrying capacity of the land.

As a result of that head count, I was able to convince him that we needed more doe days and a higher doe bag limit. Unfortunately, he said, the tags were already printed. I said *use archery doe tags for firearms season*.

He insisted that it couldn't be done.

"Anything can be done," I argued back. "Deer hunters communicate. Just put the news out. It'll be all over the state in two days."

Needless to say, I was pleased that Joe accepted my suggestion and took the idea to the upstairs people and obtained their approval. Not every state has such open-minded and dedicated personnel.

Joe put the news out to writers of hunting stories. I think it took maybe three days rather than two, but I heard the news from some dozen of my hunters in those three days.

DEER HUNTING

Season Limit: The bag limit for deer shall be no more than 5, of which 3 must be antlerless and harvested during either-sex seasons. **All 5 deer may be harvested with a firearm. The "archery-only" tags may be used on deer harvested with a firearm on legal either-sex days and hunts.**

Copied from the 1991-1992 Hunting Regulations bulletin.

His upping the doe bag limit convinced many hunters that we did need to cull does.

Today, the bag limit is up to a dozen, ten does and two bucks. Some hunters complain that we're killing too many does and that coyotes are killing does and fawns. Others argue that we still have overpopulations in some areas. Both groups are right. But at seventy-nine, I'm done with these battles. Let the youngsters do the fighting. I'll just watch the deer browse and the turkeys strut when they go through my yard.

But I still chase poachers.

* * *

One spring, newspapers from Atlanta to Macon to Milledgeville ran articles about crop depredation. The state would issue permits for the farmer to kill a certain number of deer in the off-season—but the permits were limited: The farm had to be inspected by a biologist; the biologist had to find that deer depredation was harming the farmer's crops; and ONLY the farmer had authority to do the shooting.

My land had been over-seeded for silage by a local dairyman. Richard Key used a special seeder that plugged seed into the ground in rows. Even before dusk, deer appeared in the fields. One would begin eating on a planted row and eat its way along that line, putting the two or three inch growth to zilch. The dairy was fast losing its crop to the twenty-five or more deer that visited every day.

My land and the dairyman's crop were not the only sites to suffer. Farmers state-wide were complaining. Seeing twenty-five or more deer feasting on Richard Key's planting every day was enough to get me involved.

My first battle with Joe over crop damage was about who would be allowed to do the shooting. No way for anyone to go out alone, handle a spotlight, drive a vehicle, and shoot the critters.

I pushed until that regulation got changed so that the farmer could get some help protecting his crops.

I got a crop depredation permit and Wayne and Norman and I set about to remove ten does.

Problem: The deer were feeding at night. The solution was included in the permit. We could shoot at night, and use a spotlight.

Problem: Gotta field dress the deer, hang it to chill, cut it up, wrap it and freeze the meat. Two deer in one evening took the rest of the night to prepare for the cooler. The next night would be a repeat—with little or no sleep. With the freezer full, we gave the wrapped meat to some of my neighbors.

Big problem: Bucks had shed antlers and there was no difference in the spotlight between a buck and doe. We killed more bucks than does. Six bucks make no difference in population growth. Ten does would have been effective in reducing the herd the next year. One doe can produce two fawns annually; a doe fawn can breed at six months, so will give birth when only one year old.

I wasn't the only one discouraged with the system. Letters to the editor from others showed their distaste for killing excess deer. Many carcasses were being left in the fields and woods to rot. What a waste of quality, heart-healthful meat.

I argued that the night-hunting crop permit was ineffective, and that the doe tags should be increased.

Newspapers reported that in some counties as many as 65% of traffic accidents were caused by deer.

I photographed browse lines and sent the pictures to Joe.

Deer ate these bushes, in the middle of a field, as high as they could reach.

I argued with my friends at Game and Fish with one hand and supported them with the other, and never did we lose the friendship or the mutual support.

*   *   *

When we lost Joe Kurz at the age of fifty in 1996, we lost the man who set the standards for future Game Managers not just in Georgia but nationwide. Georgia has named a wildlife management area the Joe Kurz WMA in middle Georgia. The National Wild Turkey Federation presents the Joe Kurz Wildlife Manager of the Year Award to the outstanding game manager in the nation. The Turkey Federation so honors Joe because he was instrumental in the wild turkey trap-and-transfer programs across North America.

DEER PICTURES I ESPECIALLY LIKE

Even from the time that the only camera I had was a point and shoot, I loved taking pictures. Today I have a Nikon 14-pixel digital and I photograph everything from daffodils to deer to turkeys and anything I see in between. I do not, however, use any of the computer programs to enhance my pictures. I keep 'em as I get 'em.

My yard plays host to numerous deer who visit the feeder, and often the fawns take a nap while mama feeds. And sometimes they flee when they hear the camera click.

Sometimes they hang around long enough to check out the local yard decor.

Other times they come in close enough for a portrait.

They always put their best foot forward when curiosity lures them.

A surprise the day I caught a bird landing on a doe's head.

"You may be bigger, but I'm meaner."

I have seen whitetails mate but never when I had a camera in hand. On one of my trips, I did have camera in hand when a Père David's buck consummated his marriage. Unfortunately, the breeze ruffled the lake, so the picture was not a perfect reflection.

Me, Willie Mae, the deer she claimed was half hers and Nellybelle.

My neighbor and close friend Willie Mae Bryson often went with me in the Jeep while I scouted the land or did whatever. She would take a bucket and shovel to bring home wildflowers. But three days before this picture, she rode with me to Larry's Ridge and helped me put up a climbing stand between two fresh scrapes in an oak thicket. And this day, when I came to the house for the Jeep, she wanted to join me—after all, she said, the deer was half hers since she had helped with the stand. Not one of the biggies, but still, it was an opening day harvest that freed me up to walk the land and not worry about getting another deer.

Spring morning. I was perched in the truck, window down, trying to shake off the late March cold and listening for sounds of a turkey poacher when these does came to the eastern edge of the meadow. The clicking camera ran them off.

When fall comes, bucks become teenagers and challenge each other. Sometimes it's a pushing match.

Sometimes the pushing becomes mutual suicide.

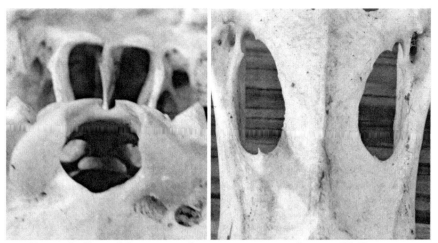

Deer skulls and bones can become sources of art or Halloween decorations.

The boss buck and the boss doe state their positions to other deer. The buck was fussing at a doe that was out of the viewfinder. The boss doe chased off not only the one in the foreground but two others as well.

These three mule deer bucks didn't run from the camera clicks.

Texas Ballet on an exotic game ranch.

This fella posed with the sun highlighting his antlers.

**His antlers were red from fresh blood—he shed velvet just
a short time before he posed for this picture.**

The unpredictable Montana buglers always make fun subjects.

THE JAMES R. DARNELL
OUTSTANDING-RANGER AWARD

In the early 1980s I was fortunate to meet James Darnell, an exceptional wildlife artist who worked in both two- and three-dimensional media. Over the years I amassed quite a large collection of original paintings and prints as well as original sculptures and duplicate sculptures that he released in a numbered series.

One of my favorites is the *Fawn*, a sculpture of a bedded newborn. When I visited Jim and purchased the fawn, I stopped on the way home to see a businessman. I walked into his store with the sculpture wrapped in my arms as if it were alive, and everybody in the store ran over to see the fawn—Its realism convinced them on sight that it was alive.

I gave a duplicate fawn to the Department of Natural Resources in 1988 to be presented annually to an outstanding ranger. The ranger's name was to be added to the sculpture's base; the ranger would keep the sculpture in his home for that year, and it would rotate annually. Eventually it will be retired to the State Museum in the Capitol.

THE CHUFA PATCH

Two meadows on the land were sandy, not the typical red Georgia clay that packed hard as brick in summer unless the farmer kept it turned. When I learned about chufas, I thought, yep, those two fields are perfect.

One field ran alongside a Jeep trail and covered perhaps a half-acre. The other, about four acres, lay at the northern end of the land and sloped. It required contour plowing, whereas the smaller field could be plowed from end to end. But direction of furrows did not matter—chufa, like clover, could be scattered by hand, not dropped into plowed furrows. In these two fields, the seeds grew like mad, and the turkeys weren't long in finding them.

I had purchased a 600-mm, f 2.4 Nikon lens the year before the turkeys were stocked on our land. I used every opportunity to take pictures of wildlife. Especially our new turkeys. I set up Pop Top tents overlooking the small chufa patch, several clover patches and other food plots.

I needed a luggage carrier to get that lens (weight about twenty pounds) and all the camera gear to my hidey-hole. Before we had a turkey season, I spent many late-winter days perched in a folding chair inside one of these tents, with that camera. A number of the gobbler pictures in this book were taken from these locations.

I didn't try to call birds to me. I just sneaked out before light and waited for them to come feast on the planted crops.

When turkey season arrived, I figured I might as well set up in one of the tents. The small chufa patch, situated on one of the Jeep trails, was easily accessible. So there I went.

I set up everything I needed the day before the season opened. The tent had been there for the picture taking, so all I really needed were decoys and calls and lots of camouflage to hide me. I decided on a Redi-Hen, a hard-bodied decoy that could be stood a few inches or almost a foot above ground—her height depending on how deep I stuck her one-legged stand.

Opening day, I was on site well before first light. I positioned the

Redi-Hen and crawled into the tent.

As daylight came, I *yelped* a couple of soft tree *yelps*, and when a gobbler answered just down the road, I knew I would go home with my turkey.

Only he flew down and went to the flock of hens that roosted with him.

Okay, I'll give 'em a while and yelp them up this way when the hens won't accept his courting.

Something moved in the thickets across the trail and down to my right. Not a turkey. Too light. Brownish. A dog?

Nope. A coyote.

The breeze moved the tent a little.

He looked at the tent. And slipped back into the woods.

I readied my shotgun. *You just come up here, buddy, and I'll teach you about eating baby turkeys.*

I *yelped*. Twice.

Here came the coyote. He stalked my hen. Moving as slowly as a cat slipping up on a bird, he locked his sight onto the decoy.

I ruined my hunting day when I shot. I also ruined his day. One less predator for the birds to dodge.

I let the area cool down a couple of days before I returned. The only luck I had elsewhere was as bad as that opening day. On day three, I went back to the area to listen to the birds roost. Both hens and gobblers flew up about fifty yards off the small chufa patch.

Yes. Come back tomorrow!

Again, my calling was as attractive to the birds as a scratching fingernail on a blackboard. Old Redi-Hen waited with great patience for a tom to visit her. I propped my chin on my hand and went to sleep.

A harsh clawing woke me. I jerked awake. Where the heck was I? Inside a tent somewhere.

The noise came again. I peeked through one of the windows.

A yearling tom. The stupid jake had tried to mount the decoy. I swear he looked puzzled, and if he coulda talked he would have been cussing that hen. He tried one more time to mount her, and this time, she fell.

I nearly fell over laughing.

He left. So I did, still without my first bird.

RANGER MARION R. NELSON

Marion Nelson became our senior local ranger in 1977. Like previous rangers, he was Johnny on the spot whenever I called for help—mostly in the middle of the night when the night riders were active and their shooting woke me up. Eight years later, I decided that our ranger needed recognition, so in 1985, I wrote to Leonard Ledbetter, then DNR commissioner, and requested that he present a token of our thanks to Sergeant Nelson, but to keep the donation anonymous. (See Appendix XII for the entire letter.)

On our behalf, Mr. Ledbetter presented Nelson with a framed copy of the print *The Guardian* by James R. Darnell, the noted wildlife artist.

The *Union-Recorder* carried a story on October 18, 1985, page 2, with the headline: **Nelson Honored**:

Conservation Sergeant Marion Nelson of Milledgeville was recently recognized for his work in ceremonies at the Georgia Department of Natural Resources.

Nelson was presented with a limited edition framed print of *The Guardian*, a painting of a white-tailed deer in the Middle Georgia woods. The award was given to Nelson in recognition of a job well done in a professional and competent manner by an anonymous sportsman in the Baldwin County area.

DNR Commissioner J. Leonard Ledbetter, who made the presentation on behalf of the donors, said, "We are extremely proud of Sergeant Nelson and the job he does for us. There is no greater honor for a ranger than to be honored by the citizens he serves."

Nelson is a veteran of thirteen years with the Law Enforcement Section of the DNR's Game and Fish Division and is assigned to the Macon Law Enforcement District.

J. Leonard Ledbetter (left), commissioner of the Department of Natural Resources, and Leon Kirkland (right), game and fish director, present conservation sergeant Marion Nelson with an award given by a Baldwin County sportsman.

When the presentation was made, because it was anonymous, Nelson said he could not accept it; too many bad guys might be involved and be using the gift as an anonymous attempt to implicate him in a bribery plot. When he was finally told that the award came from my group of hunters, he accepted it because he realized it was indeed what it was presented to be, a thank you.

* * *

Five year's later, local political events caused problems for both Ranger Nelson and myself, so I wrote another letter, to the new Commissioner of the Department of Natural Resources, about Nelson. All the rangers supported me; I supported them when the need arose. That letter stressed the problem Nelson faced:

Nelson once charged a man with a wildlife offence and that

man's relative is now sitting as judge here in Baldwin County and hears all Game and Fish cases. This judge is known to bear grudges, finding people not guilty when the evidence is indisputable and even refusing to recuse in a case in which he was obviously prejudiced.

These revenge problems ended when the judge (my distant cousin Bob Green) was voted off the bench after he threatened a superior court judge with a pistol—in the courthouse, no less.

MORNING AT WHITE CLOUD LODGE
OF THE 777 GAME RANCH

Predawn, **before** the birds awaken or the night prowlers return home, when Orion pierces the sky like four eyes searching for his game before the glittering ice of the stars begins to melt.

I stand on the cabin porch with coffee cup in hand and with the camera at my feet. The darkness begins to lighten and small feet whisper through the leaves as a shadow blacker than the night moves by. A ringtail trots in the light falling from my window, a mouse clutched in his teeth. He scampers up the mesquite tree beside my car. The last I see of him is his tail slipping over the cabin roof.

Moments later a cottontail starts across the road, looks my way, freezes, and then scurries into the underbrush.

Human noises drift from the barn as workers stir. Sheep, used to early breakfast, *baa* their way toward the barn. A dark form moves between me and the lake, for a few brief seconds silhouetted against the dawn reflected in the lake; the yard buck, head lowered as if to hide his trophy rack, sneaks toward the barn for a free meal with the sheep.

Peafowl and yard turkeys drop from their roosts into the barnyard for breakfast, their wings flapping like blankets on a clothesline. One peacock yowls like a cat, and a goose answers from the lake.

Sunrise over the lake is not spectacular today. Clouds, drifting in from the Gulf, extend the dawn and add a cool dampness to the early breeze.

Two rams slam their heads together from somewhere in the mesquite behind the cabin. My mind watches them as they continue their dispute and I wonder if they are giving each other a headache.

Ducks flock overhead, circle the pond and begin to swoop down, their legs extended for the landing, when they suddenly spook, roll as a unit, quack their distress, and fly off to look for a safer lake.

Peafowl stroll from the barnyard, the cock with his tail fanned and the hens bugging their way across the field.

The dawn explodes with animals.

A dozen ibex trot between me and the lake. Then the Père David's buck materializes behind the ibex and stands broadside, as if challenging me to photograph his best side. I scrabble for the camera, but as I lift it to my eye, he vanishes into the shadows, and even the ibex disappear.

Camera in hand in spite of the lingering darkness, I slip along the trail from the cabin toward the headwaters of the lake. A patch of white moves, stops, moves, and I freeze. All I see is the impression of palmated antler as the white fallow buck disappears into a thicket.

Fallow buck in yard at White Cloud

I ease on and try to blend from one bush to another and to watch 360° around me, but I miss the shadow until it lurches into a trot, head thrown back, antlers laid against his shoulders. Knowing he is not hunted, the Père David's buck runs only some thirty yards, stops, turns his white face to me and stares.

A smaller shadow stops with him—a Sika buck, his antlers like black ink against the sky, also stares at me. But the Sika doesn't wait; in a second, he jumps into a thicket.

Sika buck

Spooking through the small patch, the Sika rousts out the white fallow buck; another fallow deer jumps out with them; it is half-white, half-spotted, as if someone had thinly white-washed a spotted fallow. All three plunge across the power-line opening and disappear.

Another day has begun at White Cloud Lodge.

This chapter placed second in the Hall Bernard Memorial literary contest at the Southeastern Writers Workshop in 2010.

ATTITUDES CHANGE WITH EXPERIENCE
(PART I)

From my earliest childhood, hunting was not forbidden, but deer, our most precious wildlife, were certainly not to be disturbed.

Somewhere in the back storage of my childhood mind I knew people hunted for food; just as we killed our chickens, turkeys, hogs, and cattle, so some people went to the woods and fields for rabbits and raccoons, quail, and possum. But these were the country people who needed food for their families, not the well-to-do city dweller who today seeks recreation and solitude at a financial cost higher per pound of harvest than filet mignon would cost at the corner market.

But when I left home to work in New England, I discovered two men in the office went deer hunting. Their stories of their kills were abhorrent and I nagged at them constantly as I remembered the first deer I had ever seen in the wild—the two bucks and doe that visited our pasture near the barn.

I was not yet ten years old when Dad awakened me and my sisters to go to the meadow by the barn. Two bucks with massive racks stood in a ditch, a doe nearby. My sisters and I, who devoured Felix Salten's *Bambi* and *Bambi's Children* (long before Disney turned Bambi into an American deer), were enthralled with Bambi's American cousins.

So I had grown into an anti-hunter (except for possum and raccoon), partially from children's literature and romanticism, and partially from plain ignorance of the facts of nature's balance that should have been drilled into me at school, but weren't. These same facts applied to the mixed timber/livestock farm of my youth: We had to limit the number of livestock to the food available.

For some years, I spoke my opinions loud and clear, arousing anger and antagonism of co-workers and friends.

In 1964, everything changed.

I moved back close to home to be able to visit the farm each weekend and holiday. That deer season and the next one my mom and I prosecuted each poaching hunter we found on our land. In our first year, we raised the county's income from the fines, and I learned the value of wildlife rangers and the protection they provide to both wildlife and people.

Then, opening morning in 1966, I crawled into a sweetgum tree and huddled into myself to stay warm while the stars faded and frost settled on the golden-red forest around my small meadow. I was so cold I swore I'd never repeat the experience—until a deer walked out and buck fever hit me harder than an eighteen-wheeler. By eight that morning, I had become an addict. I spent every spare moment since then either deer hunting, picture taking, scouting for deer, reading about deer, or preparing for the next season.

As the seasons progressed, I accepted the attitudes prevalent in my community about hunting: If a wild dog chases a deer, shoot the feral dog and let the deer go. And **never** kill a doe.

These attitudes stayed with me for years, and when I watched a highly emotional anti-hunting propaganda program on television, I found one gruesome segment affecting my attitudes and I added another negative belief:

—Exotic animal ranches are terrible places where the game is cruelly slaughtered in the name of hunting.

One by one these attitudes fell as my knowledge increased. I've been exposed to wider experiences, and conditions have changed.

In some areas of my state, hunting with dogs has been standard procedure for generations but I still remembered the fourth deer I had ever seen. It had been torn to shreds by a pack of dogs. In those days of my youth, packs of feral dogs attacked livestock. Twice, they went after my father. I had to kill dogs that were attacking our cows. Our pets were sometimes killed when they ran with these packs, as happened to our collie.

In my early years of hunting, feral dogs were common and often chased deer. One weekend when I was scouting before the season opened, I found a litter of puppies huddled in a creek bed, against the bank; babies that they were, they growled and tried to bite. Even from a distance, I saw ticks matted on them; their bellies were swollen with intestinal parasites. Their mother was another feral dog, perhaps dropped off in the country by someone tired of feeding her—pathetic, but an impossible situation to allow to continue, and we had to dispatch the puppies.

A friend from the South Georgia flatlands joined our hunting group and told tales of hunting and dogging deer in her youthful years.

Every deer she had killed had been busting through a small opening in the undergrowth, dogs in pursuit; every shot required quick judgment: Buck or doe? And then a sure and quick aim because there'd be no tracking deep into the swamps for an injured deer, not through those thickets. She told us of the excitement of listening to the hounds howl their prey across the swamps as she sat hunkered against a tree on the edge of a logging road or firebreak. Thirty years later when she was hunting with me she needed only one shot to down a deer that was running flat out.

From her stories I slowly learned that dogging deer can't be all bad just because I didn't hunt that way. She explained people had hunted with hounds in the flatlands of the Southeastern Coastal Plains for years because humans don't normally try to penetrate the thickets, marshes and river swamps; as long as people hunt these flatlands, the hounds will flush the bucks to the waiting hunter.

Many hunters still feel as I once did about killing does—if we remove the female, the mother of the next generation, we will eventually kill off the herd and will have no more hunting. Right? Wrong! If we **don't** kill some does as well as bucks, if we don't keep a low buck-to-doe ratio, if we don't keep the summer population **below** the carrying capacity of the land, we might not only lose our good hunting but also lose our deer habitat and the deer. If the herds increase beyond the carrying capacity of the land, they will eat the available food, destroy their own habitat, and decrease in size until they are not worth the bother (or cost) of butchering. They would die off from diseases and starvation.

My attitude about killing does changed slowly, however, even as the laws were changed to allow us to take does. At first, I limited myself to only one doe per season. When our area suddenly exploded with deer, not only did I forsake buck hunting entirely, but I also demanded that my own small group take only does and encouraged other hunters in my county to follow suit to help reduce the population back to the land's carrying capacity. Thus my second *wrong* attitude changed as conditions changed and my knowledge increased.

The third negative attitude I developed about hunting has also fallen, not as a result of my own hunting for the freezer, but as a result of my hunting with a 35-mm camera.

One TV program provided my only knowledge of exotic game ranches—I believed that the hunter walked into the equivalent of a barn lot, picked out his prey, which was as tame as a farmer's milk cow, and shot it. Two weeks on two exotic animal ranches in Texas showed me it's not that simple, at least not on the ranches I visited.

When I made arrangements to go to these ranches to photograph whitetails, I expected to walk out into a small pasture, something like a zoo, and take close-up photographs without needing a 500-mm lens.

How wrong I was! Their smallest pastures were more like a couple of square miles. Getting a picture there was not much easier than photographing in the wilds of Montana or Nebraska or South Dakota or New Mexico, where I'd photographed deer in 1985. Back home on the farm, I knew where to find the deer and get close-up photographs, but my deer were babies compared to the trophies on these ranches where the animals were fed supplemental, high-protein diets.

Located about 100 miles apart, the two ranches were quite different topographically. The Triple Seven near Hondo was mostly thickets that only wildlife could penetrate because the thorns would shred a man's clothes—and flesh. On the Texotic near Kerrville, the land was more open, some rolling hills and cedar growths not too tight for walking or driving.

Many exotic animal ranchers have special interests in their herds; the Triple 7 has a small herd of Père David's deer, on the endangered species list and protected by the ranch. The Y.O. Ranch (the first of the exotic animal ranches) raises longhorn cattle to ensure that the bred never dies out.

Although the State of Texas does not regulate the harvest of the exotic animals on the ranches, it does control the exotics that have escaped, adjusted to Texas wilderness, and reproduced. For example, the aoudad sheep is now established in some counties, thanks to those that escaped, bred and raised offspring.

My objective when I went to Texas was to photograph whitetails, but I found myself taking pictures of whatever animal I could get close to. Safari-style hunting (from a vehicle) is allowed in Texas, and while there, I hunted from a Jeep at times and in blinds other times. I discovered that although the fall hunting season was not yet underway, the animals were spooky, and taking pictures safari style in Texas was no easier than from my Jeep or blind back home in the Southeast.

These two bucks slipped out of the brush soon after I was set up, camouflaged, at the edge of the woods, overlooking a food site. The camera's clicks sent them flagging away.

As I left Texas, I felt that exotic animal hunting on a game ranch is like all hunting; the garden is planted, whether by God, by the State Game and Fish Department, or by an individual rancher who imports the animals. The garden may be our back yard, a state-owned hunting area, or a game ranch that is *not* a cattle pen.

We all want to harvest what is available and will continue to go to the garden of our choice for the crop of our choice.

These two articles about attitudes were written for the national magazine *Deerhunters United*, but it folded before these were published.

ATTITUDES CHANGE WITH EXPERIENCE
(PART II)

"These are the animals you may eat: The ox, the sheep, the goat, the hart, the gazelle, the roebuck, the wild goat, the ibex, the antelope, and the mountain sheep." Deuteronomy 14: 4-5.

And so God's Word tells us to harvest the deer for our tables, just as we harvest tomatoes or cattle that we've grown to eat or sell. Many hunters use this quotation to explain our harvest to the nonhunter, but how many American hunters look at the entire quote—that He intended for us to also harvest the more exotic animals such as the gazelle and the ibex.

Just as some deer hunters consider exotic animal hunting to be wrong, so does the nonhunter often consider deer hunting to be wrong. Both groups must remember that neither act is of itself *wrong*; we must keep in mind that some actions are considered *not acceptable* and others are considered *expected*. The difference lies within each of us and in our attitudes.

For anyone who has not experienced the excitement that can be found on an exotic animal ranch, such hunting may be *wrong*, but many of our fellow hunters consider it as American as the '55 Chevy.

As a landowner/hunter, I deer hunt on about one square mile of family land. Each year, before the season opens, I explore and scout so that I know where the natural food is and where the deer are. I have averaged better than a deer per year, and have passed up many a deer to guide another hunter to a stand or area for an almost-guaranteed deer.

After a couple of weeks on exotic game ranches, I realized that their system is really not so much different from mine. The only real difference is that their pasture fences are game-proof.

Now don't get me wrong. Some ranches do have small pens for the customer to just walk out to the animal and dispatch it. The two game ranches I visited did not—their animals had more acres than my own personal hunting area covered; they had more than one square mile (sometimes several miles) of refuge inside their fences. The hunter doesn't just ride out to a pasture of tame, unafraid animals, pick out the one he wants, and slaughter it as if he's in a packing house yard. At times, the hunter goes home empty-handed; other times, he must spend several days hunting his game. And, true, sometimes he lucks up and gets his game in a couple of hours—but, then, so have I, hunting unfenced whitetails in the Southeast.

To hunt on a game ranch, you must have a guide; sometimes you hunt from a stand and sometimes safari style (from a vehicle, as in Africa, which is legal in Texas).

Many hunters travel to Colorado, Wyoming and Montana to seek elk, antelope or mule deer. Often they are required to have a guide or outfitter, who does the cooking, provides the horses and tent, and leads the hunter into the hills. The outfitter also locates the game, so all the hunter does is fire the killing shot.

So it is with game ranches. The game are limited in range, true, but an area of one-to-five square miles is large enough for an animal to evade a hunter for quite a while.

Recall the experiment with penned whitetails and several hunters? The researcher placed transmitters on all the bucks and all the hunters so he knew where each was at all times. Although hunters came within a few yards of deer several times, not one deer was seen, much less killed, in that square mile.

On game ranches in dry areas, water holes could serve as bait for any animal. Ranches in these areas have to dig wells and create streams and pools for the wildlife. Water is piped into various areas and allowed to flow naturally through open areas and thickets, to form ponds and a lengthy—perhaps a mile long—system to give the animals a variety of choices for watering.

I rode one day with a hunter seeking a trophy-sized fallow buck (the deer native to Sherwood Forest and Robin Hood's victims). After searching about an hour, the guide spotted a sizeable buck, on a distant ridge. He and the hunter glassed the animal for a few minutes while I tried to get photographs with my 500-mm lens. Even with that magnification, the deer was only a white speck. The massive palmated antlers were barely visible. The buck walked into thickets and we rode along our ridge and finally came up on the road the buck had crossed.

Thickets made hunting on foot impossible. The Jeep tires were filled with a rubber-like substance so they would not go flat when punctured by a plant's spikes. Openings and roads in the semi-desert jungle were carved out with machinery.

The buck stared at us from only yards away, but he stood in such a thicket that the hunter had no shot. Both guide and hunter managed to get their binoculars on him before he silently vanished, not to reappear on our side of the thickets or downhill into a larger opening.

The mesquite and other brush were low enough that if the buck lifted his head high we would have seen him. From our uphill perch we could see about fifty or so acres in the area where he hid, but the wise old trophy kept his head down. We circled the thicket, but still no sign of him. After more than a half-hour, we left, not expecting to see him again that day.

In fact, that hunter was not able to collect that buck. The deer was pastured in 1500 acres but took refuge in a fifty-acre tract. I could only compare his chances for survival with that of the whitetails back home, where 75% of the whitetail bucks were killed by the age of eighteen months, and every fifty acres of hunting land had at least one hunter. On the game ranch, the bucks had a longer life.

Those who object to game ranch hunting most often oppose the fences that limit an animal's range. But those fences serve other purposes. They allow the rancher to shift animals from pasture to pasture as food supplies and populations vary. By using a small catch pen connected to various pastures, the rancher can open the catch pen gate to allow animals from one pasture to enter; once the animals he wants to move are caught, he releases them into the pasture where he wants them.

Fences also help the rancher control the food supply. Knowing how many animals are in a given pasture, he can supplement food to produce magnificent animals. On one ranch, for example, some of the deer I saw were not available for hunting because they were too small, and their food supply was being supplemented to produce real trophies for another year. (Every hunter I know would have been thrilled to have collected one of those "too small" bucks!)

Here are some of the bucks I met in Texas:

A trophy collected on a game ranch cannot get into the Boone and Crockett records if the animal is killed within the penned area, no matter the size of the pen, since the Boone and Crockett Club does not consider hunting on a game ranch to be fair chase.

The Boone and Crockett Club gets its name from, of course, Daniel Boone and David Crockett. It is a hunter-conservationist organization dating from 1887 and has been instrumental in protecting wildlife and expanding national parks and eliminating commercial sales of wildlife. Today it is most widely known among hunters for its method of scoring (e.g., measuring a buck's antlers) big game animals. Only animals of a certain score are entered into the record books, along with the hunters' names.

What constitutes *fair chase*? To some, fair chase is moving the animal out of thickets with dogs; to some, it's using a Jeep to ride the thickets; to some, it's sitting in a tower or tree stand to ambush the animal when it walks by; to some, it's hunting only on foot and only with a longbow and arrow. Turkey hunters also have a strong definition of fair chase: They consider ambushing a gobbler to be legal but sinful—the only way to kill a gobbler is to make like a love-sick hen and call him to you.

I found it interesting that the hunter I traveled with as he sought his fallow deer had taken a Dall sheep on a game ranch a couple of years before. He needed seven days of constant hunting to get his sheep on the game ranch, but only three days to collect one on the wild, open lands of Alaska. So what is fair chase?

In the Southeast, our wildlife is not limited by fences, but the whitetail deer limit themselves. They usually don't travel more than a mile from their birth sites. Most hunters I know use some transport—a Jeep or other four-wheel-drive or even an off-road four wheeler—to get close to a deer stand. Hunting from the vehicle itself is not legal in many states, however, and these laws would have a negative influence on someone first introduced to safari- style hunting.

Only the deer hunter who has not heard of its advantage fails to use a sex lure during the rut.

We all take what advantage we can in pursuing our game. Some of us want a whitetail, however small, in the wild. Some want a deer in front of the hounds; some want an exotic animal from a game ranch.

Whether in the wild or on a game ranch, many game animals now depend on man for survival. Without game laws and rangers to enforce them, many species could be lost, like the passenger pigeon. Man provides supplemental food in some areas to prevent mass starvation. And we harvest the game of our choice under the appropriate laws and regulations and under the conditions we prefer. We must each remember that no matter what our own choices, someone out there thinks his hunting methods are better.

A TWO-BUCK DAY

The deer season had been dry for our entire group, with only four deer in the freezer after a month-long hunt. My group usually had at least eight in the freezer by the end of November. That special hunt between Christmas and New Year's was not productive the first days.

So sure I'd get a deer in the November hunt, I had sent different guests to the stands that usually produced for me, and I'd taken a nearby stand. Four guests had scored, and now that the final week of the season was here, I still had both my tags.

Sitting in my stand, I wondered how the boys fared in the wind. They had to be cold too. I had carried extra clothes, but now, even with them on and it still two hours before dark, the cold got to me. Wind walked through the pines gently at times, sounding for all the world like a deer browsing in oak leaves. Silence for a moment before a hearty gust slapped limbs together and threw pine cones onto the ground with so much force I turned my head to look for the deer that had to be jumping through bushes.

With only two more days of the special Christmas bonus hunt, only one hunter had collected a deer, a small yearling doe yesterday, the first of the three doe days. Tomorrow would be cold—the meteorologist's prediction of 7° F was enough to send us out early today. We all hoped to get a deer before that cold wave kept us in the house and by the fire.

Already it was below freezing, and the wind took the chill factor much lower. I wiggled my toes, hunkered over and got still.

Was that a deer, off to my right? The ridge sloped downhill, through scattered pines and hardwoods, to a wet-weather stream that spread across the valley. Halfway down, something moved. An outline etched in white appeared—a tail. It switched once. Leaning far forward, I barely made out the doe, easing along, browsing as she went. She was the third deer I had seen here this week, but the boys claimed nothing had moved on this ridge when they sat here, one a day, for three days.

The deer took another step, and I leaned back, to look around the other side of a pine. Long minutes passed and then without a sound the doe stepped into sight again, head down. She was much too far away for my shotgun and I could only watch. She fed a few minutes, switched her tail, and then spun around, head high, ears cocked, as the wind whipped a dead limb from a pine uphill from me. I looked that way too, and when I turned back, I couldn't find the doe. Had she gone? I squinted, trying to remember where she had stood, trying to separate her from the brown-gray woods. Only when she moved her foot did her outline become obvious.

As much as I have hunted, I am always amazed at the camouflage Nature has provided its animals; apparently solid colors blend easily into a variety of colors, patterns and shapes. That deer was invisible in pine trunks against a background of needles and oak leaves and some scattered honeysuckle.

She moved again, this time disappearing behind a clump of honeysuckle. But for another half-hour I listened to the doe rustle leaves as she worked her way along the ridge. I kept my head turned her direction until my neck felt locked into pain. I expected another deer to appear at any moment on the upper trail, as one had only three days before.

A glance at my watch told me it was 3:45. Three days ago it was almost 5:00 when the other deer worked its way along the closer trail toward this stand. I was not worried about her small size—our lands were getting striped by too many deer and not enough food, and any size doe would mean two or three fewer mouths to feed next year. If that second doe came my way as she had earlier, it'd be an ideal shot, some twenty-five yards to my right, perfect for a left-hander. I shifted slightly in my stand in anticipation.

Somewhere to my left, over a ridge or two, a shotgun blasted away once, and again. Was that my nephew, Rusty? My mind traveled over the woods, up and over the ridge, down to my other stand where he sat at the junction of two streams where I had gotten three bucks in four years, instead of this tree where I had always seen deer but never a buck. Maybe he had one; he wanted a buck badly after going with only does for the last two years. Strain my ears as I would, I heard nothing but the wind walking the trees, trying to imitate a deer slipping through the brush. Well, it was after 4:00 now; if he had a deer, he would find me for help, although I had said I planned to be in hearing distance.

Then another shot, a rifle. Again, again. Was that the other boy? From all the noise he was making he must have his limit. That boy just didn't miss.

For the next few minutes, I was torn between staying there, waiting out the last couple of hours of light, and going to the boys, both beyond two ridges. Suppose they hadn't fired? All I'd do was spook deer if I tromped over there—besides, I thought, the shots *might* have been off the land. Not likely, but possible.

I was still in a state of indecision a few minutes later when something crunched the ground over my left shoulder. I eased my head around. A gray form moved slowly downhill, his right antler light against the dark woods. Easing that shotgun around was simple for a right-handed shot. He lowered his head, browsed on honeysuckle, ambled along.

A deer moved behind him. *Is it a doe?* I saw only part of a body. I'd wait, jut in case it was a doe.

Scattered and high up the bushes, out of reach of the extending noses of deer, honeysuckle swung a curtain between me and the deer.

Their brown-gray coats blended into the tree trunks and gray limbs. The buck moved into a jumble of haws and disappeared. If he followed the trail he was on he'd step from that jumble, into range. But where was the second deer?

Back up the hill it moved again, head down, antlers almost white against his neck. No doe. Well, I'd settle for a buck. At least it would be meat for the freezer. And if that second deer would just move down a little, into easy shotgun range, I just might be able to fill that freezer.

My calmness surprised me. Had I hunted so much, had too much success with hunting, that I no longer cared? No excitement welled up in me. That first day I hunted and the buck walked into the field, I shook so hard I missed and missed again. If these walked by, it did not matter. All that mattered was eliminating mouths.

I eased the shotgun to my right shoulder, felt it strange against my wrong shoulder, my arms and hands out of place in the unfamiliar grip. But with a dominant right eye, I knew I could hit. The first buck stepped from the haw thickets and stood with his head up high to look down the trail. I put that little bead on his neck, held tight, and looked for the second deer. Buck Number Two had entered the haw thicket. *Oh, well, one is only half as good as two, but lots better than none.* I turned my attention back to the first buck.

I found that small slot on the back of the shotgun barrel, lined it up like a rifle sight, and squeezed; the gun jumped; the deer dropped. I didn't I see a white flag bounding off. Where was the other buck? Only stillness as the ridge and valley echoed the sound of the shot.

My semi-automatic was ready if that second buck was still around. I kept the shotgun half up to my shoulder. Excitement surged within, reached my stomach and tied it into a knot. Where was that buck?

He bounded from the haws in two jumps, stopped, looked at his traveling companion lying flat on his side, and presented me with a perfect target. The second shot was perfect and in half-a-minute I had filled my tags.

From twenty-five feet in the air, a deer looks small; for a woman who's never field dressed one alone, they looked like monsters when I approached them to contemplate where to begin.

After a week of not taking my gut kit with me, what had possessed me that day to be prepared for this, I'll never know. But I wrestled those bucks onto their backs one by one, tied them in place with the spare ropes, and field dressed them without help.

I had forgotten about my nephew in that long hour of blood and guts and fighting the hill's slope on the first one, only to use it to my advantage on the second.

When I met my nephew, he had a five-pointer, and this time I had help with the surgery.

BROADUS, MONTANA

Little did I know what a trip to Deadwood, South Dakota, would lead to: A bump on the head, a physician who was a hunting nut, a trip to a grocery store in Broadus, Montana, and more deer than I could count.

When my traveling companion smashed her head against the wall-mounted TV that night and bled all over the hotel room, I decided to play it safe. I drove her to the emergency room.

The doctor walked in, lifted the towel off her bloody head, and said, "You'll live. Whatcha doing in Deadwood?"

I said looking for deer to photograph. "Go west," he said. "To Broadus, Montana." As he plunged into a discussion about his favorite deer country, his excitement was contagious. I ran to the car for my map, but Broadus was not shown.

Before he bothered to patch up the bleeding head, he drew me a rough map. And come morning, westward I went. Through backroads, where cowboys were working the cattle and boots hung upside down over fence posts. Where the roads were dusty and rocky and bumpy. Where the air tasted dry and smelled of dust and cattle manure. Where strange fences leaned against mounds of baled hay. Where a warped board with hand-painted letters and a crooked arrow directed me along the dirt road to Broadus.

I found the town.

Its population of some 600 (in the county in 1985) never locked their doors except during tourist season. Local ranchers' sons have a calf roping contest in town every week, and deer go where they please.

The best motel in town (and the only one I found) was the C-J (Cee Bar Jay), and Jean Hough, who ran it, knew everybody in the county, not just their names but where they lived and their children. When I told Jean I had come to photograph deer, she gave me outstanding directions.

One road led to the river bridge and the flatlands that stretched along the banks, through scattered brush and trees. Another road would take me into a spread of several sections (one square mile = 640 acres = one section) with the river in the distance across alfalfa fields to my left and buttes and meadows to my right. Ask the ranch foreman about taking pictures—everyone would treat me like family, the hotel manager told me.

While my traveling companion stayed at the motel and caught up on her TV soap operas that afternoon, with evening approaching I took the road to the ranch. Deer? They were in the alfalfa fields off toward the treeline near the river. Not just a few scattered, but dozens of both whitetails and mule deer—a hunter's and photographer's paradise not just of deer but of trophy deer.

Finding the ranch foreman was no problem—I stopped at the only house I'd seen within a mile, and the foreman gave permission to venture anywhere "for eighteen miles of our road frontage. Just be sure to fasten the gates to keep the cows in."

"I grew up in the country," I said. "I know about gates. I'll be sure they're closed. What're those funny fences leaned up against the hay?"

Slatted panels of what looked like fences leaned against the stacks of baled hay.

"It's to keep elk off the hay stacks. They get on top to eat and then defecate and urinate on the hay. Then the cattle won't eat it."

He went on to tell me that they did not officially have elk in the Broadus area, but he'd seen a few and wasn't taking chances.

Bless Pat if I didn't see two bull elk feeding in the fields as I headed back to the motel as the sun dropped behind the buttes. Naturally, the elk were too far away and darkness too close for even my 600-mm f/5.6 Nikon lens to capture an image.

Breaking dawn found me back at the McEuen ranch and crawling through the fence with tripod, camera and stool to await full daylight. I settled beside a tree (don't ask me what kind—it just provided something to break up my outline), with camera on the tripod, and waited for the deer to come feast on alfalfa.

The wait was short. The deer appeared from the shadows of the treeline along the river and scattered across the fields. Even with the camera clicking, they didn't bother to look my way.

These deer were nowhere as skittish as the Eastern whitetails. I set up the camera and tripod day after day in the open, sometimes snuggling close to sagebrush, sometimes standing against a tree, but not needing the full blinds or elevated stands needed back home in Georgia. Ironically, however, they'd spook from the car because it was a stranger on the roads.

Back at the C-J, when I asked Jean about the deer not being afraid of us, she said not to worry, they got plenty shy when the shooting started and the land was invaded by hunters from *back East*.

I shopped at the local grocery for supplies—I had a microwave and fridge in the room. At the store I discovered a carved meadow lark on display. When I asked about it, I was referred to the artist, Keith Stevens of Ashland, a few miles up the road. He also happened to be a pilot who flew the game management rangers for their deer counts.

I called him, went to visit, bought one of his carvings and made reservations to fly, with my camera. Keith introduced me to his friend Buzz Tartar, an artist. When I saw Buzz's work, I immediately said, "You remind me of Will James." I couldn't leave without one of his drawings of a cowboy riding a bucking mustang, which hangs near my computer.

Keith kept three planes on his personal runway, and flew to visit neighbors rather than drive the gravel (to me, dirt) roads.

A Piper Cub can fly as slow as, maybe, 55 mph, but taking pictures from the back seat, as the pilot slows, turns, and points out the deer or antelope, is not easy. I finally learned to put the camera on *automatic*, the motor drive on *continuous* and the focus on *infinity*. When he dropped to below sixty feet, the close-up pictures might be out of focus, but the distant shots would be sharp. I had plenty of film and would take lots of exposures. Since he was not one to harass the animals with numerous passes, I was happy for the pictures I got during the single run.

Once, he did make three low passes for me to get pictures of one buck. The animal was with a herd of does, only yards from the end of the runway. The does loped away from town, leaped fences and the road and were headed for the hills. The buck, however, hunkered down in a gulch (a coulee) and Keith had to fly over him several times to spook him into the open.

Off we went, above the Powder River, where whitetail bucks looked up at the noisy bird and wild turkeys scurried from the fields to hide under the trees along the river.

How different the land was within only a few yards—the river bottom gave way to alfalfa fields and to buttes and sagebrush where the deer bedded in the heat of the day.

On we flew, across buttes and a plateau where only a few hunters ever ventured. Six mule deer bucks galloped down into the coulees to hide from the loud bird. To see a group of trophy bucks together, watching us approach, gave me as bad a case of buck fever with my camera as I'd ever had. I wanted those photographs as much as I had wanted my first deer.

I was able to get a shot of three of the big muleys.

I told Keith I had seen two elk the day before our flight, and he said I was lucky, that elk were rare around Broadus.

One morning, Jean Hough drove up as I opened the tripod along the gravel road to photograph does in the flame of fall colors. Usually I'd ride for several miles, sometimes sit near the road for a couple of hours and see deer but no people.

She stopped, rolled down her window, and said with a smile, "Well, I see you really are taking pictures. Getting some good ones?"

I told her I hoped so, I was sending them back to Atlanta to have them processed. We chatted a few minutes, and then she was on her way.

Antelope herds speckled the flatlands between buttes, their white and orange standing out vividly compared with the gray/browns of the deer that so closely matched the sagebrush and ground in untilled areas.

The mule deer were insistent cusses. If a deer decided to go somewhere, it went, no matter that a stranger blocked the road. One morning two small bucks off in the distance strolled toward the fence and road. I left the car and spooked the deer. But I figured they would be back—they hadn't gone far. So I stood beside the fence, leaned against a tree and waited. And within five minutes both yearlings were back, to cross the road. I snapped pictures. One had the courage to cross the fence near me.

If this fella could read, he'd know from the sign on the left no one could shoot him here. No mention of the camera, though.

When I ran out of film, I intentionally spooked the other one off and reloaded as fast as I could. The second buck came back, but this time he brought a big doe to help him get past this strange thing that clicked at him. They both ran off rather than face the clicking camera.

Everyone I met treated me as a friend. One lady invited me to wander over her ranch and directed me to her flocks of wild turkeys. Another rancher, Lawrence Giacometto in nearby Boyes, Montana, turned me over to his son Ron (with a broken leg from calf-riding!) to drive me over his ranch, and then the family treated me to supper. They were as eager to hear about Georgia as I was to learn about Broadus and Boyes. Lawrence had been to Georgia on vacation once, but left because he couldn't see anything for the trees.

Montana has views beyond words or imagination.

Montana is called *Big Sky Country* for a reason—you can see to infinity. Here a mule deer buck shows off the gait I call the *bunny hop*—all four feet off the ground at once,

One of my favorite picture-taking spots was the bridge over the Powder River. Wide and shallow, it is known to be "a mile wide and full of dust powder." One morning, in three hours lots of deer came along, but only one vehicle—the school bus.

I shot one of my all-time favorite pictures from the bridge one morning.

Water is scarce in southeast Montana; ranchers with water rights to the river can irrigate with river water. Others must drill and use windmills to raise underground water. Rain storms with fine shaft lightning dropped curtains of water, but none reached the ground. The humidity was so low the rain often evaporated before it hit earth.

As a deer freak, if I should die and go to Deer Hunter's Heaven, I'm sure it'd be called Broadus, Montana.

A Broadus courting couple at the McEuen ranch.

I am delighted that I have been able to get back in touch with Jean Hough and her son Steve Held. We've e-mailed about Broadus of 1985 and how it is today. I have learned that the C-J Motel got its name from the family ranch brand. They raise black Angus.

Steve says elk, unofficial residents in 1985, are definitely official now. He has graciously allowed me to share this picture of some local residents—his neighbors:

For information about Broadus, visit Jean and Steve at:
www.broadusmontana.com
www.site.twinheartsranch.com
Steve's personal site: www.steve.twinhearts.googlepages.com/home

THE POSSUM COP AND THE CB RADIO

Robert Joseph Sires
1946-2016

Christmas, and the Citizen's Band (CB) radio was on everybody's want list. What fun to ride up and down the road, listen to the chatter about Smokey and think about Burt Reynolds and his adventures in the movie *Smokey and the Bandit.*

I had a base unit CB as well as a hand-held unit, and I purchased three extra hand units so at least four of us would have 'em when we were in the woods. A friend had put up the antenna on the roof of the house—two stories with twelve-foot ceilings, where I was reared. We could chat with CB folks who were miles away.

December 26, Warden Bob Sires came by to visit on his way to stake out a baited stand. He wanted to let me know I could reach him on his new toy any time he was in his ranger truck. His handle: Brer

Possum.

"Why Brer Possum?" I had to ask.

"Don't you know poachers call us Possum Cops? I thought it'd be fun."

So when I started this book, I had to include that nickname in the title.

I was delighted to be able to reach him by CB; my hand unit had ten channels and I'd be able to reach Brer Possum at quite a distance. I hoped.

When Bob had driven about a mile, he called to check the reception on my hand-held radio and the home base unit. Reception was almost too good—modulator needles almost flew off the base's display. When I signed off the base, I called him up on my hand unit and got him easily. I told the Possum I was happy to have him in good radio contact, and signed off.

The CB wouldn't reach the world like a phone, but it sure beat having no way to communicate.

I checked reception one more time, just in case: "Catbird to Brer Possum."

"Brer Possum here. What's up?"

"Just checking in. What's your twenty?"

"About fifteen miles up the road from your dead end," he replied.

My dead end was the junction of the state road through the family lands and the Macon highway. So he was about twenty miles away by road, maybe about a dozen or so across country.

"Reception's good here. Your system seems to be working okay."

"Ten-four. Have a good night." And we signed off.

I kept my base radio on in the house to listen to chatter and got some directed to me.

"Catbird? You got a copy?" An unfamiliar voice, and only a few of my hunters knew I had a base unit.

I picked up the mike. "Ten-four. You got the Catbird."

"What's the twenty on that possum cop?"

Ah-ha! Somebody's up to no good. Maybe I can find out what. He musta thought I was a fella.

On the phone, because my voice is close to tenor if not baritone, strangers say "sir" to me all the time.

"He's over toward Jones County. Going after somebody baiting. What's your handle?"

"This is the Deerslayer here. Thanks for that comeback, good buddy. He won't be over my way now, and I can turn my dogs lose this afternoon."

"Well, now, I sure do wish you luck. How'm I coming to you there?"

"Loud and clear. What's you twenty?"

"I'm off Highway 22. How about you?"

"We're up here at Sinclair, on the Putnam-Baldwin line. You sure are coming in clear."

"Well, that's good to know. You had any luck hunting this year?"

"None today. But I got three bucks back in November. You done any good?"

Oh-ho. One over the limit.

"Yeah, I got me a nine-pointer back in November. Don't tell it, but I got me a good eating doe, too." *Maybe that will get him to bragging some more.* "Say, you going out this afternoon, I reckon?"

"Yep. They got the dogs ready now. We're down and out."

Well, that ploy didn't get me any more information. At least he said "down and out" instead of "ten-ten." He must be turning off his radio.

Maybe.

Did Bob hear the Deerslayer's half of the conversation, when apparently the poacher hadn't heard Bob when he and I talked? I went to the phone to call Bob's supervisor in the Macon office.

No dial tone. Typical.

Only one alternative. Back to the CB. The Deerslayer ought to be in the woods without his ears on by now. If he were on a base unit. And if he meant "down and out."

Maybe I better wait at least a half-hour.

Time dragged. I went out to the back porch and sat in the rocker. I passed the time letting my mind wander to the activities of rangers who had worked my county and what the poachers had left in the woods and along the road.

—A buck with his guts shot out, still on his feet as dogs snarled and attacked, found by a hunter who shot the buck, ran the dogs off, and fell to his knees and wept over the deer.

—The doe skeleton I found where a poacher killed her and left her to rot.

—The man on his lunch break who shot from his car toward

several does in my field. When we faced him down, he swore he was shooting at a buck. But my hunter in a stand near the road saw it all, including all the does. He went to jail.

—The shot at 2:30 a.m. in bow season when the telephone did work and our ranger caught the three poachers, with one bow and a 30.06. We all lost a night's sleep, but they lost a *lot* of cash, and their vehicle.

—The game warden who stated matter-of-factly: "My only goal in life is to be half as good a warden as my sergeant."

—The friendly competition among the rangers to catch violators, and their hiding in the bushes all night to protect the deer they love but do not have time to hunt themselves.

—The group of white men from Atlanta who pushed their way

onto a black neighbor's land, built stands and baited each with salt and apples—and got caught on opening day. They paid a fine then, and another one later when Smokey caught them speeding up I-20.

—The six deer skeletons I found within yards of the highway, shot by night hunters who did not even bother to stop to collect their kill—a fawn, one young buck, and three does left to rot, plus the trophy buck with his antlers cut off.

Thirty minutes finally went by while I mulled over the past. Time to call Brer Possum.

I didn't say his handle, or mine, just used his call numbers and invited him to another channel. Without handles, maybe even if he was listening, the Deerslayer wouldn't have a clue.

"Bob, you hear that conversation a while ago?"

"Sure did, Catbird. I've passed the word on and we've got two men on the way."

"Terrific. Let me know what happens."

We cleared the channel, but before I turned off the unit, the Deerslayer said, "We got ears, too, Catbird."

Yeah, maybe so. But Brer Possum clued in Possum Cop Mark Payne who pinned their ears back that afternoon.

SHARING MAKES FOR QUALITY HUNTING

Sheila Key scored a big one on her hunt with us.

Neighbor Shelia Key and her husband, Richard, joined us for some quality hunts.

Having spent three days swapping tall hunting tales with one thousand other deer nuts at the 1986 Buckarama, I found myself thinking about what makes for quality hunting. I could only think of adventures shared with friends.

At sixteen, Greg had never killed a deer, although he had spent several weekends of three seasons beside his aunt in the November woods. Everyone in the club wanted a deer for him as much as he did. On the final day of last season, we all had expected him to get one—It was our only doe day, but the lands were full of does. All he had to do was walk from the house, cross the main road to the meadow and crawl into what's known as Herbert's Hilton. The does would be all over him by 8 o'clock.

But that day, when the does came by, they were stretched out, pushing for all they were worth, and he had no clean shot through the brush; we'd taught him to never take a chance shot that would lead to injury and slow death or a painful crippling recovery.

And an hour later, his aunt's 30.06 busted the morning. In a few minutes, she and I drove up to get Greg. He didn't say much as we went across the fields, but when we reached her deer (measured at 136 7/8 Boone and Crockett), boy and aunt looked at the buck and then at each other. "I'd never have shot him if he was coming your way," she promised him. They hugged and cried on each other's shoulder.

The buck had been only yards from the no-man's land at the edge of my property line, and it was take him, or leave him for some other hunter across the way.

This year, Greg was due for his deer, and we waited at the house all morning with our ears cocked toward the hill where he was perched on Norman's favorite stand. When we heard the shot, we didn't bother to wait for him to reach the house—we immediately went for him and his deer (was there any doubt?) in the Jeep, and met one happy boy running off the hill, waving and yelling his joy.

That was quality for the season, in spite of the punishment we inflicted on Greg. We'd never cut off shirt tails or rubbed it in if someone missed his shot or got down too soon and spooked off a buck. But that day, Greg got some special treatment we'd saved for two years and threatened him with constantly. Norman, who had yet to get his deer that year but who had given up his favorite stand, did the honors while Dad held his son—the boy got a champagne shampoo in the yard.

For me, it was quality to see these two young men friends sharing joy, unafraid of being unmanly, willing to hug each other and cut up like children. It takes a special fellow to give up his stand when he hasn't gotten his deer.

Greg remembered, and later that year, he repaid the favor to a younger hunter, who, without Greg's willing sacrifice, would have gone without a deer.

Doe day in early December, Greg put his sights on a doe with a crippled leg, knowing that if the doe didn't go to the freezer she would probably fall to dogs over the winter. But something made him hold his finger lightly on the trigger and not fire. Instead, he watched her hobble into the woods and out of sight. Greg came in that day to tell us he had made a mistake, that he knew he should have shot that deer— he had a tag left and she was in easy range—but somehow he just couldn't.

The *why* became clear after Christmas, when we came to the last day of the bonus hunt week. My nephew Russ was home for the holidays and eager to bag a deer. He'd gone two long years without one and the itch was like a raw sore. But the week slipped by rapidly and no deer for Russ. The last day dawned, with Russ scheduled to leave his stand at 9:30 a.m. and leave the house for the airport by 10:00. So he picked an easy-in-easy-out stand where deer often fed in early morning.

But 9:30 came. Russ squeezed out another minute, and then another. The doe hobbled out of the brush into the field, to stand broadside.

Greg reached Russ before I did, and when I arrived, the boys were pounding each other on the back, Greg proud that he'd left that doe for Russ and my nephew showing his gratitude in return.

Quality is also sharing what you know about hunting. One of the best *still-hunters* I know is Norman, who returned from Vietnam and had seen so much killing he refused to hunt for a couple of years, but after he spent some time with our club as a nonhunting guest, he decided to try this crazy stuff we were doing.

He got his first deer while he was having a coughing fit in the stand. The buck dropped; Norman started down from his perch; the buck kicked; Norman scrambled back up the tree. Our city-boy hunter, afraid he'd be attacked by the frenzied animal, shot it again from the safety of the stand. But today that city boy can cross a field of deer and the deer just look but don't bother to run. Well I remember the day he asked me to help him to learn to walk quietly. I told him simply to use his toe to test for a solid footing, then ease the rest of his foot down. I followed ten or fifteen feet behind him along trails in the woods, through pines and hardwoods, in fields and hollows and along ridge tops. I made my bootfall coincide with his, and every time I heard his boot fall louder than mine, I said, "I hear you."

He quickly learned to avoid sticks, rocks and leaves while watching the area for deer—and he learned the patience to wait five minutes between steps.

Today when he shares hunting adventures with me, I remember our learning-walk and his beginning years as a hunter. I know how a teacher feels when a student wins an award. For Norman today, the reward is the experience of the hunt with or without a deer in the cooler.

I always felt I have given visitors a quality hunt if I let them use my stand and they collected a deer. Each of these fellas enjoyed one of my deer stands that morning, and I enjoyed their success. Nephew Rusty on the right and his guest Keith Hamm on the left.

At the 1986 Buckarama, a landowner told me of an experience that would certainly **not** qualify as quality. A man wanted to share his hunting experience with his girl friend's teen-aged son, so the two went hunting together, on private lands without the owner's permission. The older man told the youngster about his poaching adventures, how many deer he'd killed illegally, how long he'd poached from the deer stand overhead. He shot at a shadow—and almost hit the landowner. That man was passing his illegal habits on to another generation, but we can hope that his arrest put a halt to the youth's desire to poach.

I reckon the most quality I've experienced as a hunter came several years ago, when an old friend and a hunter since her youth joined our hunting group. She wanted a big deer so bad, but big deer are scarce in our area. Everyone in the group had gotten a deer that season, and day after day we'd see deer (mostly does, and some spring fawns) but she saw none.

I went to my favorite stand one morning—I'd gotten a spike and did not intend to kill another deer, and in that stand, I'd be close to Lois if she fired. But shortly after daylight, a deer came down the hill behind me and to my right. All my eyes could focus on were antlers, more antlers than I had seen in the woods in a long time. Oh, the temptation was there, tugging at my heart—actually, about to throw my heart through my chest—but I thought of the pleasure Lois would have if she were to collect that buck.

One of the few times I carried the load of a firearm and a camera.

I watched the buck walk off, wondering if I were seeing him for the last time, if he would cross the land line and get himself mounted onto someone else's wall. But at least, I thought, maybe the picture I took would come out okay and I would have myself a walking trophy.

Lois had to work a little for her deer—morning after morning passed as well as long afternoons. We were all getting discouraged. Then one afternoon when I was half-way up a pine in my climbing stand, I heard her shoot.

I waited for her to whistle. Silence. I yelled. Silence. I whistled. Silence. So I worked my way back down the tree and hurried to the hollow where I found her, knee deep in water in the creek, trying to hold that dead buck's head up so he wouldn't drown.

That day was tops in quality hunting.

Originally published in "Georgia Wildlife," official publication of the Georgia Wildlife Federation, Vol. VI, No. 2, August 1987.

IMPATIENCE CAN BE COSTLY—OR LUCKY

Day two of the season, and after sitting three hours in a stand and listening to squirrels and jays and other alarm birds fuss at me, and no deer in the neighborhood, I decided to stretch my legs. Patience was not one of my virtues.

Sneaking around in the woods is just about my favorite activity, whether it was off-season to scout or deer season to dream on my feet. I unloaded Ole Betsy, my favorite shotgun, lowered her to the ground, followed her down, reloaded, and slipped up the ridge. I had probably scared the dickens out of every deer on that side as I scampered down the tree, but I hoped not.

By this time in my hunting years, I'd learned how to *still-hunt*: You stand still more than you walk. After an hour, I'd worked my way over the ridge top and about a hundred yards down a footpath. At the forks, I stood against the sweetgum sapling and debated which fork to take. I thought of Yogi Berra's advice, "When you come to a fork in the road, take it."

A slight rustling noise, down in the hardwoods, to my left, out of sight in the dry hollow, caught my attention. I eased around the sapling until it was between me and the sound of footsteps. I closed my eyes and pictured the feet—too slow and steady for a squirrel, for even the trio of black fox squirrels that lived in that hollow. It had to be a deer.

I watched through the brush and brought up the .12 gauge. With my thumb wrapped around the hammer, I held it ready.

The deer stuck her head out of the brush. I exhaled. A doe.

She looked to her left, away from me, for a moment and then turned my direction. I cut my eyes to look beyond her, off to the side, but felt she was staring at me. If we locked eyes, I knew she would see me as predator and flee.

She glided across the road into the thickets of an island circled by the forks of the path. The white outline of her tail remained visible.

There has to be a buck behind her.

I had not been along these trails since the season opened, but I'd seen scrapes here about ten days ago, three down the right-hand fork and two on the other side. I was in the midst of buck country.

Waiting for him to show, I began to get nervous. Even a spike set my heart to racing and my hands to trembling. *Where are you?*

More than thirty yards down the path a bush shook. I squinted. Where was he? Was that another doe? I didn't see antlers, only gray-brown deer hair.

He grunted, like a soft mooing or a subdued pig grunt.

He had crossed the path out of my sight.

The buck thrashed a cedar, its top waving with the violence. I could mentally picture him stripping the bark. The slight breeze blew the Christmas smell of sap to me.

I eased to my right, desperately looked for a view through the bushes to be sure I shot only the buck and that I had a killing shot.

Two ears flicked toward me. No antlers. The doe. Head high, she played peep eye with me for a few seconds, her head bobbing for a better view. I made a mistake—I looked her in the eyes. She leaped away, tail high, and made enough racket for a herd of deer.

The buck's most likely gone too. Or maybe not.

I sneaked down the right-hand path about ten feet, to a large pine, where I had a view down that branch of the trail to three scrapes, only a few feet from the hanging stand in the oak. I backed against the tree to break up my outline and waited. For movement. For him to grunt or thrash another tree. For her to blow at me or him. A couple of minutes became five and then stretched to ten.

Nothing.

The deer were gone. I had no doubt.

The stand hadn't been checked for soundness this fall, so I put the safety on the shotgun, let it hang from my left hand, and walked to the oak. All three scrapes showed fresh pawing—two under limbs of the oak itself and one under a bush on the other side of the trail. Leaves and dirt had been thrown more than three feet from the scrape, and the buck had shredded the limbs overhead.

I checked out the stand—the ropes were in good shape; the chain didn't wear any rust, and the board was still level and steady. A good spot to be tomorrow.

Back on the ground, I looked at my watch; it was almost 11:00. Might be a great place for somebody in the morning, but no way I'd sit there from 6:00 o'clock to after 10:00. Somebody else could have it.

I picked up my shotgun and struck out for home. And spooked the doe from the middle of the island of thickets. I froze. Did she watch me climb up and back down that tree? Surely not.

I sighed in disgust and stepped out again. At my third step, waving his massive rack at me, the buck charged after his lady.

That evening at supper, I offered the stand to one of the other hunters. "You'll have to sit there maybe until noon. A long time. And he may be off with another doe," I warned her.

She didn't have to wait. In the stand before 6:30 a.m., she hadn't even fastened her safety belt when he grunted his way into sight. She dropped him as he pawed the scrape across the path. He weighed 210 pounds field dressed; his rack had a 19-inch spread.

I still claim half credit for that buck, as I do for several others.

My nephew came down for our first Christmas bonus hunt, and I sent him to my stand, known as the BBB stand, for the *big-butt-buck*. We'd never seen his antlers, but had spooked him from the scrapes in front of the stand on several occasions. This stand, too, was in an oak, overlooking a Jeep trail and three scrapes. Rusty came home with a trophy.

Rusty with his mom Thulia Bramlett.

When you love someone and want him to love hunting, you send him to what you consider the best place to get a deer. Today, Rusty takes his vacation to deer hunt and has come to love the land and the wildlife as much as I do.

I had a stand in a tall sweetgum where I'd hunted only once. The next fall in bow season, I sent Norman there, and he got his first bow-kill. In firearms season, I sent Greg to that sweetgum. Again, he had to put his books down to take the shot.

Greg and his trophy

I never did learn patience—as many years as I hunted, I never could sit for hours in a deer stand. My feet itched to walk the land and see what was on the other side of the ridge. But one time, it paid off for me.

I was perched in the platform stand in three-legged turtle hollow. I faced east with the soggy bottom to my right, and on my left the Jeep trail and a pine-hardwood hill.

About the time I got tired of sitting, I spotted a buck ambling along the edge, just across the Jeep road. *Ah-ha. Enough antlers to qualify for the freezer but not the wall.* Now, if he'd just wander over this way a little.

All I had was my shotgun, and she couldn't reach that fifty yards.

If the buck wouldn't come to me, I'd go to him. Maybe.

First, unload the shotgun. Next, lower it to the ground, butt first so as not to get crud into the end of the barrel. Then get myself down to the ground. All without spooking the buck, without flashing the rising sun from my blaze orange vest into his eyes.

Took a few minutes, but I managed. I reloaded and crept along the path to the edge of the road. Waited until he lowered his head to feed and I took another step. And another. He ambled. I moseyed. And closed the distance to forty yards, then thirty.

And put him on the ground. My first ever stalked deer. And perfect for the freezer.

WHEN THE DEER IS ON THE GROUND

Took me a couple of years to learn what to do once I had my deer on the ground. Field dressing techniques were bloody, messy, stinky, and not exactly easy. I had teachers aplenty, and I queried every hunter, every hunting guest, and every social guest who hunted elsewhere. And searched magazines.

I soon learned to take supplies with me. Lots of supplies. A hunting knife with a serrated blade, a pocket knife, paper towels, plastic bags if I wanted to save the heart and liver, two feet of string, and two four-foot lengths of rope.

One friend taught me to remove the musk glands to prevent contaminating the meat with urine, which a rutting buck pees down his legs, over the musk glands and into a scrape. Wash up the pocket knife and my hands after that surgery before I began to field dress. No matter where I hunted on the land, I knew where to find the nearest creek or spring.

A guest showed me how to peel back the genitals, ream out the rear end and tie off the genitals and rectum to prevent spillage into the body cavity. And to castrate him before I opened the belly.

The castration procedure left an opening in the hide, the perfect place to begin to open the belly. Slide my fingers under the skin, place my knife, blade up, between my fingers and rip it up the belly hide to the neck. Pull the skin back a few inches on each side. To open the belly, *very carefully* nip an opening in the abdominal wall where the inner lining shows at the rear. Keep the knife blade pointed up. I got an *oops* a few times when I nicked the gut. With the blade up, slice the membrane open to the breast bone. I use a special serrated knife to open the breast bone. That's one tough bone to tackle with a pocket knife or a regular hunting knife unless you have strong arms.

I cut the diaphragm free from both sides, down to spine, and pull out the insides, including the tied-off urethra and rectum which I pull through the pelvic opening and dump with the guts.

We originally would hang the dressed deer to a pecan tree in the yard to skin it out slowly with a skinning knife. After I read about someone using a golf ball to skin the deer, I used a rock and the Jeep.

With the deer hanging head up, I cut the hide around the legs and slice it up to the opening in the belly. Cut the hide around the neck and down the front of the neck to the opening in the belly. These cuts will make the hide one piece that will pull free.

Tie a rock *into* the hide on the back of neck and the other end of the rope to the Jeep trailer hitch.

I drive off slowly, and pull the hide off with nary a nick in the skin. The deer swings out away from the tree, so someone has to keep the body from slamming back into the tree. Perfect, especially if you're going to send the hide to a tannery. I had two jackets made from undamaged hides.

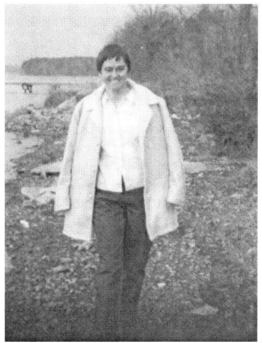

Me on a stroll in my deerskin jacket.

May be a lot more work to field dress a deer my way than simply to turn it onto its side, slice it open and pull everything out. But my cleaning procedure sure did make a huge difference in how good the resulting venison tasted. No wild, rangy, urine or musky taste.

HUNTERS SHOULD KILL DOES TO THIN HERDS

In 1987, the deer population had expanded to a level I feared the land could not support, and I responded with a plea to the local hunters to take action to reduce the herd.

Union-Recorder
December 1987

To the Editor:

Doe days are upon us again and hunters are wondering: Should I take a doe or wait for maybe that monster buck that might be behind her?

Hunters in Baldwin County, don't wait for that monster buck. We need to eliminate a lot of does this year.

As you know, lots of folks are unhappy about our deer population (me included). We've got to reduce the herds to a much lower level to pacify the folks who're getting their cars smashed, who're losing crops to deer and who want a trophy but see only small deer with small racks.

When the herds grow to more than the land can feed, the deer get smaller and bucks have smaller racks. We have no choice but to kill off a lot of does to reduce the herd. Remember, the number of deer can double in two years if the hunters don't control the herd.

So when you go out this week, don't depend on the other hunter, don't think that only sissies kill does, don't expect to find a trophy deer later in the season—use that doe tag. Remember, the game biologists gave you that tag for a reason, to put on a doe. And don't tell me you don't want the meat—any hunter who kills only for a trophy and doesn't eat what he kills is not a sportsman.

When I hear shots this weekend, I plan to be counting does, and I am sure that your shot will echo all the way to the Game and

Fish offices in Atlanta when you use your doe tag. Let's improve our herds so that down the line we can join other counties in Georgia that can produce deer for the record books; we for sure can't if we don't kill out some does this fall.

Susan Lindsley
Milledgeville

THE NURSING BUCK

I keep a feeder filled near my farm home so I can watch all kinds of wildlife. Raccoons and foxes check out the corn but mostly, however, it's deer and turkeys that wander by, check for food, and eat the natural supplies—persimmons, acorns and the heavily-fertilized cattle fodder in the fields.

I have seen both deer and turkey mate. I've seen does beat up on antlerless bucks and even on other does over a tidbit of food. I have watched toms strut across the fields behind a flock of hens who paid them no mind.

With five producing persimmon trees, I have to laugh at the fawns who try to outrun each other to get to the next tree for the fallen treats. As many as four raccoons have raided one tree at the same time.

On August 29, 2004, my friend Pat Blanks stood by the window to watch the animals while I perched in the living room.

Several does, two spring fawns whose spots had almost faded away, and one four-point buck whose antlers had hardened came into the yard for the feed I had scattered near the kitchen window.

The buck stood a couple of inches taller at the shoulder than the does. Several times, a doe would slash at him to chase him away.

Pat called me to the window. "Quick. Come look! One of the grownups is nursing."

The nursing deer was on its knees, mouth turned upward, and the doe stood patiently while the other adult nursed. After about a minute, the doe stepped forward, and the four-point buck stood up from kneeling.

He licked the last drops of milk from his lips, and Mama returned to foraging.

WHICH COMES FIRST:
THE BUCK OR THE BOOK?

I love to read, to write, and to hunt. Too often, I tried to mix the hunting with the reading or the writing. Especially as I got older and tired of sitting. *Still-hunting* required me to move in spite of being still, so books and pads for writing poetry got left at the house.

One October afternoon I went to a favorite leaning ladder stand. In a clump of hardwoods it overlooked the merger of two streams. To my left stood a mulberry tree whose golden leaves lured deer as surely as gold called to the prospector. The dry fallen hardwood leaves gave warning of any critter coming along from any direction, so I knew it was a good place to take a book. I picked out a Stuart Woods novel and stuffed it in my pack along with a pad and pencil and my always-handy gut kit.

I wouldn't get bored if no deer showed. And I was ready if one did wander by.

I clambered up the ladder, got myself settled and my safety belt secured and pulled up my pack and rifle. I double-checked that the safety was on, chambered a round and laid the rifle across my lap. I sat beneath a camouflage hood wide enough that the carbine would not touch the cloth and spook away the deer when I lifted it.

No deer would be along for a least a half-hour, I figured, with all the noise I'd made walking through the dead leaves from the Jeep road. So out came the book and I wiggled my butt more comfortably on the cushion, pulled my feet up onto the ladder's top rung, propped the book on my knees and read.

Noises in the leaves behind me. I pushed the book under my right thigh and tilted my head. Turkeys. Spooked and clucking a warning. Did they see my feet? Surely they didn't see me. I tried to peek out the window of the blind, but the sun slapped me in the eyes and I had to lean back.

From the front opening, I saw the *spooker*. A buck. A nice buck. An easy shot. *Get the rifle up. Move easy. Don't shake the camou-flage.* As I snugged the rifle against my shoulder, he pulled a deer's favorite trick: Step behind a tree and walk straight away. My last sight of him was a flash of his tail as he dropped into the creek bed and worked his way downstream.

I cussed awhile. Listened awhile. Used my bleat call to try to lure him back. He kept on his way. The turkeys went off somewhere too. The only company left for me was Stuart Woods. I returned to his words. But I kept an ear cocked for sounds other than the slight afternoon wind that tickled the leaves.

Ah, put down the book. Another something in the leaves. Never mind. It's just a squirrel. I didn't even close the book. The noises got a bit louder, and I finally looked out—to see two does going down the same creek crossing the buck had used.

Under my leg went the book. It wasn't doe day, but maybe, just maybe, a buck followed the ladies. I waited, hands on the rifle. No sounds except the ladies scrambling up the bank across the creek.

I reached into my shirt pocket for the bleat call I always carried while deer hunting. I grunted once. They both stopped. One looked directly at the blind. The other browsed as if she had not heard me. But the listener got antsy. She walked down the creek a few yards, turned and came back to the crossing.

She walked back and forth for almost a half-hour, and I wondered if she were in heat and looking for the buck that she and I both thought would never show. Something spooked her. She snorted once and took off toward the food plot some 300 yards down the path.

I hadn't found my place in the book when another sound caught my attention. From my left, down the hill and across the small stream came a buck. I fingered the window of the blind for a better look, and up came his head at the motion. How could he have seen that one-inch movement?

He spun, leaped the creek, and bounced his way up the hill.

Oh, well, I'd try again tomorrow.

Tomorrow came, and I went out again, with a book, but to a different stand, in a small meadow where I had planted wheat and crimson clover a few weeks back. To where I had carried a bedded doe decoy, and left her hidden under camouflage beneath the leaning ladder. I placed her midfield, where the ground humped up a little, so she could be seen from any direction from the woods. I sprinkled her with doe-in-heat urine.

The seeds had sprouted and turkeys had found the fresh food.

Seven fed in the field as I approached—two with long beards—but they got on the road into the woods as soon as they saw me.

The birds came back to their greens, twice, and both times I lightly shook the camouflage over a window to run the birds off. About an hour before dark, he grunted twice off to my right, in the woods. I put down the book, picked up the rifle and waited for him to come out of the woods—I just knew he would see my doe decoy and come out to her, but he didn't.

I bleated to him, and he grunted twice more, about another fifty yards down the ditch/creek. And went silent for more than ten minutes while I fretted over whether or not to bleat again.

He grunted somewhere to my left. He was circling me, trying to smell the doe. Maybe. The grunts were soft and tender, like a cat's purr.

The sun had gone behind the western hill. Only shadows covered the clover and wheat. My decoy was itself becoming only a shadow. I began to consider the long walk back to the Jeep and getting home for supper. It was almost too late to shoot.

A buck stepped from the undergrowth, his head bobbing as if he were unsure whether or not the decoy were really a deer. Ten yards into the meadow, he froze, head up, his body dark, his antlers bright and almost white in the approaching darkness. I eased the safety off, lined up on his neck and squeezed off. He fell in his tracks.

I reckon books and bucks can go together, if you read the sounds as well as the words.

TURKEY ROOSTS AND DECOYS

So many turkeys roosted near me and wandered around me when I was deer hunting the previous fall that, come spring, I decided to pile up brush and hang camouflage netting to make myself a blind near my deer stand at the junction of two creeks. All I needed to do on opening morning would be get there before the birds flew down, and one would land right in my lap. Or at least, close.

I had another option, another roosting site. I had heard turkeys fly up many evenings when I fished nearby. So to follow the famous motto "Be prepared," I had piled up a circle of brush near that roost. If no luck at the deer-stand site, I'd try uphill from the fishing hole another morning.

I no longer had the endurance to turkey hunt *properly*: That is, owl hoot as day lightened the sky, run toward the answering gobbler, perch on the ground against a tree and flirt with the tom with my call until he was so love-sick he would strut to the end of my shotgun. Both of my legs and my back scream, "No way!" Besides, I couldn't hoot worth a hoot.

Thus, on opening day, I hustled to get across the meadow before first light so I wouldn't spook the birds from the roost. I crept through the dead leaves and underbrush as silently as I could, slipped through the small opening in the blind, and draped the camouflage cloth back over the doorway.

With my butt on a cushion, my knees pulled up, and my .12 gauge resting on my knee, I placed my box call near my right hip and pulled on camouflage gloves and face mask. I was ready. I hoped the big tom I'd seen last fall would cooperate today and drop from his roosting pine.

No *gobble* nearby as the day begin to slide in. One sounded off far up the ridge, but I knew Norman was up there somewhere. I couldn't go chasing after his bird. *Mine* roosted here, and here he'd be.

A *yelp* nearby got my heart rate faster. *Hen, where are you? Where's your lover-boy?*

The sun touched the upper limbs of the pines and gleamed them almost white. She *yelped* again. I didn't need to think about my box call—she would pull in a tom for me.

I looked every which way I could without moving my head. No sign of the hen. No sound after her second *yelp*. I forced myself to wait. And wait. My hands were below the edge of my blind, and I glanced down at my watch. I let another ten minutes go by. Still the hen didn't show. No gobbler called. Even the one on the ridge had gone silent. Or gone down the other side so far his voice wouldn't reach me. I'd have to do something to get some action.

I scratched my box call with a soft *yelp*.

The devil cackled and flapped out of the tree over my head. Terror lifted me two feet into the air.

The hen flew about twenty yards out front and clawed her way onto a limb. She *yelped* and *yonked* her own terror. But I too had landed back on my seat, out of her sight.

What a way to start the morning—an alarm bird in front of me who had probably scared off every turkey for a mile.

I waited her out. She soon went quiet, fluffed herself, *yelped* twice, dropped to the ground, and walked away.

I debated moving, but remembered all the birds that walked through the area last fall. I waited. No need to call after all that racket. Her last *yelps* might entice somebody to visit.

Her *yelps* did so. After about a half-hour a flock of jakes sashayed toward me, from the direction the hen had gone. I wondered if the hen were actually one of these jakes.

I wasn't fussy. If they wandered close enough and separated, I'd take one. They crossed the creek, and my fever began to rise. They turned parallel to the creek bed—they would walk right in front of me. I was gonna have a shot.

Not quite. They cut behind a small island of thickets. Too many heads too close together. Too much brush. I tried to ease the shotgun to my shoulder. Too much movement—by me.

One *yelped*. They flew across the creek. I cussed.

A shotgun blasted.

Norman got one. I'll go help him dress his and come back to this area tomorrow.

Norman always had an interesting tale to tell. He was slapping at no-see-ums when several hens came to his call. A gobbler followed, in full strut. Norman stopped swatting the insects and sat still. All the birds kept moving along—and apparently did not see him.

When he pulled up his shotgun, the gobbler came out of his strut, looked at Norman, and Norman simply squeezed down with perfect head shot. He had a twenty-pounder.

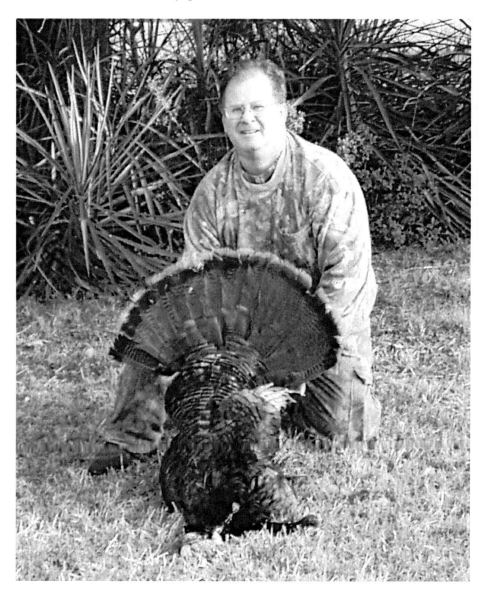

NEXT DAY

The morning was cold, but still as the dead. I bundled up an extra wool shirt in case I sat a long time, tied a cushion to the back of my belt, grabbed my old faithful shotgun and a handful of number 2 birdshot, and off I went into the darkness. I was gonna walk the rails as a shortcut to the roosting area on a nearby ridge.

Not a long walk, and the train would whistle from more than a mile away if it approached from either direction. Plenty of time to get off the tracks. Just in case some frisky tom opened his eyes early, I used a tiny flash that illuminated a three-square-foot circle for me to see where I walked. When I reached the creek crossing, I looked for the white marker the railroad had put on a crosstie to indicate it was to be removed. From there, I counted 120 ties to my path.

When I had set up my blind, I'd kicked out trash on a deer trail to make the path easier to see and to keep my footsteps silent. In less than two minutes, I had the decoy out of the brush blind and staked out about fifteen yards in front. Then back at the blind, I settled in on my cushion, placed my calls by my right thigh, pulled my knees up to serve as prop for the shotgun and waited.

Facing east, I was able to watch the day birth—the sky lighten, the pines become silhouettes, and naked hardwood become black fingers that scratched at the sky. No matter how much I squinted through my face mask, I couldn't see any bulk of gobbler perched overhead.

But I knew they were here. They had sounded off from that cluster of pines for four years. A friend and I had camped out in a meadow nearby two weeks ago and the gobblers hollered us awake. I shoulda been here yesterday instead of over at that deer stand.

A soft *yelp* from overhead, in front of me. Then another. Feet scratched pine bark as the birds shifted. A gobbler called, and while his voice echoed, three hens *yelped* and another gobbler whooped his welcome to the ladies.

A jay screamed. Crows cawed. Small birds began to wake. Turkeys shifted, called, and began to drop to the ground, their wings announcing their arrivals. Some simply drifted from the roost. Some flapped as if eager to greet the lady that beat them to the ground.

Here came the toms. They lit almost a hundred yards away, in a wide opening, once a roadbed, under the pines. The boss began to strut toward the hens, the decoy, and me.

His movements became a dance, one foot forward, body thrust forward and turned slightly, the other foot forward. The two other toms flared their tails and then deflated as if they didn't dare show out with the boss tom around.

Boss Tom strutted like a teenage football hero at the prom. Sunlight filtered through the overstory to highlight the bronzes, reds and greens on his side as he turned.

I managed to pull Old Faithful to my shoulder without alerting the birds. The gobblers had their minds on only the hens and the safety of their home-town roost.

Boss had cut the 100 yards in half. A few more dance steps and my shot would reach him. But he remained in full strut. Merle said never, but never, shoot one in full strut, the flared feathers would stop the shot.

I waited. Waited. Got impatient. The shotgun got heavier. Sweat ran down my face. My hands began to tremble, from the weight and from the same illness known as *buck fever*. I'd even suffered the same shakes the first time a fox walked in front of my camera lens.

I lined up the bead on the big bird, half-whistled a soft sound, and up went the boss bird's head and down when the strut.

I squeezed off.

He and the entire flock flew.

All others hit the trees. He hit space—a long flight from the ridge and across the creek. He became a silhouette against the green of a meadow. And vanished.

I cussed. No way to track a flying bird.

Was he dead? Or did he get to the meadow and just walk off? I had to find out. Had to find him if I'd killed him.

I put away the decoy, pocketed the calls, strapped on the cushion and extra shirt, shucked a new shell into the chamber, double-checked the safety was on, and set off to find the gobbler.

To track a deer, I always began at the last place I saw him. Would the same system work with a turkey that left no sign on the ground? I lined up with the oak tree at the bottom of the ridge, where I'd seen him pass on the left. I headed out that way. Then slopped across the creek and up its six-foot-banks and followed a deer trail toward the tree.

Beyond the tree, at the edge of the field, only empty grass greeted me. I turned back, checked the location of the oak, and moved more to my left as I started into the field.

There he was. All twenty-four pounds, ten-inch beard, ¾ inch spurs.

I had to go home for the truck—that skeester was too heavy for me to tote with all my gear.

Roosting sites and decoys—my best aids in a turkey hunt.

* * *

About my strolling along the railroad—don't you do so. That stretch of land where the rails lie does not belong to the railroad, but to me. The Jordan family, who owned the land, never deeded it to the railroad, and when that family sold the plantation property, the land under the tracks went with it, and down to my father when he bought Westover Plantation in the 1920s. So I was walking along on my own land, not trespassing.

POACHERS STEALING FROM EACH OF US

Union-Recorder
October 22, 1988

To the Editor:

Thank you, Ranger Vernell Jackson—you caught the poacher hunting turkey over bait.

Thank you, too, Judge Hugh Thompson. When the evidence was in and the verdict was guilty, you imposed a sentence strong enough to deter future poaching: a $1,000 fine and eighteen months on probation during which he cannot hunt in Georgia.

Our judges are in a position to eliminate or to encourage illegal killing of our nongame and game animals. No one wants an animal badly enough to chance a $1,000 fine and loss of hunting licenses. But many return to night hunting or hunting out of season or hunting over bait when the financial cost is low and they do not lose hunting privileges.

Until all of us consider that the poacher wants to steal from each of us, until we think of the poacher as a criminal (not as a man who is trying to feed a hungry family), until we realize that everybody does not poach (just as everybody does not snort cocaine or drive under the influence of alcohol), until we are willing to tip the ranger to poaching (just as we would tip the police to someone stealing a car), and, yes, until our judges all follow the example set by Judge Thompson, we will lose our wildlife to the greedy few, those who steal tomorrow's animals from their own children, their neighbors, you and me.

Susan Lindsley
Milledgeville

WAYNE AND NORMAN: "THE BOYS"

They have passed sixty and retirement, but I still call them "the boys" for they are younger than I am and we have shared so many years of hunting, fishing and chasing poachers. We have gutted deer together—well, most of the time. I have to admit a few times they headed for the bushes to upchuck as I pulled out the guts.

They toted heavy loads for the woodpiles and helped flag land lines and toted my loads in and out, to and from the car into the house. They have sharpened my knives, shown me some Marines' secrets of cleaning a firearm, and helped set up deer stands and hide-a-ways for me to turkey hunt and photograph.

We have scouted the land together in the fall, watched gobblers go to roost in the spring, and fished together when we weren't hunting or doing all the off-season chores to get ready for the next hunt.

They taught me how to skin a catfish, and I taught them how to read deer sign.

If one of us got sick, the other two came to help. They chauffeured me when I was on crutches. When one's family member got married on opening day of turkey season, the other two went—not to the woods, but to the wedding.

When something needed doing, they just did it.

No one could ask for better hunting buddies.

This was one of Norman's happiest days as a hunter.

"He came from that-a-way."

Little did Norman know he would get an even bigger buck some years later:

Norman killed this thirteen pointer about a half mile from the eleven-pointer killed by Cindy Key Sanders a few years later. Same genetic pool—same bunched-up ear guards.

Wayne with his seven-point piebald.

Another day, Wayne came home with a buck and a doe.

Wayne's recent buck was a nice trophy for our county.

Wayne with one of his gobblers.

Wayne and guest Jeff Hunsucker both scored one opening day.

Another buck that made Wayne smile.

In 2014, on the coldest morning of the fall, with a hard frost turning the food plot into a look-alike snow field, Wayne was in a predicament. Should he give up the hunt and go tend to his screaming bladder?

Yes. Get down now. But as he prepared to exit the tower stand, two does trotted into the clover patch. Wayne gritted his teeth, told his bladder to hold it, and took the larger doe with a shot to the neck.

No time to waste. He lay the rifle down on the floor and scooted down the ladder to take care of his own personal demands.

I'll get her loaded and then get the rifle.

He was cold and looked forward to the heater.

But as he drove back into field, he spotted another deer. A buck. Nice eight–point, well-balanced rack, the spread outside his ears. Wayne cursed himself mightily for having left the rifle in the stand while he went for the truck.

He stopped behind a now-naked sweetgum and watched.

The buck trotted to the dead doe. Circled her like a coyote circling a carcass before deciding which area offered the best feast.

But food was not on the buck's mind. It was the rut, she was in heat and her aroma had him aroused to a frenzy. Back and forth he went. He nudged her with his nose. Circled her again. And tried to breed her as she lay on the ground.

* * *

Norman got the first bow-kill in the group with a recurve bow—long before anyone designed the compound. He perched in my swinging stand in a tall sweetgum where another year Greg collected his trophy.

Norman had the patience to wait for the big bucks and somehow his smoking did not deter them. Like many other men who hunted, he also grew his own camouflage.

In the picture below, note the heft of the antlers at the base of the main beams and the wide double points rising from the deer's right beam.

Wayne with our first bird of 2016.

SUMMER-TIME POACHERS

Late June, when middle Georgia endures temperatures that reach the upper nineties and sometimes push beyond the century mark on the thermometer is not a time to go deer hunting.

Only a month old, fawns are still nursing when they rise from their hidey-holes to follow mama doe for awhile.

From the beginning of time, mankind has known the time to butcher is the time of cold. Warm weather causes fresh meat to spoil quickly.

But some idiots decided to deer hunt in June, on a neighbor's land.

Visiting us was Maruta, a friend born in Latvia, who had survived the invasion of Russia as most of her family fled the Red Army. Her family made it to Germany, and she often said how thankful she was that they were in the American Zone when the war ended. They made it to America.

Although she had heard enough gunfire and had dodged strafing airplanes, she piled into the car with me to investigate the noontime gunfire.

The day was hot. We were both dirty and sweaty from working in the yard, trimming bushes, dragging off the clippings.

My trusty .12 gauge was in the house. I didn't have time to get it. I drove off, kicking up gravel from the driveway.

I roared down the paved road, slowed for the sharp curve, and reached seventy on the straight-away. As I turned into my neighbor's drive, I saw a truck in midfield, two men beside it. They saw us.

If they had killed a deer, they might have already piled it into the truck bed. They wasted no time jumping into the cab and starting across the field—toward the driveway I was blocking.

"Oh my God, they're coming this way," Maruta said from the back seat. She dropped to the floor. "Let's go. They've got guns."

I was too mad to leave. "They won't shoot us," I said. "Besides, they can't get by. They'll see the drive's blocked and they'll head off. Gads, I wish we had a phone or radio or something to call a ranger."

I pulled ten yards up the drive, and turned sorta sideways so that my station wagon completely blocked the exit. The driveway was too narrow for two cars to meet unless one ran into the shallow ditch and the driver were willing to have his vehicle clawed up by the plum bushes and scrappy brush that pushed over the ditches.

The truck approached the upper end of the drive, but rather than turning toward us it turned away.

"He's gone to hide," I said. "You can get up."

"Don't you think we should leave?"

"Naw. We'll just wait him out."

We didn't wait long. Five minutes later, "Look!" she said and pointed up the paved road. "Isn't that the truck?"

It was. They had circled around the pasture, circled the main house, and slipped back to the highway from the driveway to the barn that I didn't know connected with the main pasture.

I'd been snookered.

We were too late to catch the culprits. They had left the deer when they fled. Ranger Vernell Jackson came out to my call and was able to give the meat to a charity food bank.

THE LONG TRACK

Maggie shot, and then blew the whistle three times. Three meant "I need help with a deer."

I unloaded my shotgun, tied it to the pull-up rope, and eased it to the ground. I scampered down the spikes, gathered up everything, and headed up the hill. She stood on the ground beside the steps to the Hilton, her Remington 30.06 semi-automatic slung over her shoulder.

The Hilton, our biggest stand, can hold three people, or one person and a tripod with a telephoto lens. About twelve feet above ground, it was nailed into three pines in the edge of the woods and overlooked one end of a long field.

It was a perfect site to hunt the food plot of crimson clover and rye. Two or three deer had been harvested there annually.

"Where's the deer?"

"I dunno. He ran that way. He's a beauty."

Maggie pointed almost behind her stand.

"Where'd you hit him?"

"I shot for the heart."

"He won't be far then. Tell me when I get to where you saw him last." I headed in the direction she pointed. I found where he'd kicked dew from the grass before she called, "There."

I was still in the field. I put down my gear, shrugged off my jacket, and re-donned my red vest. Then, bending over, I studied the ground. Where the dew was kicked away, the sod was torn up. A few drops of blood speckled the winter dead grass

"Here," I called. "Come stand here."

Maggie did, and I gathered up my CB radio and shotgun. Ole Betsy is a single-shot, 1913 Stevens that feels weightless. I've carried her for several miles on some hunts and never felt her weight. I shoved a shell into her barrel—I had three more in my pocket—and began to follow the tracks.

The soft ground in the field yielded sharp impressions that led me into the mixed pine and hardwoods. Once under the trees, however, without the sun to throw shadows in the prints, I had a harder time.

The blood trail was almost nonexistent, only a few blood spatters off and on—I would have to find tracks.

Every few yards, I'd called her to move up to the latest good sign, to have an anchor to fall back to if I lost the trail or picked up the tracks of another deer.

He had veered to the left and onto a path. There the tracks were more visible and I began to stride after him.

"You wait there," I told her. "I'll call you when I find him." I was sure he'd be only a few yards ahead.

The lack of heavy blood sign gave me some doubts about where she hit the buck. The blood was bright, arterial, but only spotty and not from a major artery. If the wound closed up and he got into the pines, it'd be nigh unto impossible to trail him.

Well, finding him seemed easier when I got some fifty yards down the path. He had left good track sign—he tore up the ground—and I followed at a steady walk. When the trail dropped into a narrow hollow, I hoped he'd crossed it and gone up the other side. I didn't want to have to drag him up that hill when I found him.

Sudden crashing ahead. I pulled up the shotgun, but had no shot at the flash of a tail. I followed, and found where he had rested in grass and honeysuckle vines smashed into a bed. Blood in it.

Should I go on, or should I sit and let him bleed out? Or would he keep going anyhow? Would he cross the land line? If he did, we'd lose him. No one was supposed to carry a firearm on that land. The owner was a multi-generation friend, and I always honored her wishes.

I sat for a few minutes and listened to the woods. No deer sounds, no snort or flash of a white tail. The buck had spooked all others away for now. But a jay shrilled at me until it decided I was just another stump. A chipmunk scurried about under an oak as he gathered acorns for the colder months ahead.

I had to come out of my wool shirt. Even sitting those few minutes wasn't enough to cool me down from sweating. I decided to move on.

The deer did not cross the hollow—he cut east instead, down the hollow. I lost the trail several times and had to work back and forth to find it. Then the tracks began to go up an incline, into the pines, and vanished in the pine straw. I had to crawl to find which way he went. Only a few blood drops now as his injury began to close up.

At times, I knelt and felt in the straw for a track, and once I found it, I would stick my fingers into the toes to figure which way he was heading. When I reached a gully, his tracks stopped. Where had he gone? Up the gully to my right, or down to my left, or did he jump it? I found no sign on the bank to indicate he'd crossed.

I looked for any deer sign—crushed or overturned leaves, a spot of damp earth atop the mulch, flattened grasses or the shape of a hoof pushed into the soil.

I marked the spot in my mind and went up hill a few yards to an old cattle crossing, then returned to the spot. At last, I found where he'd landed when he jumped the gully.

I'd been on the trail for almost an hour and still had not found the deer. I didn't know how bad he was hurt, but I wasn't about to quit, for I lost a deer my first year hunting because no one else knew how to track. I determined to keep going.

So I went on, checked toe directions with my fingers and looked for blood on leaves underfoot and those still clinging to low bushes. A drop on a log he'd jumped. A few leaves kicked up where he had stumbled. Easy-to-see hoofprints in mud where he crossed the upper end of a wet- weather creek. Torn earth near the bank where runoff had eroded a six-foot ditch.

I hoped he had not fallen into the ditch.

I came around a thicket and there he stood, broadside, closer than twenty yards, his head turned to look at me.

I eased up the shotgun, whispered to myself, "I'm so sorry fellow," and pulled the trigger.

He had covered more than a mile, gone downhill and up, jumped two gullies. He would not have survived the shot, and I have forever been thankful that I did not give up but was able to put him down and end his pain.

* * *

Another day, I sat in that same stand. A dismal day, but I went out because I had not scored a deer. Mist continued long after daylight and kept the world gray. Something moved, and I blinked, staring at the darker gray line just above the weed tops. Yes, it was a deer. Out came the rifle and I carefully sighted through the 2 ½ power scope. Keeping my finger away from the trigger and the safety on, I tried to determine if it were buck or doe. The head was down. I waited for what seemed like an hour, my arms burning from the weight. I moved it back to my lap, point up, resting the butt on my thigh, and waited for that head to lift.

When it did, I knew I had my deer. A sizeable beam and tall tines glistened from the rain, and showed near-white against the pines.

I hurried, and cursed as the rifle spat. I knew it was a poor shot before the buck jumped, tail waving, to disappear into the timber in one leap. A second shot was impossible.

I planned to wait a quarter hour for the deer to lie down if he would. But before the time moved, the rain came. Hard. I had to find the deer while tracks were still visible. I climbed down with radio and rifle and walked to the spot where the deer had stood.

Nothing. Had the rain already washed out all sign? No blood or hair, a faint scratch in the wet ground where he jumped. I eased along and searched the ground to the spot where he disappeared over the ridge. Then I found a splash of blood, and I knew I hit him. The rain fell harder. I marked the spot and tried to locate another sign. After half an hour, I was at the base of the ridge, checking along a major old cow path that paralleled the stream. I stopped at a crossing and looked for tracks, but the rain had turned all tracks into small mudholes. Maybe some were his. I crossed the creek and walked face-first into a spider web.

I might not have tracks to follow, but spider webs hung heavy where I stood. I backtracked across the creek. The other path had webs, too, but they hung in ribbons.

I followed the trail the buck left in the air and found him. He had run more than 200 yards with his lungs blown out.

And left a trail that had slapped me in the face.

THE RACCOON-HOLLOW BUCK

The day I finally was able to put down Maggie's buck I was beyond CB range and had a long walk back. I did not retrace the winding uphill and down route the injured buck had followed. Instead I crossed the ditch to the worn path I knew was on the other side.

Deer sign everywhere.

Fresh tracks and droppings on the path. A large scrape beneath a white oak limb a buck had slashed with his antlers until he had shredded most of the leaves the frost had not taken down. A dozen trees horned, some with sap still wet-fresh.

Musk tickled my nose. The buck must have been around when the injured one stumbled along—I had probably run him off his scrape line.

A perfect place to hunt, but no stand anywhere in the area. I was gonna bring my climbing stand down here tomorrow and overlook that path.

The next day at breakfast, I told the others to go hunting that afternoon, I was gonna take my climbing stand out to a new location and would take Nellybelle. I loaded my climbing stand, a rope, a cushion, a crescent wrench, needle-nose pliers and a bottle of my pine scent into the Jeep.

Off I went, alone, to plot my hunt for the next days. I didn't want anybody else around to disturb the area.

I drove down the trail I had pushed through the bushes yesterday with Nellybelle's angle-iron front bumper but parked the Jeep about a hundred yards short of where we picked up Maggie's deer.

I didn't want to get too close to the fence—I wanted to locate upstream of the four scrapes. The buck might come from across the fence, but he was just as likely to come from any other direction. I wanted plenty of room to watch both ways and did not want to ambush him at the fence, where if my shot wasn't perfect, he might escape onto forbidden land.

I scrambled to the bottom of the gully, used roots and rocks to step across, and pulled myself up the other side with the help of saplings rooted in the creek. I needed to find the perfect tree overlooking those scrapes before I toted the stand over. It was a heavy load.

Finding the perfect tree became a problem. I worked my way downstream between the creek and the path to avoid laying down my scent on the trail where, I hoped, the buck would walk. But every tree seemed to be nothing but limbs, limbs, limbs. No way to take a climbing stand up these hardwoods. I hadn't brought a hatchet, so I couldn't trim off limbs.

The pines in the rich bottom soil were too big for the stand.

Ten yards, then twenty of battling vines, limbs and stumpholes. Soon I had covered half the distance to the fence. But there it was, a perfect tree. Tall, limbless for the first thirty feet, a sweetgum. It stood across the path from the stream, away from the scrapes, a few yards up the hill and would provide a semi-open view in both directions.

I would face the path and creek, and have a wide shooting lane. I hoped the buck didn't come down the hill behind me.

I went for the stand and the other supplies. I put the tools in my pocket and chunked everything else except the stand across the creek. That I separated into the seat and the foot rest and left them on the bank while I tried to balance on rocks and roots. No dice—I wound up with my boots in the water when I moved the stand to the other bank. At least they were waterproof until the water ran over the tops. They'd dry out tonight.

Oh, well, I may as well get used to wet feet since I'll probably wade the creek again tomorrow.

In less than an hour, I had the stand on the tree, the bolts holding the blades tightened down with the tools. I tied the cushion straps to the seat and the pull-up rope to the backrest, and folded the backrest down over rope and cushion. I dribbled a few drops of the pine scent on a nearby bush.

I wasn't about to go to the new stand in the dark and stumble across the creek. Maybe even take a dive into two inches of water.

Before I left the house the next afternoon, I perfumed my boots with pine scent and put a drop on the front collar of my tee shirt so that my body heat would help carry it into the air. And uphill in case the buck came from that-away. I also dribbled a couple of drops of doe-in-heat on my boots.

I walked from the house—only about three-quarters of a mile. Not much to tote, just the .44 Ruger magnum and my CB radio. And by walking, I avoided bringing Nellybelle smells back into the woods. Two days running, she had spread fumes in the area.

I climbed that sweetgum almost silently. The bark did not scream against the metal the way pine bark did. I had climbed enough times to learn how to tilt both the seat and foot sections so I could move them without touching the bark.

I settled in to wait and checked my watch. Quarter past two.

The wind stirred. A leaf crunched its way down, limb by limb, from an oak near the stream. A crow landed on a pine limb and cawed at me. A jay echoed the crow.

I waited. The sun sneaked rays between pine limbs to my left and warmed me. I got sleepy. Facing the tree, with my rifle laid across my lap, I used my elbows to push the weapon against my belly, laid my hands against the tree trunk and my head on my hands.

Naptime.

I slept to the lullaby of the breeze as the pines sang back to it.

One of the many alarm clocks of the woods woke me. *Scrabbling. Where? To my left. Up, above me. Not a deer. Okay, I can look.*

I eased my head up and looked for the noise source. *Raccoon. Not one. Four. Mama and three babies in the oak. Heading right for the scrape.*

They hit the ground and immediately began to paw in the leaves. My attention stayed riveted on the foursome as they scratched their way downstream in the woods and a bit northward, toward the creek.

Well, they've probably put an end to my chances of a deer.

One behind the other, they disappeared over the bank into the creek gully. Silence again.

But not for long. Leaves crackled across the creek as they scampered up the bank. *Must be headed for that persimmon. But I think all the fruit is gone. Hope they'll be gone soon too.*

I need not have worried. They were still making enough noise to wake any sleeping critter when from my left came another sound in the leaves—a doe. She ambled along, snatching a nibble of browse every few steps. She looked toward the raccoons once but must have recognized either the critters or their sounds. She kept on along the path toward me.

She jerked her head up, tilted her ears forward. A leafy twig hung from her mouth. She raised her tail to parallel her back bone. She flicked her ears, dropped her tail, and swallowed the last leaf.

I looked down to my right. What had caught her attention? After what seemed like years of trying to see something in the shadows of the pines, vines and hardwood limbs, I saw an ear twitch. The doe had seen company coming. And wasn't interested in any love life.

Okay. Here he comes. A gentleman caller.

His top hat caught the sunlight. Looked like eight points. Outside the ears. *Nice. Worth all the effort. He's calm, no extra adrenaline pumping to give him a wild taste.*

I eased the safety off the Ruger. *Wait. He'll see her in a minute and look her way. Wait.*

I didn't obey my orders to wait. Half hidden behind the tree, up more than twenty-five feet and in shadows, I eased the rifle to my left shoulder. It would be a perfect neck shot. I did obey my orders to *see the entire circle of the scope and put the crosshairs on the middle of his neck.*

I eased pressure on the trigger and through the scope watched him fall.

Lawd help me, I gotta get two or three fellas to drag him out of here and to the butcher.

**This one hangs in my office, in front of my
computer desk. A reminder of that day
with the raccoons along the creek**

OTHER TRACKING VENTURES

Maggie described the deer as a "monster" when I arrived after she shot. I was gonna have to track it, but I began by following the strong musk smell—for about 200 yards. Nowhere did I find any blood or indication that the deer was hit.

I returned to where the buck stood when she shot and eventually found where the bullet had gone into the ground. The rifle was sighted for fifty yards and the deer was in excess of 100 yards away.

* * *

Another morning, same shooter, different location. One shot, the buck fled and crossed the road right in front of a ranger who hit his brakes to avoid a collision. The ranger had arrived at the house just as we were gathering together to search for the buck. So down the road we went, and found the blood trail where the buck crossed the pavement.

Five of us tracked that buck for four hours and more than two miles, back and forth across the woods and over the hill and back down and across a creek and back up another hill, and then the trail stopped. Stopped dead, as if a UFO had lifted him from the earth. He had stood by a gully and dripped blood. We never found another sign. No tracks to show he had jumped across the gully. No tracks down the bank or in the gully. Nothing. Not another drop of blood anywhere. We dragged ourselves back to the house to have breakfast at 3:00 p.m. and none of us had the energy to sit in a stand that evening.

The ranger told me later that a deer hit in the brisket will survive, but the blood it leaves on the trail will look like enough to paint a house. She apparently hit the brisket and not a vital spot.

* * *

Maggie again, on a different morning, but the same location. After she shot, the buck reversed himself and bounded away. But almost instantly he returned to the field. This time, he took it in the neck and dropped in his tracks. When we gutted him, we expected a mess, but the first bullet had only slithered through the guts, damaging nothing, leaving only a tiny hole where it entered and a tiny hole where it exited. If that deer had not returned for that second shot, we'd have trailed forever to find him.

* * *

Skeeter's first buck limped toward her across the field, and when she brought up her rifle, he lifted his head, chin up, to look. Her bullet entered his chest and his heart. But the deer charged straight ahead. On her first deer hunt, Skeeter thought the deer had seen her and was attacking. She was afraid to come down from the stand. When I reached her, she still shook with buck fever—and fear.

But at least she settled down enough to direct me to where the buck had entered the woods. No blood, but a mass of tracks where the buck and the several does with him had galloped from the meadow. Twenty yards into the woods, one set of tracks veered off the trail while the path itself was torn by many hooves. I followed the one set and found a drop of blood on a yellow poplar leaf. Another step, and blood splashed everywhere. The deer lay less than another twenty yards away, his heart blown apart. If I had taken the external bleeding to indicate the seriousness of his injury, I'd not have trailed him at all.

Crippled herself, Skeeter later said the buck was special for her. He had only three legs and one normal antler.

**Skeeter with her three-legged buck with odd antlers. She herself was
disabled from a car wreck. Note the folding stool behind her. It was my
seat on many hunts in the early years.**

* * *

Again, Maggie shot a whopper one day, just before noon on the
last day of the season. The deer dropped, rolled into a gully, and she
did not see him leave but heard him scrabble from the gully.

Off he ran. We gave him a half-hour and then began to trail. Up
the ridge we followed an easy trail, then downhill into the upper end of
a long hollow. We strolled along with no trailing problem—yellow
jackets buzzed over every drop of blood. The buck crawled under a

fence and entered a neighbor's property. Since we respect property lines, we had gotten permission to trail any wounded deer across the fence, so over we went, down the hollow, and followed the yellow jackets. Some 150 yards into the hollow, we found a small pool of drying blood, four distinct hoof prints, where he had stood for some minutes and licked his wound to stop the bleeding. From there, he walked off, somewhere down the hollow, through those leaves into a jungle of grasses and brush, typical Middle Georgia bottom land. We searched for another two or more hours, found only dozens of trails crossing back and forth, all covered with fresh tracks, but no injured deer, no blood, no more yellow jackets.

Our entire club went over the next day, in hopes of finding him if he were dead or to execute him if he were lying there somewhere, stiff and dying. We spread out and walked down the hollow, covering the same area we'd covered the day before.

Norman almost stepped on a log. But that log rose up and galloped away, the forest atop his head. It had to be the same buck we'd trailed yesterday. He didn't stumble as Norman watched him bound over the thickets and leap across the beaver creek. We were all glad to see him recovering for next year.

JUDGE NOT

"If you don't get her off my back, I'll do it myself."

A ranger brought me the message from my distant cousin, Judge Bob Green. I'd been sitting in his courtroom every session and taking notes on all wildlife cases for months.

I immediately rearranged my living room and no longer sat with my back to the window that faced the paved road. I didn't want a long-distance shot coming through the window—some night hunter had missed a deer down the road at the Harrison's and the bullet had gone through the wall of their house.

He wasn't just angry because I was taking notes—his anger went back to the cattle episode. When he was in the state legislature, some of our cows vanished.

The man who drove the cattle to market told my father. The driver told me about it years later, when he was a fireman and helped put out a wildfire on our land. He'd driven several cattle to Macon from north of our place, from a cattle trap in an old barn. He thought the cattle were ours, but they were in Bob Green's name at the sale barn.

My parents went to Macon where they found the cattle, which were indeed ours. They returned with an injunction to keep the cows from being auctioned, but too late. Cousin Bob didn't auction them. He sold them directly to a meat packer and avoided the injunction. By the time we learned the cattle were sold, they had been loaded up and driven off.

Mother began a legal battle to recover the value of the cattle, but politics prevailed—after all, our "culprit" sat in the state legislature. The case never came to court. After my parents died, Bob had the case dismissed.

But the cattle incident kept him out of political office for many years. Until new people, who did not know his history, moved into Milledgeville—and voted him into office as state court judge.

I wasn't the only target of Bob's anger. A ranger had charged one of Judge Bob's kinfolk with a game offence, so he tended to dismiss cases brought by that ranger, as well as those I brought. He had the same reaction to another law-enforcement officer who arrested another of his kinfolks.

No matter how clean a case, if the culprit were night hunting or poaching on my land, the judge more often than not let 'em go.

The best example came with a case that began when I heard a gunshot one midday. I happened to be in the yard, and the shot was just down the hill, at the railroad. I drove down and arrived to find a man holding a rifle, standing on my land that spanned the railroad.

I stopped behind his truck, jotted down his tag number, and leaned over to the passenger window.

"You get 'im?" I asked.

"No," he said.

I got out and walked over to him. I smelled cordite.

"Hey, what kind of rifle is that?"

He held it up. "It's a Remington 30.06. Just bought it."

"May I see it?" A trick I'd used before.

He gave me a smile and the rifle. I didn't need to sniff the end of the barrel. The odor of cordite still drifted from it.

His rifle in my hands, I felt secure. "Tell you what. I'm gonna call for a ranger. You're hunting on my land."

"No, m'am. I'm on the railroad land."

"Hate to tell you, but the railroad doesn't own the land. You're outside the ditch, and the railroad has use of only the land between the ditches, and doesn't even own that. You are in fact on my land."

I finally had a radio-telephone in my truck. I kept the man's rifle and called the dispatcher/operator, who connected me to a ranger's home. No answer. Then she patched me through to the sheriff, who patched me though with his radio to the ranger's radio. (I felt I was really up-town!) He was on a case in another county and couldn't leave. I then called the T.I.P. hotline and was told to hang on, a ranger would be dispatched.

One was, only he didn't show up. He had been recalled because politics had changed everything. A ranger now was allowed to work only so many hours a week (or month) and would then have to be paid overtime. But there was no money for overtime.

Eventually I got help and the man was charged with hunting without permission.

But three funny things happened on the way to justice. One, the guy wrecked his truck, got charged with DUI, was hospitalized and arrived at court wearing a head bandage and with his arm in a sling and a cast. Second, the judge ordered the court reporter **not** to record the case. And third, after my testimony, he announced: "She doesn't know where her land is. I grew up in the area and know you were not on her land. Not guilty." I guess it didn't matter that I was under oath and swore he was on my land, and I definitely knew the location of my own land. It also didn't matter to Bob that as the judge he was not supposed to provide testimony, especially false testimony.

For some, any excuse is as good as another if you want to do something.

Thereafter, I sat in his courtroom, in the second row, and took notes on cases. When I asked for a copy of the court reporter's file on any case, he refused to allow her to provide it. When I brought charges against someone and asked the case be recorded, he told the court reporter she was not to record the case. Eventually, I had enough evidence to bring him before the state judicial ethics committee.

But what was the use? Politics won out. I actually received a letter informing me that the case had no foundation and that I would be charged with contempt of court if I told anyone I had filed the complaint.

Thus the threat sent by a law officer to "get off his back." Years later, he also threatened a superior court judge and pulled a pistol on him in the courthouse. This time, the world knew about his antics—the local paper kept the voters informed. Cousin Judge was again before a judicial ethics committee, one that did not yield to politics. This time, he was suspended for a month, and never won another election.

The judge wasn't the only one to issue a threat. People often stopped on the road or at the driveway directly in front of the trailer to turn around or to watch the deer in my yard. If the vehicle stayed very long, I would drive around to see what was going on.

I kept a pad and pencil on the seat beside me, and the first thing I did as I approached a vehicle was to jot down the tag number.

"Whatcha doing? Got trouble?" Same greeting I used with them all.

"Just watching the deer. You ran them off."

"Uh-huh. Well, I hope you weren't watching to pick out one to shoot."

He laughed and said, "What do you think you'd do if I did shoot one?"

"I'd turn you in to the ranger," I said and smiled.

"Well, I know the judge and he'd let me go."

"Oh, yeah? Well, I know him too." I wasn't about to let on that I knew he was right—if he drove into my yard and killed a doe, the local judge would find him not guilty.

"Yeah? You could have an accident or something."

"And you'd be the first suspect. I have your tag number, and I'll give it to the ranger. You'll be investigated if I just fall on ice this winter."

Without another word, he slapped his truck into gear and roared off.

* * *

Since he seldom found one of my game and fish culprits *guilty* I asked him to recuse on a case because of the long-term animosity between us and because I was the defendant's victim in the criminal case.

November 24, 1990

TO: Robert Green
Judge, Baldwin County State Court
Courthouse
Milledgeville, GA

COPY TO: James Watts
Solicitor, Baldwin County State Court
Courthouse
Milledgeville, GA

SUBJECT: Cases against defendants
       XXXX
       XXXX

Charged with Hunting from a vehicle
       Hunting from a public road
       Hunting without permission

Scheduled for State Court November 28, 1990, 9 a.m.

You are requested to recuse in the above cases because of your long-standing personal animosity both toward me (the victim) and toward the Game and Fish Division Wildlife Rangers (the arresting officers).

Because of this long-standing friction, I feel that you will have difficulty being impartial in these cases.

A judge should recuse if there is any doubt about his objectivity.

Sincerely,

Susan Lindsley

He did not recuse. Since I didn't remember the outcome of the cases, although I attended court, I searched the court records for this book. Ironically, I found no records of these arrests in the misdemeanor files at the courthouse.

When we later caught two fishing poachers, I knew I faced a challenge in court.

THE FISHING POACHERS

Norman hadn't gotten to the lake before he charged full speed back up the hill, yelling for me before he reached the house. I ran onto the porch.

"There're two men fishing at the lake," he shouted.

I ran inside, yelling to the others to call the ranger, grabbed up my .12 gauge, ran back out and scrambled onto the four-wheeler behind him. He took off down the hill, so fast I was barely hanging on to the shotgun and onto the four-wheeler.

As we came around the bend and saw the dam, I realized the men had fled.

"Head around behind the dam," I told Norman. "I know where they parked."

Around the lake we roared, down the spillway, and beyond one of my favorite hunting spots, to the land line between me and what used to be part of Andalusia. He skidded to a stop at the fence. I jumped off, crawled over the fence, and took off running for the driveway that the loggers had opened up when the new owners had recently cut timber.

Gasping for breath, I reached the poachers' truck. One man stood beside it. He looked at the shotgun in my hands and raised his hands, palms toward me. I did not point it at him—no need to. He was scared enough—his hands shook.

Besides, at that time I had not pointed a firearm at anyone; I often let poachers see I was armed, that I was willing to protect myself, but no poacher had ever indicated he would resort to violence against me since that fella half-threatened to set the woods on fire back in the 1960s.

The rangers were always after me to leave the poachers to them because of the potential danger. But I reckon I just got too mad to be scared.

"Where's your buddy?" I said.

"I—I—dunno. He went up the hill."

"Well, you're going to jail. How come you're fishing here, anyhow?"

The man kinda shrugged. "A buddy told us about it. He said he'd found a honey-hole. That he'd never caught as many fish in his life."

"Well, you tell him he better not set foot back here again, or he'll join you in the jailhouse."

Norman staggered up behind me then, hobbling on his bad leg, and as out of breath as I was. He was way ahead of my thinking—he reached inside the truck and removed the keys from the switch.

"Let's head out to the road, " I said. "Vernell oughta be there by the time we get to the gate. The other fella's not going anywhere."

We didn't talk on the way out. It was not a short walk. We stomped through chiggers and ticks, briars pushed down by the truck and scattered limbs left by the timber crews. Squirrels barked at us. Blue jays and crows, like the squirrels, announced our passage. A rabbit bounced away.

We reached the main roadway in the woods, strode up the hill and over the mudholes where their truck had splashed out the all the water. No drinks for the birds there anymore. A deer blew at us and then bounced off through the dry leaves. We reached the gate at the paved road just as Vernell stepped out of his truck.

I was especially fortunate, surrounded, so to speak, by rangers. Vernell lived maybe two miles away in one direction, and Nelson lived maybe four miles away along another road.

"We got one of 'em," I said. "The other one is still in the woods. Norman's got their truck keys so he can't leave."

Vernell talked to the guy for a few minutes, out of my hearing, and then they got into Vernell's truck. They went to apprehend the other poacher. With his keys gone, the culprit waited at his truck. Vernell took them to jail, where they were both charged with fishing without permission.

Now my real test would begin. What would my cousin Judge Bob do with these two men? Let 'em go?

I demanded that the prosecutor issue subpoenas to everyone I could think of who was involved: The former State Court Judge and the leading business man in town (co-owners of the land the men crossed to get to ours); Norman, who had to lose a day's pay and drive 100-plus miles to come to court; and of course the ranger, Vernell, would be there.

Surely, Cousin Bob wouldn't find these two men "not guilty" when all these folks testified.

Court day came. The judge entered and we all had to stand. As usual with him, he remained standing and led us in the pledge of allegiance to the flag. I expected him to tell us all about World War II when he sat, but he looked over the courtroom. I sat beside Sonny Goldstein on one side and Norman on the other. Beside Sonny sat Milton Gardner, former state court judge.

Bob didn't have to find them guilty. The culprits pled guilty. Bob fined each $100.00 and told them to never go there again. He also denied them fishing privileges for a year.

A few weeks later, I stopped in at a mama-papa store that catered to the fishing and hunting crowd. On their wall was a photo of a man with his truck, the bed full of fish.

"Where in the world did he catch all those fish," I asked.

"He didn't tell us where the honey-hole is," the store owner said. "He told me he's never caught so many fish in his life. I think he was poaching on a private pond."

"I think he was too," I said, "Please tell him he better not be coming back on our place."

The fella with the truck load of fish probably told the other two poachers where to fish, and he also is likely the person who stole our electric motor and battery earlier that summer. At least those three culprits did not return.

* * *

Cousin Bob gained international attention in 1960 when he went to Russia to defend Francis Gary Powers, the pilot of the U-2 spy plane who bailed out and did not bite his cyanide capsule when his plane was shot down. Powers' "spy swap" was featured in the movie *Bridge of Spies*.

WATERHOLES AND NATURAL FOOD

Posthole diggers are made for building fences, not for cleaning out springs. I didn't know they would seal up the walls of a spring until later, when I also learned they can seal up the walls of a hole dug to plant a tree or bush and that plant will die of thirst.

So I dragged a pair of diggers around with me—well, actually I put them in the back of Nellybelle and let her carry them for me. In my youth, every valley on the land had running water. And it seemed that every hilltop had a home. The residents, however, had to walk down the hill to the spring for drinking water, bath water and laundry water.

Our livestock kept the woods open, so rain became run-off water and kept the underground water table high enough to feed the springs and creeks in the hollows.

The livestock were gone by 1967, and the land grew timber, underbrush and vines galore. Although the soggy meadow stayed soggy, many springs quit flowing and rainwater was not enough to keep the creeks alive. Tilled land and pastures had grown into timber, and trees sucked up tons of water.

So I decided to dig out the ones I could find. Get water flowing again. The first one I tackled still had its original terra cotta pipe, but it had filled with dirt and trash. Took me an hour or more (after all, I did have to take a break) to dig it out down about five feet, where I hit rocks. I'd have to get them out if I were going any deeper, but it'd take somebody stronger than I am to do so. At least a little water rose. But slowly. Oh, so slowly. I decided to let it take care of itself and headed for the spring on the other side of the hill.

Mae's spring still flowed, some. It had served her family for about thirty years as a source of laundry water. They had a yard well that dried up and forced them to carry water from the spring. Now, with the family moved into a more modern home, with running water and a washing machine, the spring had not been tended to for perhaps ten or more years. It needed cleaning out.

As I approached the spring, a bullfrog *huh-rumped* and jumped from the spring drain into the small waterhole a couple of feet away.

At least he didn't go into the spring. I knelt down, getting my jeans' knees wet, but who cared? I didn't want to post-hole-dig the critters in the bottom of the spring, so I had to see who was down there. The bottom was sand, almost as white as the beach.

Crawfish flipped their tails and backed against the terra cotta pipe. Two spring lizards retreated into the shadows. How in the heck was I gonna clean the sand without harming these inhabitants?

The sand bubbled in one corner (actually, not a corner since the pipe was round) where the water came in. The flow was good. I decided leave the spring alone and work on the drain. It was filled with moss and the spring itself overflowed the low edge of the pipe, where someone had chipped out a chunk about the size of my fist.

I pulled most of the moss out of the drainpipe, and got the rest out by standing in the muck and pushing the shovel handle into the drainpipe. That act put the moss into the spring, so then I had to get back on hands and knees to pluck it out.

Took awhile. Sure would have been easier with machinery instead of my back. But I tackled the vines and weeds that flourished in the muck. I was able to open up a drain so water flowed easily to the small waterhole and, I hoped, on down the hollow.

I spotted a crawfish, in the mulch I'd shoveled up. Poor thing was struggling to move, so I sloshed back in the mire, picked it up and released him in the new ditch. I decided the salamander was safe enough in the muck and could fend for itself.

Swamp critters safe. Water flowing. Time to go have a bath and supper. And take a walk to look for deer.

Didn't walk far before I saw six bucks, all in velvet (it was May). But one buck's rack was black. Hope to see him again.

ʄ ɿʄ ɿʄ

My hunters and I used both small and large openings in the woods for food plots—garden spots for the deer and other critters. One weekend we planted a ten-acre field with soybeans. The next week, the seeds germinated and stuck green shoots up. When I went to admire our soybean field the next weekend, the deer had cleaned up the entire field.

Over the years, with more fields planted over a larger area, the food supply lasted better.

Food plots provided a hunting site, but not as good a spot as the oak or persimmon thickets. As much as turkeys like chufas, they cleaned up those plots long before winter came and went. When we checked their craws to see what they were eating, we'd find a rare acorn, but mostly greens—clover or grasses.

* * *

"You got something in your hand I wouldn't even want to say the name of," Miss Willie Mae said when I stepped out of the Jeep and sorted through raccoon droppings to recover some persimmon seeds.

We laughed together, but I continued for years to collect persimmon seeds that had run through an animal—raccoon, fox or coyote. The alternative was to pick the seeds out of ripe persimmons and scratch them with a sharp edge to simulate their passage through an animal's gut.

I would wrap the seeds in a paper towel and stuff them into my pocket when I'd go into the woods. Doesn't take long to seed a forest with persimmon trees. Kick the mulch, drop a seed, kick mulch over it, and move on.

A friend who hunted some land I'd seeded said he had never seen so many persimmon trees in his life. The fruit feeds not just deer, but also turkeys, coyotes, raccoons, fox, and any other critters that give them a try. Persimmons can also be made into a fine wine.

This kind of food for wildlife makes it worthwhile to scrabble through raccoon dung.

Every autumn, when the acorns fell, I'd beat the squirrels to some white and chestnut oak acorns and hide them under mulch in the woods, same as the persimmon seeds.

When someone told me how fast the sawtooth oak grows and the size of its acorns—they are bigger than those of the chestnut oak or the white oak—I decided I'd plant some on my land. The easy part was buying some. The tough part was getting them in the ground.

I seemed to find ground that was "poor" and the trees struggled for a few years. I lucked up and found some trees producing vast numbers of acorns and collected some of them to plant around the farm.

I reckon over the years, I planted about 500 persimmon trees over the land, and perhaps as many oaks. But my messing in the raccoon's mess earned me the nickname "Persimmon Sue."

Deer think the autumn leaves of the red mulberry are candy. I've often hunted near one with success, and so have my friends. Cindy Key Sanders killed this buck while it dined on mulberry leaves. (Have to brag on her—she found one of my favorite hunting spots and it is now one of her favorites.)

Cindy Key Sanders and her eleven-pointer, from one of my favorite hunting sites. Note the bunched ear guards.

Another tasty treat for deer is the honey locust pod. The branches, however, are loaded with thorns that will ruin a tire.

Always better to plant something that will feed wildlife for years than to throw out something that will feed only for the day or a season (such as clover), or that will feed for a few years but not replace itself (such as apple trees). Persimmons, oaks, red mulberry and honey locusts will feed the deer, turkey and other critters long after I'm dead and gone.

"GET UP, LAZY BONES"

One of those cold November mornings when the grass was frosted white and bare ground rose up on icicles that rattled when I kicked them, I returned to the sweetgum tree stand where I began my hunting years. Even the sunrise did not warm my shaking body, and my toes hurt from the cold. I lay the rifle across my knees—the built-in stand had a foot rest that gave me a level lap for the rifle. The firearm almost burned a cold blister on my legs. I had to tuck my hands into my armpits to keep my fingers warm enough to fire the rifle, just in case.

The sun hit the field, and mist began to rise as the ground warmed. But the sun did not reach me.

Three deer trotted into the meadow. Two does led a buck in. I got to shaking more than just from the cold as my usual buck fever struck, without warming me up at all.

I wrapped my shoulder strap around my right arm and pulled the rifle butt against my left shoulder. *Tight*. I leaned forward, rested my right elbow on my knee, lined up the crosshairs on the buck's neck, and eased off the safety. I squeezed down, and through the scope I watched him fall.

Neither doe ran. They looked at him. One lowered her head and poked her nose in his direction, and then pulled her head erect again. I didn't move. I didn't want to scare them away from the stand. The other doe sniffed at the ground as if she were looking for a snack.

The first one stomped a hoof. The buck did not move. She stomped again. He did not move.

She walked over to him and stomped again. Same response. She circled him and when she reached his belly side, she poked him with her nose. Probably saying in deer language, "Get up, lazy bones."

I decided it was time to ask the ladies to go away. I whooped.

They ignored me. Didn't even look my way.

I considered lowering my rifle, and then realized I'd been watching the does and forgotten to put my rifle on safety.

I didn't bother to try to soften the noise when I clicked it off, and that small metallic sound sent them tearing out of the field.

ME AND WOOT AND THE REDBONE HOUND

Woot had a new dog—a redbone coon dog. Actually, a half-grown hound that was supposed to know the difference between a coon and a jackrabbit. The pup needed some practice runs.

We had a history, Woot and I. He had taken me and my high school friends on possum (yes, possum, not opossum) hunts fifty years ago, when some folks frowned at white teenage girls being led into the woods by a black youth.

Now in our late sixties, neither of us was frisky enough to charge up and down the hills behind the dogs. But we could lean against a tree and listen—and I knew where the new puppy could tree a coon.

I called Woot, and the date was made. Seven-thirty.

Excitement filled me, like the thrill of opening day of deer season. I hadn't been possum hunting in almost twenty years.

Woot lived only a couple of miles away, so I hurried to get ready. I donned my walking boots and hunted up my five-battery flashlight. I was ready to brave the night and the woods. No heavy coat, however. Walking, even in the chill, could bring on a sweat.

Anticipation gripped me. A quarter after seven found me sitting on the back porch, my knees bouncing as I listened for his truck to rattle across the railroad at the foot of the hill. At seven-thirty, he drove up with three hounds in the truck bed. I trotted to his vehicle, piled in the front seat and off we went.

He parked alongside the road, where the land stretched out wide enough for the state to add another lane to the highway. He leashed the dogs until we crossed onto my land, and as soon as he released them, the $300.00 redbone puppy galloped toward the hollow.

The others trotted around us, sniffed at me and used the road for a toilet, as if to be sure we would step in their deposit when we returned to the truck.

The high-priced hound bellowed, his voice deep, excited. My mind resurrected nights of my childhood, nights of listening to the possum hounds and wondering how the dogs' owners distinguished the voices of each hound as well as the message relayed by the tone of its howl: "I'm just trailing," or "I got 'im in a tree," or "It's in the ground, but I got 'im trapped for you, master."

The older dogs, both female, yelped and charged toward the pup. Tonight, I had no doubt about voices. The male bayed nonstop. The two bitches yodeled and turned back to us as if undecided about why they were in the woods on such a cold night.

The redbone's voice lured Woot and me about fifty yards down the hillside. Woot said, "Wait till he barks *treed*."

He went silent.

And streaked by us, back up the ridge, ran to an oak tree, and bellowed frustration.

The dog was supposed to have been trained to track only coons and possums, but so far, Woot said, he had not treed anything.

At full tilt he headed back into the hollow and barked *treed*, only to change his mind and run uphill again.

We *treed* our shoulders on a pine for a while rather than sit on the damp ground. Howcome, with the shower today, was the hound so undecided?

On his third run uphill, he stayed on the ridge for maybe fifteen minutes. He was near a cluster of persimmon trees, where I had a deer stand.

The Persimmon Ridge stand was a favorite, where I loved to watch the woods wake up, the woodpeckers hop up and down tree trunks and *rat-tat-tat* the world awake. Coons feasted on the persimmons at twilight, their paws rustling the leaves as they scrabbled for food. As silent as a dream, a fox stopped by one morning before sunup. Squirrels bounced around the oak tree over my head and in the pecan tree in front. I saw my first buck fight there, two spikes seeking dominance but weighing only sixty pounds each.

One morning, while I turkey hunted alongside the trail, an eagle landed on a pine limb nearby. First and only bald eagle I have seen on the farm.

My first local coyotes showed themselves there.

Persimmon Ridge was never dull.

Redbone stayed on the ridge his third trip.

"He's at the persimmon trees," I said.

Woot said he had not treed, he was just running.

"Well, let's go to the permissions anyway, just to see."

Redbone was somewhere in the pines, carrying on like a courting tomcat at midnight.

"I'll tree your coons for you." I pointed my flashlight into the trees and eased the light across the limbs.

Eyes gleamed in the light beam.

Woot laughed. "Lawd, Miss Lindsley, how'm I ever gonna tell it that you done treed them coons when my dogs couldn't."

Training a coon dog well demands that the dog sink his teeth into his prey. No, the hound doesn't eat the coon, but once he is involved in killing the animal he will begin to remember that his nose is to follow only that scent and not be lured away by a more recent trail of a rabbit, fox, bobcat or deer.

With me behind him and my light shining over his head into the eyes of the victims, Woot used his ancient .22 to bring them down, one at a time. With the first shot, all three dogs charged to the tree.

Woot went home happy and with food for his family and perhaps a better trained dog. A week later, Woot came back, and even without me to tree them for him, he went home with three more coons.

From earliest memory, I have gone possum hunting. My father chaired the chemistry department at the local college, where he sponsored an annual possum hunt for the chemistry club. In the 1930s and early 1940s, the college girls weren't allowed off campus, except for the possum hunt. So the membership in the chemistry club grew. As soon as I was old enough, I joined the long walks in the night— nights filled with the excitement of girls out on a new adventure, the magic of the lanterns swinging shadows back and forth, the hurrying I had to do to keep up with the grownups. Those hunts ended when Dad retired—I was about twelve.

This chapter placed second in the Julie L. Cannon Spirit of the South literary contest at the Southeastern Writers Workshop, June 2014.

THE GREAT PEABODY POSSUM HUNT OF 1999

The moon tangled itself into the naked tree limbs like the fading smile of a ghost on Halloween, as if it were laughing at the old ladies who planned to tromp the night away in the woods. Long before the sun left us to darkness, we ate ham sandwiches and drank co-colas while laughing at stories of our youthful hunt, forty-six years ago, when the only possum we captured was black, long-haired, and wore a white strip down his back.

Steve, the reporter from WMAZ-TV, wandered back and forth, declining our food, but keeping his camera working, catching images of the puppet possum, and letting his imagination roam back over the years with us. A bunch of women in their sixties going on a possum hunt was about to make the local 11:00 o'clock news.

And one gal brought along her own possum, just in case.

Pat Blanks and her possum

Woot, our hunter-guide, arrived with darkness, his redbone hound and his Santa-like laughter. Everyone reminded him of that other hunt, when we were all teenagers, a time when racial tensions were high, but our only tension was the excitement of the hunt—until we had to flee a polecat's projections.

Unlike the previous hunt, this early winter evening was almost warm, the ground moist only from the dew. Woot said it was a perfect night.

We scrambled for flashlights, piled into vehicles and were off to the woods. As soon as we unloaded ourselves from car and truck, Woot and I lit the lanterns and Woot lead us into the darkness while Steve stood behind us, filmed the soft lantern lights and recorded our laughter.

Red the hound claimed the territory as his, bush by bush, as we ambled along the old logging road toward the first meadow. Apparently he thought with all the noise and laughter, we were just out for a walk, not to hunt, and Woot had to whoop at him a few times for him to take the evening seriously. We crossed the first meadow and plunged into the deeper shadows of the pines beside the road.

Since we were getting farther and farther from the vehicles, the two Pats (Blanks and Riner) decided to return for one of the trucks, and Woot, who, like me, is getting lame with years and arthritis, suggested they bring his. So off they went, with one flashlight, a road to follow, and no way to get lost.

But they did. They got to a fork and took the other road. Meanwhile, Red suddenly decided to put his nose to the ground, and he ran toward the creeks, his voice rising with his excitement as he barked *treed*.

Woot plunged into the thickets, June and Gail right behind him. Ruth and I took the easier way—we followed the road another twenty yards and strolled beneath open hardwoods. Unfortunately, Red was barking up the wrong tree. No eyes reflected light back to us in our flashlight beams, and in a few minutes, even Red lost interest in the tree.

The Pats reached the truck just as Red had begun barking, and now here they came, Woot's truck rattling to beat all heck as they sped though the woods and hit every mudhole in their eagerness not to miss the critters or their capture.

We reassured them they had missed nothing. Then Woot whooped Red off again, and as he headed toward the east side of the meadow, his voice rose in volume, his bass impatient, insistent, and demanding.

A hound sounding on a trail on a cold night, with the wind asleep, is a major portion of country living. Even sitting on a porch and listening to someone else's hounds sing through the night breeds excitement because the dogs' voices exude enthusiasm and joy for life and time in the woods.

Red's tone changed from, "I'll find him," to "He's here!" and we hurried off to join him. Luck was with us, for this time we didn't have to fight the briars and vines—Red was at one of the oaks along a side road. But luck was with the possum, because he had fled up a white oak, which doesn't shed its leaves until the new ones begin to nudge them off. Somewhere in that thicket of leaves hid our prey, out of sight of our flashlights.

Red tried to turn himself into a beaver, gnawing at the tree when he wasn't loudly demanding that we get the critter out of the tree for him. But all we could do was shine the lights and look. Woot moved off the road, down into the nearby ditch, looking from another angle.

A strange sound, like a cross between a cat hissing and growling, ruptured the night. Our skin crawled across our backs as we looked around for the panther of childhood legends, the mysterious creature that crept through the night to pounce on unsuspecting children. The sound came again, and I realized it came from Woot's direction.

"Was that you, Woot?" I called.

"Yes'm. Hit's de sound of a mad coon. Sumtime hit'll spit back and we kin find 'im."

"Howcome you don't climb the tree and shake him out?" Woot's whole body shook as the laughter erupted upward. "Well," I went on, "You used to climb the trees. What's the matter? You gitting as old as I am?"

Woot just laughed at our crazy antics.

He just laughed. This tree was only about three feet in diameter and rose up at least twenty feet before a limb stretched from its trunk. Woot reminded me he had seen his sixty-first birthday and doesn't climb trees any more, thank you.

With our unconquered prey watching from overhead, Woot pulled Red away from the tree and, undaunted, we tromped on into the night.

But raccoons and possums seemed to have taken to scentless feet, for Red cast first one way and then the other, but no critter aroused him to call us to follow. So we piled into the truck and moved to another area.

With the truck parked in the middle of a deer food plot, we stood shivering in the rising wind as Red ran uphill and through the trees, then again back to us as if to reassure Woot that he was really trying. The subject of fireside and the 11:00 o'clock news came up, but Woot said to give Red time. Red shook himself all over, as if to tell us he was through just fooling around and was now getting down to real business. Off he went, head high, toward the nearby land line and the unknown wilderness beyond. I secretly hoped he would not strike a trail over there.

Every once in a while, Red hollered. Woot said his barking was just to let us know he had found some interesting scents. He ran silent for a few minutes, then sounded off into the night with delight that he was doing well, to remind us not to go home, that he would fetch us a possum before the night was over.

For a few minutes we heard only the silence of the stars overhead, the loudest noise the moonlight moving across the meadow. Red barked and Woot whooped back. The other hunters of the night, coyotes interrupted Red and Woot with howls and laughter as they sought their supper.

The cool dampness penetrated our clothes as if we were in mist beside the sea. The cold was enough to cause a little tooth chattering, but the eerie calls of the coyotes added to the mystery of the darkness.

When Red barked *treed*, we forgot the coyotes. Everybody started off toward the fence line at a trot, but my foot took that moment to not work, so I halted the group. "I'll have to stay with the truck," I said. "At least, when you get lost, I can honk you home."

Left to right: Ruth Haslam, Pat Blanks, Gail Cabisius, me and June Kitchens Smith. Photo by Trish (Pat) Bass Riner

Woot allowed that was a good idea. "I dun spent many a night in dem woods," he said. "And had to wait for hit to be light afore I could git out."

Off they went, Woot, the two Pats, June and Ruth, two lanterns swinging leg shadows, two flashlights slicing the darkness. Gail allowed she'd stay with me, and we took the truck to the hilltop where we listened to Red and Woot holler back and forth. They moved farther and farther away, and the coyotes seemed to be moving closer.

So back down the hill we drove, going to the edge of the field, and as close to the back land line as possible. There, we stood beside the truck and listened. The neighbors' dogs tried to fill the night with their voices and drowned out Red. Back up the hill we drove. By then Red had traveled so far his voice was faint. Woot's whoop split the night, however, although his voice was also far, far away.

"They're lost," I said.

I sat on the horn for a few seconds. Standing in the cold, I honked and we listened.

The moon was long gone, the dew was heavy, and as I stood beside the truck I felt the cold descending deeper. Meanwhile, in their mad run through the darkness, Pat (Trish) had spilled herself flat on her face. Everyone was fighting briars, limbs, ditches and darkness to reach Red.

But alas! Again the critter—possum or raccoon—had sought refuge in a large white oak and could not be seen. And neither could a trail out of the thickets.

I honked and hollered. Woot hollered back. Hot, sweaty, tired, and laughing at themselves, they stumbled out of the woods about half an hour later.

They had come up on a firebreak and followed it a little way, but then had to cross it to reach me. Had they stayed on the fire break, they'd have walked four times as far, and made two right-hand turns, but they would have come out at the meadow where Gail and I waited. And not gotten into the briar patch. But not even Woot knew about that long-distance shortcut. So through the thickets they came, through the thickest thickets on my land, thickets of thorns and stumpholes and gullies.

They didn't wait to be asked. They all piled into the truck, where they giggled and puffed for breath and wiped sweat while I hovered over a lantern to try to catch some warmth.

Meanwhile, Red trotted proudly into the field, circled the truck once, and took off again. It was 10:30, and we wanted to see the TV program, but Red refused to return to us. Woot called. I called. We cranked the truck to make him think we were leaving. We turned the truck around. Woot finally shot his .22—the sound to a 'coon dog means the raccoon has bit the dust, and here came Red, loping with excitement.

Woot placed the lanterns into five-gallon buckets and two of the girls held them so they wouldn't fall over. The only fire we wanted would be at the lake for our hotdogs. Woot left us when we reached my truck, and he headed home, not interested in our cookout. He said he'd see himself on TV while sitting beside his own fire, thank you.

Hot chocolate was first on the agenda after turning on the TV. Then we got to admire ourselves and laugh again at our outrageous adventures in the night. Midnight found us at the lake.

We got the bonfire going, but waited for it to burn down to coals—best for cooking hotdogs on sticks. We all huddled for its warmth. Cooking time, and we managed to roast our hot dogs without burning them, and only one marshmallow tumbled into the ashes.

While we stuffed ourselves, we were entertained by the chorus of the coyotes again, this time closer, only 500 or so yards away. They all seemed to be laughing, as if they were close enough to see a group of old ladies hovering over the campfire and pretending they were teenagers and giggling at themselves.

It was 3:00 a.m. when we finally doused the fire and headed back to the trailer. Trish and Ruth staggered off to the city and to a real bed while Gail, Pat, June and I crawled into our tents, but enthusiasm and adrenaline kept us awake.

Dew dripped onto my pillow from the condensation on the tent's ceiling because we'd left the windows open. From far in the distant swamps came the infrequent call of a barred owl and the all-night *yips* of the coyotes.

I was up at six, ready for the day to begin. So was the Dooley Cat, wanting to venture into the yard and explore all the good smells drifting on the breeze. Perhaps a possum had gone by overnight?

Everyone left with her can of Peabody Possum, a copy of the *Macon Telegraph* article about the possum hunt, and the questions ringing in her ears:

Shall we do this again? Next week? Maybe next century?

PEABODY

POSSUM

INSPECTED BY

INGREDIENTS	HOW TO PREPARE
possum, water, spices, and other unknown things	ASK WOOT for a vareity of methods

PROOF OF PURCHASE

0019540055

I wrapped this label around a can of commercially sold meat, so the girls did not really get a can of possum. Woot said he ate his the next day. The bar code numbers are the graduation years of those on the hunt: 1954 and 55. The inspector's shield is the emblem for the school: PHS, with the torch of knowledge standing midway in the H.

This article, originally written to share with those Peabody High School classmates who went on the possum hunt, won the first place award for nonfiction from the Southeastern Writers Association in June 2004. It was my last hunt with Woot, but not his last hunt. He still dines on raccoons and possums.

FUNNY THINGS HAPPENED
ON MY WAY TO TURKEY HUNT

On my coon hunt with Woot and the redbone hound, while we leaned against a tree and listened to Red run in circles, my mind also ran in a circle back to the days I turkey hunted on Persimmon Ridge. Near the trail the redbone kept running up and down was a pine tree with a sapling growing beside it, a sapling covered with honeysuckle. I had pulled that bush over one morning for camouflage and to break up my silhouette. I had set up against that tree numerous times because the turkeys often roosted in the pines on that ridge, as I had learned by spooking them from their roosts several times in deer season.

No point in my hooting to get them to gobble from the roost—at best my owl hoots sounded like an old lady trying to make like an owl. I hoped my box or slate sounded enticing to a gobbler.

No morning on the ridge was boring, not even the day I went to sleep. Something woke me and I looked up.

The gobbler strutting to my decoy saw me, hushed his drumming, shrank his strut, and departed the premises. So I figured I may as well depart too.

I didn't fall asleep there again. Another dawn, I called in two coyotes that came up to sniff my decoy. Apparently a mama and a pup. I'd never realized how yellow some are—I'd thought they were mostly grayish, kinda like wolves.

One cool morning another season a gobbler talked back to me but demanded that I (the lovesick hen) go to him. He wandered back and forth just out of my sight. Maybe he was the fellow that woke me up the year before. I gave the area a week's rest and returned. I placed a decoy in the edge of the Jeep road, backed into my hidey-hole beside the honeysuckle, and waited awhile before I called. Soon as one gobbled, I answered. He called back to me and soon he came strutting along the road, headed directly to the decoy.

Wouldn't you know, that very moment was when the only eagle I was to see on my home territory chose to *swoosh* down and land on a limb just above the decoy.

I had less than a second to decide. *Would the eagle try to haul my decoy away? Should I scare him off? Give up a chance at the gobbler? Would the eagle attack the gobbler?*

The birds decided for me. The eagle spooked the tom, and the tom collapsed his strut and snuck into the woods.

I stood up and flapped my arms.

The eagle flew.

Boredom and naps were no longer options on Persimmon Ridge.

Strange events kept me between laughter and perplexity on many of my turkey hunts. One morning, an unusual looking turkey, chatting softly, approached my decoy. It had a thin beard, a blue head, a brown body and no visible spurs. Early in the mating season, and he didn't flare out his tail.

I didn't move. I wasn't ready to swear I was looking at a tom. Blue head and no waddle? Some does had antlers—did hens have beards?

Yes, I decided. This tom turkey was a hen turkey.

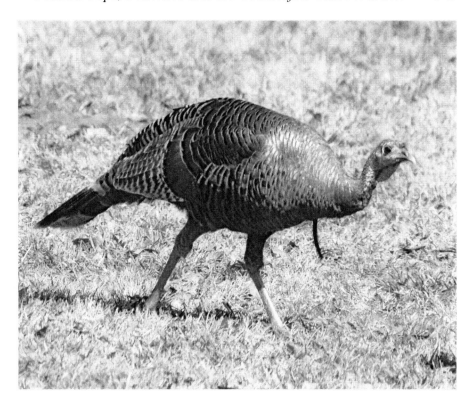

Another day, in the afternoon, I headed toward the big chufa patch, which the turkeys had scratched to a fare-the-well all winter. I planned to set up somewhere on the south side, since the turkeys roosted on the opposite side. Maybe, I thought, I could ambush one on his way to roost. Not the way the professional, the experienced or the *real* hunter collected a turkey, but I hadn't been able to call one all spring, and the season was moving along. I was willing to pull an ambush.

I never made it to my destination. As I came around the bend at the west end of the long, narrow patch, I saw a tom's fan at the other end. Since only the fan showed over the slight rise, the birds couldn't see me.

What the Sam hill could I do? What the heck, use my imagination. I had a hen and jake decoy with me, so I unloaded everything, laid my shotgun in the bushes, crawled (yep, like a good Marine) on my belly and pulled the decoys along. I made twenty yards and stuck the decoys into the ground.

And crawled back. Not the way to hunt turkeys, I knew, but I'd gone empty that spring and wanted some fall feast.

Back with my gear, I eased up. Still no birds showing their heads, but two tails fanned out in the distance.

I backed into the bushes and pushed enough limbs into others to make enough room to move my shotgun. I pulled on my face mask and gloves and took out my call. I *yelped* twice and watched the distant fan. Somebody *gobbled*. I called again. He *gobbled* back.

I put the call away.

In less than two minutes, turkey heads came over the rise. Lots of turkey heads—at least twenty, including several jakes and two-year-old toms. No long-beards. But, hey, I hadn't gotten a turkey and the season was about to end.

If they come close enough, I'll take a jake. Beats no turkey.

The dominant tom spotted the decoys—one a Redi-Hen, poised for breeding—and went into a strut, turning and inviting her to join him. But when he spotted the jake, he dropped from the strut and marched forward, ready to go to war. The flock came with him to meet the strangers.

All eyes stayed focused on the visiting decoys, and I edged my shotgun up, slipped the safety off and prepared to shoot. But which one? I couldn't risk a hen, and the toms seemed to be using them for bodyguards. My firearm got heavier, but at least the hens were losing interest in the stuck-up visitors who refused to speak to them. The ladies went to scratching for chufas. The toms milled around, ducking and nodding at the decoys. Two toms politely stopped side by side, heads up, apart from the others, and stared at the jake.

I lined up the shot—three-inch magnum, number 2 birdshot.
Can I really get two at one time?
I squeezed the trigger, and ended my season.

Two toms, one shell.

A few years later in mid-winter, I put up a Pop Top tent near a chufa patch for picture taking, and left it as a hidey-hole to hunt. I figured if I put out jake and hen decoys and called a bit, maybe a jealous tom would visit. A string ran from the hen into my blind, and if I tugged it, her head bobbled.

A broken ankle that never healed properly and a bad back that didn't like my sitting on the ground and against a tree limited my chasing gobblers up and down the hills. I had to limit my hunting to pre-determined roosting sites and food plots of clover, where I could set up a blind, have a short walk, and be comfortable.

Results were good and bad. My first visitor slinked in as I watched. Halfway across the field, he stopped, crouched, and debated attacking the decoys. They looked at him and I pulled the string to make the hen's head bob up and down. The wind blew from me to the coyote, and as soon as he got a whiff, he leaped up, spun and fled.

My next visitor came a few days later while I napped. He woke me up when he clawed at the hard-body hen as he tried to mount her. I didn't bother to try to shoot. It was too much fun to watch the frustrated fellow as he finally knocked the lady to the ground. My laughter ran him off.

Never a dull moment in the woods when you want to take a nap.

BEARDED HENS

Bearded hens are not common, but I have been fortunate to see and photograph several. Inexperienced hunters might mistake them for a tom because of the beard, but the head is blue and the spurs are only knobs.

These hens carry less risk of being mistaken for males than the antlered doe. The antlered doe is considered fair game because of the antlers. The beard, however, is not the only trait the hunter must consider when looking at a turkey—the tom's head is red during mating season (usually also hunting season). His spurs are longer, sharp and visible. And he struts.

SPRING POACHERS

A gobbler sounded off almost over my head. Another answered across the small stream to my left. A third welcomed morning from halfway up the hill to my right.

Opening day. I had watched these birds fly up at twilight the night before, as well as nightly for almost a week. I couldn't be happier. I'd have a bird in the freezer before lunch.

I'd done everything a newbie hunter who was a poor caller could do to improve chances of bagging a turkey. I had built a blind near the roosting site. I had kicked trash from the path for the last hundred yards to the blind. I had stuck decoy posts in the ground twenty yards from the blind to mount a Redi-Hen on one and a jake on the other before I settled down. I was hunkered down in my blind a good half-hour before the stars began to fade. Even if my call were to be awkward, the decoys would, I hoped, lure in the birds.

With three gobblers close by, I got the shakes, a serious case of buck fever, before even one bird became a possible target. A hen clucked overheard, and then others chattered their good mornings. I didn't have to call. One sailed down, wings spread, to the hen decoy.

I closed my eyes, clenched my teeth, and eased the safety off. No audible click. The hen talked to the decoy and when it didn't answer or move, the real hen began to scratch in the oak leaves—one foot scratch once, the other twice, head down to look for acorns or bugs, then head up, look at the decoy, purr at her. Repeat.

The air became alive with chatter and wing beats. More than a dozen hens landed around me. I didn't dare move and breathed as shallowly as I could. I didn't want even my breath to show. Here came the gobblers.

Across the creek, three strutted along the bank, back and forth as if trying to decide whether or not to cross. From my right, a jake flopped down beyond the hens and attempted a strut. The big guys crossed the creek and one ran at the jake. The jake fled.

The biggest guy strutted toward the Redi-Hen. Wings down, head tucked, tail feathers spread and body feathers fluffed, he took a step forward, turned, another step, turned, and danced his way toward the decoy, and toward me.

His life and my Thanksgiving meal depended on pulling that shotgun to my shoulder without spooking the birds. He was to my left, turned slightly away. The other gobblers watched him. The hens paid him no mind but seemed annoyed because the decoys didn't talk back. I was already scrunched down and needed only to ease the stock up a couple of inches and the barrel down a few.

Ever so slowly, I moved. No one noticed my movements. The gobblers were too busy dreaming of a quick marriage.

But my target remained in full strut. *Remember what Merle said. Never shoot when one is strutting. The shot won't go through the fluff.*

With the shotgun lined up on the bird's head, I clucked as if to tell a horse to gitty-up. The head shot up, eyes beaded at me. I pulled the trigger and the bird flopped once.

In the seconds before I reached him, another shotgun blasted the morning.

The poacher was back. Sounded like near the feeder. *Across the meadow, up the hill. A quarter-mile. No way I can get there in time and still save my bird from a coyote.*

This was the third year I'd hunted that tract on opening morning, and the third year I'd heard a shotgun only minutes after light. *Has to be the same man. Maybe I ought to quit hunting birds and just hunt him. Yeah, right. I could walk right by him and not see him, same as I walked right by Merle that time, not five feet away. He stood still and his camouflage blended into the oak so well that I didn't see him until he spoke.*

Two years later, the poacher came back, but on a day other than opening day. My sister heard the shot and had a cell phone. She called the ranger. The ranger who came had a tracking dog, and he went after the villain.

The ranger went to the site where poachers usually parked to trespass on us, and the dog trailed the man from his truck to the kill site, where feathers lay scattered and blood marked the spot. No one around.

The dog continued to track—but went a different route back to the truck's location. The truck was gone. But the good possum cop had the tag number.

The Department of Motor Vehicles provided the owner's name and address from the tag number when the ranger called. At the man's home the ranger discovered him dressing the turkey for his client. Two men were involved: The client from out of state and the guide, who was collecting about $500.00 a person to lead them to a gobbler. He'd been collecting the fee for several years—and some of the turkeys had been killed near a corn feeder. One client had left his box call beside an oak tree alongside a path, only thirty yards from our feeder.

Turned out the guide had previously been charged with wildlife offences. But this event cost him a hefty fine, his job with a nationally known hunting and fishing guiding company, and his right to hunt for awhile.

He is now a convicted felon and can not hunt with a firearm.

In another incident, I was backed against an oak tree about twenty yards from a trail. I'd pulled a honeysuckle vine off a bush to my right to break up my silhouette, placed a Redi-Hen on the trail and waited for daylight. Before I made my first call, something moved to my right, behind my honeysuckle pile. I didn't dare move; I'd spook the bird.

The honeysuckle began to tremble, then jerked away and flipped back against me. Something was eating it. Moving slower than the tree I was leaning on, I turned my head. A doe was eating my blind. If I ran her off, she'd snort a warning to the hillside. I let her feed, and when she finally wandered away, I felt it was safe to call.

Because I gag on mouth calls, I used a box and a slate; both lay on the ground beside me.

I lifted the slate and poised the striker above the surface. Before I could *yelp*, a *hen* did so from the hollow to my left. *Okay, lady, you just wander on up here and bring a tom with you.*

On her third series of *yelps*, **she** made a mistake. *Well, lady you ain't no lady a-tall. Just another poacher. Let's see if you are as stupid as I think you are.*

Not caring now if I scared off a bird, I pulled my gobbler call from my pack and gave it two hard shakes. The poacher answered. I waited about ten minutes to gobble again. He immediately answered.

I made him wait and wonder if the gobbler would come to him or if he would have to slip in closer and closer, hoping to call the bird the last few yards. We talked turkey back and forth for more than a half-hour.

The poacher kept moving toward me, lured by my fake gobbler

calls. When I figured he was less than 100 yards away, I hollered, "Better get outta here, buddy. And don't come back."

Not another sound.

I gave him time to escape—I didn't want to blindly walk up on him—then went to explore the area. I found a pair of dark glasses and a beer can (empty of course) beside a tree where he had brushed out a spot to sit.

I was pretty sure I knew the poacher. A nongentleman who leased adjacent property had been slipping onto our land in deer season. About a week later, I ran up on him and told him I had found his dark glasses. "I hope they're not prescription," I said. "I threw them away."

He got kinda pale and walked away. We never had trouble from him again.

* * *

My sister Lil set chase after a turkey poacher when she heard the shotgun fire. Into her car, down the driveway, onto the highway south, into the next gate, and back as far as the woods road went. Then on foot to the land line.

A few yards across the fence, a man in full camouflage and carrying a shotgun walked away. She yelled. He kept walking. She yelled again. He stopped, turned and asked, "What?"

She explained that he was hunting without permission. He was not allowed on her land, and he was standing and now hunting county park land, where hunting was not allowed.

His response was typical—"I didn't know. I thought I was on the Ennis land."

Strange place to think he was lost. The Ennis land was across the hills and even across a road. No way was he lost. Lil called the ranger, who met the man at his truck which was parked on the dirt road that we had begun to call the "poachers' parking lot."

The man's son-in-law from out of state also appeared at the truck. The ranger checked both men for hunting licenses. The fella from out of state had none. The older man, who turned out to be the athletic supervisor at a local school, did have one.

Because Lil had not seen the man on her land, he could not be prosecuted for hunting without permission, but the son-in-law got charged for not having a license. A few years later, in the courthouse, I got to chatting with a young man and learned that his father was the man Lil had talked to. I asked him if his dad were still poaching. The son seemed shocked, so I explained his father's lack of respect for property rights and his brother-in-law's illegal hunting.

Don't know what it is about physical-ed coaches. Another one, also highly respected in the community, got charged with hunting deer over bait.

HUNT BY INVITATION

Two weeks before firearms season, a friend asked that I check on his property for illegal hunters—no one was supposed to hunt his lands. I was happy to do so, especially after opening morning when I collected a buck and just wanted to sleep in.

So the next day, I strolled across the friend's lands. I was familiar with the layout, having walked it many times before. Although I wasn't hunting, I wore my orange vest—no camouflage, however. Just blue jeans and a warm jacket and the vest. I did not go unarmed—I carried a pistol. I never walk without a firearm, not with poachers and various other folks in the woods, as well as coyotes and the possibility of rabies.

When I was in my teens, a rabid fox invaded our yard, killed our flock of turkeys and attacked one of our horses. The mare developed rabies and fought several of the other horses, which then needed the prophylactic shots. Of course, the mare died, but the others survived okay.

Day Two of this season was cool and brisk, a day that makes you want to dance with the breeze and reach up to catch the sun. I diddy-bopped along the trail, stopping often to listen to the birds or to the wind whisper in the leaves. Acorns popped to the ground, and squirrels galloped from place to place to collect and store them for winter food.

A red-tail hawk soared overhead and I stopped to watch the sun highlight the bands on its tail. I wondered if it were the one that came across to my fields when Richard cut hay—he always saw one or two hawks diving for the field mice he stirred up with the mower, the rake and the bailer. I often saw them too, perched atop a dead pine to overlook two fields. The friend's lands were close enough this bird might be one of my pair.

From the path I could see off to my right into the tall pines that had shaded out the understory. The view to my left was only the top of the oak ridge. Some twenty feet off the path, the hill dropped to the boggy origins of a large creek. Only a few pines grew among the oaks—white oaks, water oaks, chestnut oaks. With persimmons also scattered over the ridge the land was ideal habitat for deer, fox, wild turkey, squirrel and coyote.

As I strolled along, I looked to either side, not expecting to see deer or turkeys or fox, not even coyotes, so mostly I'd check the trail for tracks. A mudhole showed raccoon tracks; a deer had run the road during the night. A hawk had left a few jay feathers as evidence of its yesterday's meal.

The ridge sloped and curved. To my left, the creek gurgled, and I stopped to watch for anything moving along its banks.

Something trotted, out of sight, somewhere between me and the creek. I turned toward the sound, and froze.

The biggest dang buck I'd ever seen trotted into view and then slowed to a walk. I could-a hit him with a rock. Twelve points rising tall and fat; main beams that overlapped in front after circling wide around his ears.

"Oh, Big Boy, aren't you glad I can't take you home with me," I whispered. He did not hear me, never looked my way. Just ambled on.

That evening, I called my friend and told him what I'd seen. I got fussed at: "Why didn't you take a gun with you?" was his major theme. With permission to hunt, I headed out the next day. This time, armed, for my walk in the woods.

And what a wonderful time I had!

I slipped to the top of the ridge before full light and didn't bother to look for a path down into the hollow. I headed over the ridge and through the bushes, toward the headwaters of the creek.

I found it. Marsh, roots that served as steps, hillocks of dry land, evidence of beavers. I allowed I needed to get out of the wet, even with my waterproof Ted Williams boots. A few yards back up the ridge, I came to a path paralleling the hollow.

Time to *still-hunt*. Take my time, let the deer announce themselves. Hide beside a bush, listen, watch, take only one step. Repeat and repeat. I would need all day to *still-hunt* my way to the spot I encountered that most beautiful buck the day before, but he had come from around this area. Maybe he'd come here again.

Thirty minutes into my walk, I spotted a skeleton. Deer. The bones had bleached white, even the antlers —that is, what remained of them. Rodents had gnawed out half-circles. Probably last year, I thought. Poacher kill? Most likely.

I was still bent over the bones when I heard running hoofs. A doe came at me, directly on the path I stood on. I stepped off, barely in time. I smelled her breath and felt the wind as she charged by. She didn't bother to run from me—she was busy running from the deer behind her. A small buck with short, almost invisible, spikes.

They tore from the path, down to my left, into the swamp. I was still hearing them when up the ridge came another pair, running parallel to my path. The doe in front fled from *the* buck, his nose extended, his antlers laid back over his neck and shoulders.

No need to shoot. Who can hit a shadow moving faster than the wind? I knew I couldn't, even in the open, and certainly not in these thickets. I couldn't move the shotgun fast enough to follow them—my eyes could barely move fast enough to keep them in sight.

I had not taken another step when here came the first pair, and again I had to scurry to get out of the way. The doe passed, her mouth open, breath heaving. The buck saw me and stopped, but only for seconds and off he went after his lady love.

That was enough dodge ball for one day. I went home.

THE PARKING LOT TOMS

The small meadow got the name *Parking Lot* because whoever hunted the stand down the hill to the south parked there. We planted every open space on the land with a variety of wildlife food, but mostly with crimson clover, rye and wheat. The Parking Lot was not an exception in spite of its small size

When turkeys came to our place, we planted only clover in some spots, and the turkeys claimed them for their own. I scattered the seeds about at thick as I'd pile up black-eyed peas on my plate. Too thick, I think, for some seeds to find enough ground to germinate.

But the turkeys loved it. They turned these spots almost white with droppings as the clover turned the red dirt green. I kept up the heavy planting to keep the birds in our area and away from possible poachers. And to keep them close enough that perhaps when the season opened in my county, I would be able to call one in.

The first season came and all I did was scare the dickens out of every turkey that heard my inept calls.

That fall the Parking Lot became a loading dock for timber cutters. The logging crew cleaned it up enough for us to plant, but had left one thirty-inch diameter log, considered unusable, nudged against a large pine that served as climbing pole for honeysuckle and muscadine vines. Enough cover for a good hidey-hole for me to hunker down into and be unseen, and perhaps call in a gobbler.

So opening day of season two, I leaned against the pine, a cushion under my butt, my .12 gauge propped on my knee that I pulled up to make the gun rest. I was ready. As the sun tipped the tree tops, I *yelped* with my box call. It must have sounded like a love-sick hen because off to my right, down the hill a bit, in the pines and hardwoods, a tom *gobbled*. I *yelped*. He *gobbled*.

I didn't know better. I kept up the *yelps*. He didn't know better. He kept up the *gobbles*.

And in full strut he walked in front of me.

I unloaded into the fluff.

He flew and I cussed.

I thought I could trail him, as I had tracked deer so many times. But flying toms don't leave tracks, and although I wandered back and forth over the hillside where he flew, I never found him.

When I told Merle, he gave me a lesson on gobblers: ***Do NOT shoot a tom in full strut. That red head is buried in feathers that the shot pellets aren't going to penetrate.***

So later that year, here comes Dave Waller. He walked the mile or more from the house as the sun lightened the east. When he topped the first ridge and called, a gobbler answered, way off, over the next ridge. He *yelped* a time or two, and the tom answered, so he headed to meet the bird.

When Dave reached the Parking Lot, he huddled against an oak, *yelped*, and waited for the gobbling tom to come into view.

One shot, he had the first bird off my hunting land.

Howcome I couldn't do that?

I tried a few mornings later. When I *yelped*, however, one *gobbled* way down slope to the north. Okay, I thought. Follow Dave's example and go to meet my prey. The trail dropped off to the west and then turned to the east. I found an oak and hunkered down. Not too comfortable. I had perched on an acorn and had to struggle to get it from under my butt. With hands and face camouflaged, I *yelped* again.

The bird answered. I stayed quiet. Maybe it'd come on up the hill.

I waited. Got antsy and nervous. Where was that bird?

It scratched just beyond the bigger oak off to my right. And then stepped around the tree.

The hen whispered *yelps* as she sought the unknown hen who had ventured into her neighborhood. I exhaled.

No tom today.

She kept me company for more than a half-hour as she fed on last fall's acorns and sought the other hen. The tom never showed, and I couldn't call again with the hen almost in my lap. I was ready to go home when she left.

But I wasn't about to give up on the area. The clover in the Parking Lot seemed to collect turkey droppings. I figured if they weren't coming to my call in the morning, they were too busy courting to visit with a mystery hen. Maybe one would come to see her in the afternoon. Especially at a food plot.

So back to the Parking Lot I ventured one afternoon. It was *hot*. If I killed a tom, I thought, I needed a Number 10 wash tub of ice to keep it from spoiling before I got home.

I backed up against my pine and *yelped* a few times.

No *gobble*. I forced myself to wait another thirty minutes and tried again. Still no answering *gobble*.

Another almost half-hour, and feet rustled the leaves to my right. The dry spell had the leaves as dry as cornflakes and even the toms crackled out their approach.

The sounds came from where I had conversed with the hen under the oaks. Had to be turkeys from the *scratch* pause *scratch-scratch.* I got ready.

Maybe a soft *yelp*. Very soft. Just enough to tease, like that hen had whispered. One strike on the box call and then a second.

A half-throated *gobble*.

Black shadows moved along the trail, visible through the greening leaves. Blue heads. Hens? No, jakes.

They entered the meadow and walked steadily to the shade across from me.

Would my shotgun lay one out at that distance? Maybe—since the shotgun barrel had been squeezed down to hold a tight pattern, the shot was No. 2, the shell three-inch magnum. But I didn't want to injure one and lose it. Besides they were jakes and maybe a tom would come along.

I waited.

I was in the sun. Sweating.

At least the camouflage net over my face and hands kept off the no-see-ums that flocked around my head like gulls over a shrimp boat.

The jakes were in the shade. Panting. Their bills hung open and their bodies heaved with heat.

No way I would shoot one that was cooking from the heat even while it stood in the shade.

I could only outwait them.

Fortunately, after almost an hour, they answered the lure when a real hen *yelped* from somewhere in the hardwoods to the south. As soon as they disappeared, I removed myself, soaked clothes and all, from the sun and headed for the truck and home.

My fourth year hunting I just knew I'd collect a tom from that clover field. Morning after morning, I was there—and the birds were far enough away they didn't bother to come to me.

On the first Tuesday afternoon I tried again. Perched my Redi-Hen in midfield and myself against the pine. *Yelped* a few times. And fell asleep. Head back against the pine, knees pulled up, camouflage net on hands and face, shotgun propped dangerously on my hand that rested on one knee.

This getting up and listening for courting toms had me plum wore out. Don't know how long I slept, but something woke me.

Ahh-rummm. Ahh-rummm.

Off to my left. On the other side of the log that rose to my shoulders. A sound I had never heard.

I eased my head around.

A long-bearded gobbler strutted toward the decoy. *Drumming. He was drumming.* With each forward thrust of his body he drummed.

I got buck fever so bad I shook all over.

I don't know how I brought up the shotgun. A lefty, I had to shoot from the right shoulder. And I did. Somehow. I think I did something that made him raise his head from the full strut, because he went down without flapping his wings. "Cemetery dead," as Merle said.

That tom paid for all the extra clover I spread over that food plot last fall.

UNDER THE SPREADING WHITE OAK TREE

Heavy fog turned the four deer into postcard-pretty silhouettes as they ghosted into the field from my left and headed to the white oak tree that dripped moisture and acorns.

No antlers showed. And it wasn't doe day.

Three headed for the oak, kicking dew from the winter-dead grass and leaving a sharp trail behind. Their hooves might as well have been cat feet for all the noise they made.

The largest doe remained at the treeline to search out danger. She turned her head toward the road in the distance, lifted her nose to catch any strange scent, and checked the edge in my direction.

Apparently my pine-oil smell soothed her nerves even though I'd not had any timber cut in several years. Or maybe what wind stirred lifted my scent up with the rising morning air.

I perched on a ladder stand propped against a pine, with a sweet-gum behind it, whose limbs I had draped with camouflage cloth. It fell low enough to break up the shadow of my legs. But I had no wind shield around me, and the 38° F dampness sneaked into every opening in my clothes. While the does fed, I just got colder.

When the quartet had eaten their fill and wandered back into the woods, I decided it was time for me to head for home and the fire. Early? Yep, too early I soon learned.

I departed the woods at 8:45, and at 10:00, Wayne came in with news. He'd run to the store and driven back by the field, visible from the road. And seen two deer under that oak. Not just does. "One was a doe, but the other a *huge* buck."

Impatience and the cold had done me in again.

Well, I told myself, I'll try again in the afternoon. I have more patience waiting for dark than waiting for some unknown time or the cold to send me home in the mornings.

I skipped that afternoon. The next day, I crawled into the stand better than two hours before dark. I didn't get bored.

A black fox squirrel began the parade to the oak soon after I got settled. It brought to mind my father's story about how he introduced the fox squirrels to our area back in the early 1930s. He'd seen an ad somewhere—I couldn't remember where—and had bought several from somewhere in the Midwest, perhaps Arkansas. Now fox squirrels abounded on our lands—some were white with black heads, some were solid black, and some were black with white heads. Today one of the solid blacks showed up.

I'd seen one of the white ones in my yard back in the summer, at the concrete bird bath. A female, she stood on her hind legs, wrapped her front legs against the pillar, and licked the concrete. Somehow, she was getting needed minerals from the fixture.

Silent as its shadow, a spike slipped from the woodline to my left and joined the squirrel. A deer crossed the road in the distance, a lone figure lifting over the fence. It broke into a run, eager to reach the tree before the acorns were gone. Another spike, it eyed the earlier arrival as it walked the final few yards. Deciding there was no need to worry, he still stayed on his side of the tree to eat.

The tree itself spread over more than thirty feet, and the wind had scattered acorns another ten feet in all directions. Acorns a-plenty for everybody.

Behind me, the leaves announced another squirrel. No—not a squirrel's *hop-hop*, but a *rustle*, a slight shifting of leaves. A deer? I rolled my head against the pine trunk. A doe ambled up the path.

She froze, head up, eyes locked on me. *Don't look her in the eye.*

I closed mine and held my breath for what seemed like minutes. If she ran, so would the others. Only silence. Was she still looking at me? Did I dare to breathe?

Leaves spoke. She was walking by. I cracked open one eye. She was headed to the oak—I was forgotten.

Five minutes later, a fawn whose spots had not faded loped from the woods to my right, only to vanish into the tall Johnson grass for several minutes.

Surely the big guy'll come back. All this activity, he'll feel safe

Antlers caught the falling sunlight in between shadows to my left.

Here he comes!

I pulled in a deep breath and prepared to shoot: Eased my feet up to rest on the top rung, slipped the safety off and propped my arms on my knees.

I let my breath out. It was a six-pointer. Not the big guy.

My watch indicated time, like its hands, did not move. The deer chomped loud enough for me to hear the acorns crunch. Probably be another dry hunting day. The sun pushed shadows across the field, toward and finally beyond the oak. Darkness would be sending me home in another half-hour.

Eight points rose wide and high, almost white against the trees. I swallowed. He must weigh 150 pounds. My heart thunked and my hands trembled. I gritted my teeth and tried to stop the fever.

He was too far to my left for me to attempt a shot from my wrong shoulder. My stand was too small, too narrow, for me to turn around.

He stepped from the black twilight shadows, his head down as he challenged and stomped at the others. One by one, he approached them, his head shaking, and one by one they trotted off about twenty yards. Far enough for Big Boy to turn his mind to feeding.

He faced away, offering me a perfect left-handed Texas heart shot, but I didn't want to send a bullet into him from rear end to heart.

I snugged my Remington 30.06 against my left shoulder, steadied my right elbow on my knee and waited, my finger on the trigger guard.

He turned to his left, sideways to me, and looked back into the woods. Another buck coming? I didn't wait to find out. I lined up on his neck and squeezed off.

He crumpled and did not move again.

I glanced toward the others. They stared at the buck. The six-pointer bobbed his head a few times and then started toward my buck.

Don't tell me he's gonna attack.

The other deer watched. So did I.

The six pointer sniffed the dead buck and then lowered his head as if to butt him.

I snorted through my nose, a kind of half-snore.

The suddenly brave warrior paid me no heed. He kept on half-nodding and half-threatening to attack.

Nobody paid me any attention.

I whooped. No reaction

I clapped. Still no response.

I didn't want a butchered-by-antler deer. Time to go. Besides, darkness was creeping in.

Although I knew I had slid the safety back on, I double checked it, then tied my rifle onto the pull-up rope and lowered it.

Everybody skedaddled.

TWO POACHERS NAMED IN *GON*

Georgia Outdoor News (GON), a monthly magazine headquartered in Georgia, has a "Hall of Shame" in each issue. Persons charged with game violations have the *dishonor* of having their names made public statewide.

GON reported:

Baldwin County: On October 21 XXX and XXX, both 27 and both from Gordon, were each charged with hunting deer at night. (One) was also charged with hunting from a public road. His fines totaled $535. (The other) was fined $155.

The incident occurred near my home site and the deer was in my front pasture, only a few yards from my driveway, when he died. When the men returned to pick up the deer, a ranger greeted them. This is the latest incident in my neighborhood. Maybe the word has gotten around that it's not wise to *mess with that old lady. You do, and you go to jail—if you survive.*

These men were fortunate—the local fine used to be a minimum of $500.00 for each of these charges. Now the State requires the fine for night hunting to be $500.00.

OPENING WEEK: 1994

By 1994, I had almost no problem with poachers. No need to spend opening day down at the jail house with some culprits. Wayne, Norman and I plotted our season, and I prepared my two favorite ladder stands. I was still able to get up and down ladders, but had to limit my walking because of my painful and failing ankle.

A week before opening day, I scouted the area. Pine scent on the boots and the hem of my pants legs would, I hoped, not warn the bucks that I had been back into the woods.

I left my truck at the gate and walked the ridge road. I probably could have walked that road blindfolded since I walked it in my mind so many times. Just inside this gate was where I sat that night and listened for the road hunters while the ranger hid a mile or so down the highway. I had planted chufas in the first field, where the road forked. The right-hand branch led to a large food plot and continued, to curve back and rejoin the main road at the small clover plot where my first ladder stood.

Nothing exciting along the road until I reached the small chufa patch. Turkeys had visited. The soft tan dirt had been turned since the last rain. Turkey droppings splashed white across the ground. I picked up a gobbler wing feather and stuck it into my cap brim.

The patch stopped my scouting for a few minutes while I scanned the ground. Raw dirt often meant arrow heads, even if they didn't show up when we plowed. Rain often *lifted* arrowheads to the surface of soft soil by packing the dirt around them. But not today.

A few yards beyond the small chufa patch a buck had pawed out two scrapes, one on each side of the Jeep trail. He'd followed a path that crossed the road, and had horned trees along it on both sides. I stood in the middle of the road. A step to either side would land in a scrape.

Ahead, I saw a thrashed limb with shriveled leaves, and beneath it, raw dirt.

He was a busy boy.

I needed another stand. Right here. Actually, back up the road about twenty yards. And right yonder, the perfect pine, maybe forty yards from the scrapes.

What else lies ahead?

I continued down the road. A cluster of four scrapes, and bless Pat, another tree overlooked them, and just behind the tree, to the left, honey-suckle had swallowed a sapling to add cover for me. Another stand needed before Saturday.

The food plot I had hunted for several years was surrounded by scrapes. One to my right as I entered. My stand was to the left, so it would provide a perfect left-handed shot for lefty me. I crossed the meadow, and immediately saw the buck had pawed beneath the small oak where the road entered the woods and crossed a wet-weather creek. I'd found a scrape there every year for about six years, and even last March the scrape had been freshly pawed. This wasn't just a hopeful buck—this one was the king of the woods, or in the terms of Felix Salten, Bambi's father.

I walked back to the house and loaded up my truck: Two ladder stands, the camouflage hoods, and extra camouflage. Putting the stands up without help was a rest-of-the-day chore, but before dark I had them ready. Extra camouflage draped behind the ladders themselves, to break up the silhouette of my legs, as on all my ladder stands. I also draped the windows with camouflage netting thin enough for me to see through but bunched up into wrinkles enough to keep my movement from catching the attention of a nearby deer.

I double-checked the tie down ropes by standing three steps up on the ladders and wobbling back and forth to see if the ladder was steady. Both were.

My magical pine scent again helped mask all the human scent I had brought to the woods.

Opening day, I would sit in the nearest stand. Move down the next day, and by Monday, if I hadn't collected the buck, I'd move to the meadow.

Saturday, opening day, came. Well before light I was perched in the first stand. It was unusual; I'd never seen another like it. An extension ladder, it had a fold-down seat and an attached hood. I had bought it thirty years before, in Atlanta's most prestigious department store, Rich's.

It was perhaps the first major store to accept returns without question. People were said to buy an expensive outfit, wear it to Easter church or a wedding, and then return it because it "didn't fit right." Rich's never questioned the customer. L. L. Bean used the same principle to build an internationally known mail-order outlet.

Opening day wasn't warm, but my patience was low. I was only a few days from my sixty-eighth birthday. I huddled in my stand like a hopeful hovering buzzard, but I soon lost the vulture's high hopes. I made it only three hours after light that morning until I decided the buck had found a lady love for the day. But I came back four hours before dark and sat it out. I had some entertainment—squirrels hopped through the dry leaves and chased each other up and down the oaks. An owl carried on awhile just before dusk. Several turkeys wandered by, stopped under the oaks to scratch, and then moved on. A chipmunk saw me and didn't shut up his warnings for a half-hour but never showed himself.

But no deer came near.

Sunday, I ventured deeper down the road, to the second ladder. Repeat the day before. That evening, my two (also deerless) hunting companions left for home, to go to work on Monday.

Day three, Monday, I slept in. What the heck, I figured. I'd killed more bucks over scrapes in the afternoon—maybe because I have more patience in the afternoon. So I caught up on my sleep. Besides, it's not as much fun to get up way before light and head out to the woods alone. Lots more fun to hunt and also listen for a friend to shoot and wonder what he may be seeing.

Norman always came in with tales of adventure, like the time an owl perched on his shoulder or the chipmunk stood up on his boot. And Wayne, one year while turkey hunting, had seen a doe drop a fawn only twenty yards away.

I'm glad now that I decided to save my patience for the afternoon.

In my area of Georgia (in standard time) in October, the sun goes down about 5:30, and the wind usually drops with the sun. The woods go still. Any animal that moves announces itself.

The buck announced himself, not with footsteps, but with grunts. To my right, in the woods. I couldn't see him, but I followed his movement by his grunts.

He must be behind a doe.

I watched the woods for any sign of him as the grunts moved along from right toward the road where the two scrapes were. But he might as well have been invisible. A gray body showed for seconds. I eased the safety off my .308. She stopped dead center in the drive, lowered her head, sniffed the scrapes, and stepped forward, only to disappear again.

The buck followed, but he was around the bend in the road, out of sight. He continued to voice his approval of her as he moved more and more to my left. I just knew they would cross the stream and go up the hill. I slipped the safety back on.

Seconds became minutes and minutes seemed to stretch to eternity. Would they turn around? They had gone far behind me, but had not gone up the ridge, just gone straight away, parallel to the trail I'd walked in on.

The doe snorted. Hoofs trotted in the dry leaves. My direction! I slipped the safety off.

Silence. Where was she? Where was *he*?

I pulled the camouflage netting at my left shoulder back a little and peaked out. Nothing in sight.

A rustle of leaves. She was moving again. He kicked leaves behind her. Had they made a U-turn to retrace their steps?

She crossed the Jeep road again, between me and the scrapes at the far end of the meadow. This time, she didn't stop to sniff them. I reckon she knew they were his. She disappeared into the woods again.

If only he'll cross this side of the woods. Better get ready. Just in case.

My feet were already perched on the top step, and when I slid the stock of the .308 against my left shoulder, I settled my right elbow on my right knee. Night was almost here. *Would he show himself before dark? Or stay in the woods?*

Bucks don't walk into sight. They materialize. He was ten yards into the meadow, antlers white against the background of the young pines, before my eyes sent the message to my brain that he was there.

I lined up my scope, whistled softly. He stopped, raised his head, looked my direction. I put the crosshairs on his neck and squeezed. He dropped.

One close-up look, and I knew I needed help to handle this deer. I called my friend Richard, who came with truck, strong back and sharp knife. And the insistence that I have this deer mounted cause, Richard said, it was a trophy for our county.

THE BUCK ON LARRY'S HILL

When the alarm sounded, I turned it off and almost rolled over to go back to sleep. But the boys expected me to join them for the morning hunt.

I slipped onto the front porch still in my pj's and checked the temperature. Only 26° F. Brrrr. I quickly stepped back inside. Too cold for this old lady, I thought.

But the light flashed on in the boys' cabin. *Crud. They're up. I guess I'll stay up too.*

I pulled on three layers of long johns. Two pair of wool socks made my boots almost too tight, but with the right ankle giving me fits, I knew the tighter boot would help my walking. And my climbing that pine in the portable stand.

After a quick bowl of cereal and cup of hot chocolate, I loaded up for the trip to Larry's Hill.

In my childhood, we called the ridge "the limbs" because the 100-year-old white oak's limbs drooped enough for us youngsters to climb onto them and play our games of wild horses—before our parents let us ride the real ones we raised. When a fella named Larry hunted with me and had his stand on that hilltop, everybody referred to it as "Larry's Hill," or "Larry's Field."

Funny, we never referred to the east end of the ridge, beyond the field, as "Norman's Ridge." But I reckon we should have—he hunted the ridge from the first day he joined me as a hunter, and he claimed his first trophy deer from his pine stand there.

My climbing stand was on a pine at the east end of the field, where an old logging road entered the food plot. And where a buck had a scrape the previous spring and had freshened it up several times already this season.

The pull-up rope was tied to the stand, so I needed only my .308 and a loaded clip and my warm gear—heavy insulated gloves, face mask for the ride on the 4-wheeler and to hide my light face from the deer. I would convert the pull-up rope to a safety belt.

I headed out to their cabin to check on the boys before I left for the hill and another cold wait for a buck.

They were on the same schedule and stepped out their cabin door as I crunched ice toward it. We wished each other good hunting. I headed for the barn and the four-wheeler and they rode off in the truck.

If I put my vehicle in high gear and tore up the hill, I'd scare every deer away for the next two ridges. I eased it along at not much more than a walking pace, slow enough and quiet enough that I didn't even wake up my neighbor as I drove by her house.

Down the first hill, into the flat bottom, I had to stop. A bird sat in the middle of the road and made no attempt to fly from the noise or the headlights. Since it faced away from me, I wondered if perhaps it thought the sun was brightening up its world. I studied it. About the size of a large quail, but not a quail.

If it'd just turn.

It turned to look my direction and its long beak identified it. A timberdoodle or woodcock. The first I'd ever seen.

I eased forward. The bird whirred away.

Only a few feet farther along the trail last year I had met a barred owl. It perched on a dead limb of a young hickory, at eye level to me. It flew at my approach.

I kept the four-wheeler in low gear until I reached the leaning oak, almost to the top of the ridge. I backed it into some bushes so it'd not be visible from the meadow. The 300-yard walk across the field was enough for my bad ankle, especially since I had to take a climbing stand up the tree.

With my rifle slung over one shoulder and two jackets over the other arm, I walked up the trail to the edge of the field. The food plot was white with frost. My breath added white mist to the air. *Frigid. No wonder the first electric ice boxes were called Frigid-Aire.*

Cross in midfield or stick to the edge? Lay down a scent trail on the edge and spook off anything that came up from the bottom I had just crossed? No. Take the short route, straight across to the far corner.

Frost sparkled on my boots.

Might as well have brought an ice bag for my feet.

I began to sweat before I was halfway across the meadow, and stopped to tug my shirts open at the throat. Sweat would evaporate and chill me more if I didn't cool down before I got into the stand.

I slowed my stride, too.

At the tree, I tied my extra jackets onto the middle of the pull-up rope and looped the rope's end through the rifle strap and tied it off.

The cushion I left the afternoon before was white with frozen dew. I turned it over before I climbed onto the stand, so at least I'd be sitting on the dry side, even if it were as cold as the wet side.

Once I sat down, I strapped my feet onto the foot section. Climbing with a two-part climber sure did beat the original hug-the-tree-and-pull-up-your-feet stand that was the only climber available back in the 1960s. Those stands demanded a lot of muscle—the two-part stand required only caution and the ability to stand up.

Stand up, pull up the seat, sit down, and pull up the feet.

With care, I climbed quieter than a squirrel or a raccoon.

I had purchased the stand from the GWF Buckarama two years before, and chose it because the seat was mobile—I could stand up and move the seat toward the tree so I could lean back on the tree. Or I could leave it in place and sit behind the tree to look over the field. I had it attached behind the tree so that I was half-hidden by the pine trunk. The bar holding the stand to the tree served as a gun rest. I settled down facing the tree and the field.

As soon as I hauled up my rifle and gear, I pulled on my extra jackets but left them open so I could again cool down after the efforts of climbing.

I'm getting too old for all this. A couple of years ago, when I collected a nice buck from this field, it was a lot warmer.

A buck from Larry's Field two years earlier.

From behind me, the rising sun threw glitter on tree tops and brightened the pines across the field. A shadow moved across the frost—too small for a deer, and its bushy tail flowed. A fox.

Cold deepened. Eight o'clock was a long time away. And until then, the temperature would continue to drop. The frost decorating my boots, held in place by a rim of stitching, had not begun to melt. Even in heavy insulated gloves, my fingers tingled. I thought of the men I worked with in Boston, who hunted in the snow of New Hampshire, and wondered how they stayed warm in that much more severe cold in the years before Patagonia longjohns.

As the day opened, the frosted clover and wheat merged into a field of snow. I saw the trail I made, kicking frost aside as I had hustled to my stand. A set of tracks crossed mine, smaller, where the fox had trotted homeward after a night of, I hoped, successful hunting.

Seven. Seven-thirty. Eight would be here soon, and with it the morning would begin to warm.

I looked to my right, no deer thataway. Back to my left. Nothing.

Back over my right shoulder toward the Jeep road. Nothing. Back to my left.

He stood forty yards into the field, broadside, head up, ears flicked forward, watching something in the woods.

I slid my left hand under my right upper arm and pulled my hand from the glove. Brought the rifle up. Eased the safety off slow enough to avoid the metallic click. Stock up to my cheek, hands steady.

No buck fever anymore.

He stood, as frozen in place as the frost around him. I lined the crosshairs on his neck, snugged the stock hard against my shoulder, propped my right hand on the edge of the blades holding the seat to the tree, and squeezed the trigger.

He dropped. Dead before he lay down.

I had a beautiful ten-point buck.

It was so cold I forgot the camera. A picture would be nice, but memories are truly treasures.

LOST—AGAIN

One evening my third year deer hunting, I was perched in the honeysuckle hollow where in the 1950s, before we even had a deer season, my mom had found a shed antler. Almost to big for my fingers to circle at the base, it bore seven points. Surely, I figured, his grandson could be around.

He was—and he was a dream buck. I shot. He ran. Darkness was close—the sun tipped the pine tops.

I scampered down, shotgun in hand, and went after the deer. He went east, and I followed, without a flashlight and with no way to call for help or directions. Cell phones and even CB radios would be in my future, but not in that present.

I followed. And followed. I should have known, but didn't, that if I waited he'd bed down and likely die. But, no, I went after him like Woot's redbone hound on a possum's trail. I'd hear the buck crash bushes and off I'd go in that direction. Before long, night fell and didn't leave a moon overhead. Clouds hid the stars.

I had long ago crossed the fence onto a neighbor's land. I was lost, with no idea as to which way the land line was. Even twilight was gone. I was too deep in a hollow to see the light pollution from town.

I heard a horn, a faint beep way off. I headed that way, hoping it was my good ole Nellybelle and the other hunter was signaling me in.

It took me less than a half-hour to get that deep in the woods, and more than an hour to stumble and fumble and creep my way back—and to find several barbed-wire fences with my pants' legs.

I was *toah up* by the time I got to the Jeep. So were my camouflage pants. I never went hunting in the afternoon again without a flashlight. And a CB radio when they became available to the public. I got one when I had to have a federal license and call letters.

My sisters and I got lost in that same area when we were kids, but we were on horseback. Give a horse his head, and he will go to the barn. Too bad I wasn't born with that same instinct.

THE LAST DOE

When I went to my stand that afternoon, I had no idea it would be my last hunt. Larry's Hill food plot was the afternoon snacking grounds for many deer over the years. And every year one or more deer fell to a hunter there.

It was late November, the Sunday after Thanksgiving. Frost and rain had long pushed down the leaves. Trees stood winter dead against the sky. My only cover in the tripod stand was the camouflage cloth hanging from the waist-high rail, and the skimpy young pine limbs. I had a mask and cap to hide my face, and net gloves for my hands.

To my right and across the old logging road stood the pine where I sat when that ten-point buck sashayed into the field two years ago. The scars the stand had sliced into the bark still showed. On the far end of the field, a pine provided a great place to hunt in the afternoons. But mornings there meant facing the rising sun.

Since I'd decided to surrender 4:30 a.m. getting-up time and the morning hunts to younger folks, I stored the stand away last year. The tripod was hard to climb into, but much easier than the climbing stand, and it faced northward, with a view to the west, and overlooked the three main entrances to the field. Its chair curved to fit my bottom, as its back supported mine. When I got sleepy, I could lean both forearms on the railing and lay my head down to nap.

The logging road to my right, where my biggest buck had his scrapes, was where a doe walked into the field several years ago on the last doe day of the year. I had been in a climbing stand in the hollow to the north of the ridge and the silence told me nothing was moving in the dry leaves. Near sundown, I had decided to walk up the hill.

My path took me to the west end, and I had moved into the thickets just off the field, where loggers had left dirt piled up. Now grasses and weeds grew over the mound. I snuggled down behind it and watched for activity.

Three hundred yards away a doe stopped in the trail and checked out the field. Her ears forward and head erect told me she was cautious. I wiggled down behind the dirt mound, clicked off the safety, wrapped my carrying strap around my right arm and pulled the .308 tight to my shoulder. I put the crosshairs on her forehead. If it's three hundred yards, I have to go up three inches, I calculated. I raised the crosshairs three inches above her head. And squeezed off.

I had pulled that rifle so tight it did not move with the recoil. I watched through the scope as the doe fell, dead in her tracks. The bullet hit between her eyes.

My best shot ever. From Larry's Field to Norman's Ridge.

One of my other best shots there was also from the west end, many years ago, long before I owned a climbing stand. That day, I sat on a wooden stand built fifteen feet up on a pine. The buck stood broadside, and I took a heart shot. He ran. I knew I had not missed, but I feared I had gut shot him. I didn't want the poor thing to run off and die a slow death.

I fired again. And again. He dropped. I had not missed. Each shot hit. With his heart blown, he had run one hundred yards. That day I realized I had lacked confidence in my aim. Those were my only shots at a running deer, and I had hit with each one. A confidence builder.

That confidence stayed with me. A couple of years later, when I sat in that same stand, a doe appeared from the same path that buck had. When I shot, I knew I had hit her heart, but she too took off at a dead run. Not across the field, but back downhill. And into a mess of gullies and vines.

I didn't keep shooting. Down I came from the tree, and walked into the woods.

Oh, boy. Here I was, alone, with the others not due in until dark. Two hours away. I brought up the four-wheeler and backed in as far as I could toward the doe. With rope in hand, I scrambled and stumbled down into the gully. I wrestled her around until her head was uphill and tied the rope to her neck. It barely reached the four-wheeler. I cranked it up and in first gear moved forward. Slowly.

Something caught. So back down I went. It was an up-and-down venture: Up the hill to pull her some, then reverse the four-wheeler to release tension; down to untangle her from brush. Took me almost an hour to get her into the open.

That year, I took heed of the best advice I ever got about shooting a deer. It came from Norman. Never shoot at *a deer*, but at a *spot on the deer*. Best is to shoot for the middle of the neck. You either miss or drop the deer in its tracks. I never had a deer run again. Not only that, I discovered a tremendous difference in the taste. When the injured deer runs, his body pumps adrenalin into the muscles, which will create a strong taste. Without the adrenalin flushed into the meat, the venison is much more tender and tasteful. I have been shocked to see on the special TV programs about hunting that these hunters shoot for the chest and the deer always run off.

So today here I sat in the tripod stand, ready for another deer to put into the freezer. You can't beat venison for taste if it is properly field dressed and butchered.

From a path across the field came a doe, and another, and three more. I picked out the largest and waited for them to browse on the clover and wheat. They covered more than half the distance across the meadow to me before they all stopped and started to eat.

A perfect fifty-yard shot with a 30.06. I eased the safety off, pressing it on both sides to prevent any metallic click. Brought the rifle to my shoulder, with the forward stock secured in the palm of my right hand which I rested on the rail of the stand.

Crosshairs on the neck of the largest doe, I hesitated. Did I want to field dress her?

No. I don't want to do this any more. I just don't want to kill her and have to pull out her insides. I quit.

I clicked the safety back on and lowered the rifle. It was my last hunt with a firearm.

Buck fever still attacks, however, when I aim a camera at deer or turkey. Or when I'm after a poacher. I measure my success by a sharp photograph and harsh penalties in the courts.

TIME CHANGES ALL

Time changes all—hunting methods, deer seasons, deer populations, deer predators and deer regulations. This chapter deals with hunting methods. See Appendix XIII for changes in regulations dealing with seasons and bag limits.

When I first hunted, in the 1960s, deer were few and far between. One man who hunted my land went ten years without killing a deer. The land was lush with honeysuckle, sawbriars and a world of browse thickening the woods. Visibility was nil through the timber. Today, I can see a browse line from my home—I've seen the yard deer stand on their hind legs to reach higher for food. The yard persimmons and acorns call them like Sirens.

I studied hard to learn about deer and hunting. After a ranger told me about scrapes and about deer not feeding if the cows were chewing cuds, I studied deer behavior anywhere I found information.

I read at least five wildlife/hunting magazines every month, and clipped special articles to build up a file to study again and again. Any weekend I could escape the city, I was on my land, walking the trails, looking for deer signs. Finding a fresh scrape in February or March would tell me where to put my stand for the fall.

In those days, we had to build a stand or sit on the ground. Many of my early hunts were on a stool or the ground with a tree for a backrest or on my feet. I'd hunted several years before a fellow hunter introduced me to the early climbing stands. The *belly scraper* required more muscle than I had.

Nellybelle became our ladder and platform for building stands.

Later, I designed the hanging stand that became the dependable stand for us all. The design was similar to that of the single-board climbing stand. I used the special waterproof plywood that we used in our permanent stands. We could make the stands as wide as we wanted them. With a contraption of rope, eye bolts, and chain, I made more in a day than we could hang in a weekend.

Norman perched in one of the swinging stands I designed. Usually the chain angled higher and swung from a limb or a ten-inch long, 3/8-inch diameter spike (as shown in the next picture). At first, we used only a rope for a foot rest, but soon learned a board was more comfortable for the ankles. In the picture below, LaVerne Bramlett, Rusty's grandmother, checks out the stand Rusty placed for his fall hunt. Note the large washer beneath the eye bolt where the chain is attached to the stand, which keeps the eye bolt from pulling through the wood. Here, the chain is looped over a spike nail behind the tree. The foot rest was attached later. We had two linesman's belts to use for safety during the work.

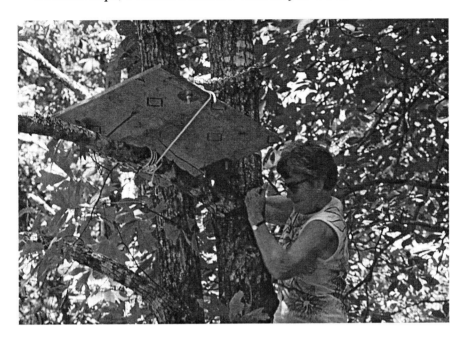

The hunting magazines carried ads for cover scents, but the predominant odor in my woods, other than deer (which I smelled when they had walked a path ahead of me), was pine. I researched pine smells—long before computers or Google or any easy way to garner information. But I discovered Siberian Pine Needle Oil and a diluent.

I ordered samples of pine, oak and other natural scents and decided on the pine oil. Then, bottles, artwork, labels and a quantity of material to mix and bottle. The challenges began. First, the plastic bottles lacked the solidity of glass, and the scent seeped through the plastic. I ordered glass bottles. But then discovered if you got it on your hands and touched the firearm stock, the mixture removed the finish.

Although it was years before anyone else started selling the pine scent, I produced only one batch—but it was about 100 dozen. Some I sold at the Buckarama in Atlanta, some I wholesaled to Ma-and-Pa stores, and some I sold directly to fellow hunters. Most hunters, I discovered, wanted the doe-in-heat lures, which soon flooded the markets.

Even the clothing has changed. No longer the broken pattern of greens to hide us in the woods. Patterns with such names as Tree Bark and Mossy Oak describe the appearance, and of course, there is the leafy camouflage that turns the hunter into a pile of leaves.

I hid my face with a black dickey pulled up over my nose. Today, various companies produce a variety of camouflage face masks, some that cover the head, others that hide only the lower portion of the face.

Hunters now have free-standing towers, warmers for the feet and back, cover to hide the face and body, climbing stands designed for hunting or napping.

Deer populations in Georgia have risen state-wide so that few hunters now spend weeks before the season scouting the woods to pattern the deer, to look for fresh and old rubs, to locate the persimmon, oak and mulberry trees and other sites where the deer feed. Nor do many hunters look for fresh scrapes in the spring to learn where the big boys court after the season closes.

Many plant soy beans or turnip greens or wheat or clover and hunt the same stand year after year without doing the homework we did fifty years ago. Some incompetent *hunters*, unfortunately, pour out corn and shoot any deer that comes to the bait.

For many people today, deer hunting has become a *deer shoot*.

What thrills so many young hunters are missing!

WHAT LIES AHEAD FOR THE HERDS?

Today, in the twenty-first century, the coyote population in my county has increased and these predators have discovered they can catch and kill deer. The feral dogs we had to contend with fifty years ago seem to have disappeared—or perhaps interbred with the coyotes.

Hunters statewide now complain that the deer numbers have decreased and many put the blame on the coyotes, not on overhunting. A lone coyote was seen as it chased a doe across my yard. Three coyotes pursued another deer just up the road a bit, in front of one of my hunters. So the deer have for sure become prey to more than just the human hunter.

In my neighborhood, however, the deer herds have not been reduced enough in number for the understory to recover—*yet.*

A fox in my neighborhood took a newborn fawn to its den to feed its babies, but I believe the fox found a stillborn—foxes usually depend on small prey such as field mice and grasshoppers.

Thirty or forty years ago, I seldom heard or saw a coyote. But by the 1990s, three packs yowled in hearing distance of my home in one night. Another night, a pack yelped its way across my yard. Now, however, I see them in daylight in my yard.

If coyotes have forgone smaller prey such as rabbits and quail in exchange for venison, and if the packs are not controlled, the deer population will decrease. A fawn cannot outrun a coyote, and a single coyote can run an adult deer to death—as feral dogs did in the 1950s and 1960s.

If we as landowners and hunters do not control the predator population, deer populations could return to the scanty numbers of seventy-five years ago. Low populations would allow the understory to recover. With the enhanced food supply, deer would increase in size—if they did not fall to the coyotes.

Our deer must depend on the natural food, not on temporary food plots or cattle feed to survive long-term since those who provide man-made food will not be around forever to provide supplemental nutrition.

We lost the deer herds in Georgia more than a century ago from overhunting. I hope the coyotes do not decimate the populations again.

I also fear a severe decrease in deer numbers will mean an increase in poacher numbers.

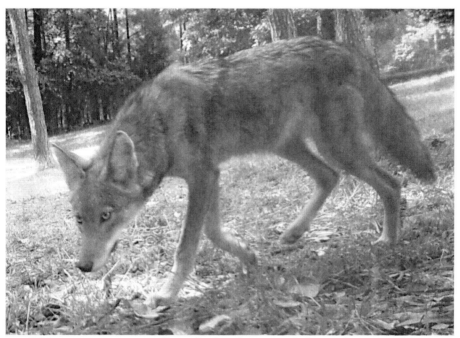

This coyote was one of a pair that journeyed through my yard in daylight.

WHY I DID IT AND WHY I KEEP ON

I reckon I got started chasing poachers because of the cattle rustlers. During World War II, we lost numerous cattle to rustlers who had to make a living stealing—or making likker. When deer were brought into middle Georgia, the focus changed: Deer were not owned by individuals, so some folks thought the deer were theirs for the taking.

My family began leasing to deer hunters and using the rent money to pay the land tax. As the taxes went up, so did the hunting fees. If there were no deer on the land, there would be no hunters interested in leasing.

If there are too many deer on the land, they will eventually wipe out all the vegetation, so hunting helps control the population and protects the land.

Poachers get into my pocket. Everyone who shoots along the road, who slips in to steal a deer, who crawls the fence to poach literally steals from me. Who's going to rent the next year if the criminals get all the deer this year? By stealing deer from the state, they also steal from me.

It's ironic that over the years, the men who hunt under these contracts have always called me rather than face the poacher. I reckon they figured a poacher's not likely to pull a weapon on a woman.

But I've always tried to be polite when approaching a potential poacher. I roll down the truck window and ask if they need help. Of course, they never do. But that starts a conversation, and if there's a deer on the ground, I would make a to-do over it, get out and admire it, and ask what happened. Did they hit the deer? Are they hurt? Is their vehicle damaged? And by then, whoever stayed at the house has reached the ranger or a deputy and he is driving up.

That approach did not work once. A black man had hit and killed a ten-point, 200-pound buck that lay in the ditch. A white man had been driving behind the black man and he took the deer, although I insisted that the deer belonged to the black man. But this was the 1960s. There was no way the black gentleman would lay claim to the meat with an armed white man saying it was his.

A similar event occurred in the early 1970s with a black neighbor. Two white men drove up to his house and said they wanted to deer hunt. He was afraid to say no. But he told me about it.

The two poachers built some stands, and when I checked them out for my neighbor, I discovered corn and apples scattered around each one. Both men went to the jail house on opening day, and Ranger Bob Sires advised them not to return.

One bitterly cold night, after midnight, a gunshot woke me. I yelled for the other hunters, slipped into blue jeans and coat over my pajamas, and rushed to my car. At the end of the driveway, I turned one way, my other hunters behind me turned the other direction. One person stayed at the house to call for help.

I reached the fork and saw tail lights to my left. I followed.

A mile down the road, the truck pulled into the drive to a gate and stopped. I drove by. In the rearview mirror I watched him turn around. I hurried to the next gate, turned and headed back, headlights off.

I was in no danger of driving off the road—there was enough moonlight to drive by. I wished the ranger would hurry. The night-hunting culprits would be in the truck in front of me.

The tail lights brightened. They were breaking, stopping, turning sideways across the road to pick up the kill. Lights came over the hill in front of us, but the truck stayed there and three men got out.

I turned on my lights. The approaching vehicle swerved in, onto the shoulder of the road, and blocked the truck.

As I piled out to join the ranger, I realized that the three men were my hunters, from the nearby camp who were also out looking for the culprits.

They too were only half-dressed. Not the ranger, however—as usual, he was in full uniform.

We didn't catch the bad guys that night, but at least we found the deer they shot and the ranger was able to take it for processing and would give the meat to a charity to feed the homeless.

Will I quit chasing poachers? Not until I have permanently turned up my toes. From the first two men I arrested, who said no one told them they couldn't hunt on my land, to the last two, who killed a buck in my yard, I haven't let up. Now I am after someone else—someone who must be hunting over bait on land adjacent to mine.

That slob has generated a deer graveyard on my land.

THE DEER GRAVEYARD

I found the graveyard because I picked some wildflowers and walked to the passenger side of the car to put them into a bucket on the back floorboard—and saw, not two feet from my back tire, a four-point antler, tines up.

Wow! I coulda run over that thing. I thought of the long drive I faced and my tight schedule. If I'd driven over that antler, the tines would have gouged holes so big in that tire that I'd be stranded until Triple A came to the rescue. I'm too old and dilapidated to change tires anymore.

But, I thought, as I put the antler into the car, W*here is the other one?* Had the buck dropped it nearby? I had once found a matching pair together, both dropped when the buck lowered his head and the antlers stuck into the ground, tines first.

I cranked up and eased across the field. A food plot on the other side of the field would be a good spot to check. But I didn't have to go that far. Only about twenty yards away lay the second antler. It joined the first one in the car, as did a third from the next field.

While I ran errands, two friends who cleaned up some of the mess left by an ice storm stumbled over three more sheds. First week of March, and the bucks were dropping them as if in a hurry to go into hiding with their naked brows.

Those six shed antlers in two days had me searching for more on day three. But what I found shocked me.

Patches of fresh deer hide, the flesh side still bloody red, had been scattered over one of the fields, almost like a trail. Where was the dead deer? I'd found numerous carcasses left in the woods by poachers, as if the scoundrels left the bodies to dare me to run them off.

Poacher-killed spike shot out of season and left in the woods to rot.

I followed the bits of torn skin to the east for some 100 yards, but the trail disappeared into a thicket. I blundered through the brambles but found no carcass. Back across the field I went, toward a large wooded area. Thickets at the edge, where sun reached, blocked me except for the opening into an old abandoned road bed.

And to the graveyard.

Fresh and old skin lay torn and mostly rotted. A rib cage glistened white against the oak leaves and pine straw ground cover. These bones were fresh, the spine held solid with ligaments not yet decayed.

Nearby lay a buck skull, five-pointed antlers surrounded by rotting hide.

Coyotes don't leave much meat behind when an animal dies, and these remains told me the deer had died late in deer season or in early January. This was early March. Rotting skin still clung to some skulls. Antlers had not bleached white. Spines remained intact with ribs circling upward.

Another rib cage lay about twenty feet away, so I walked over to it, and then looked around. To my left lay a bleached doe skull, and just beyond it lay another. And another. Up the slope a short way I spotted another skull, topped by antlers.

The skull had been cleaned to bone, and seemed to be propped up. But instead, it lay on a lump of mulch. An almost trophy size for my area, the eight points were tall and wide enough to be outside the buck's ears, but lacked the heaviness necessary to score high on the Boone and Crockett scale.

I picked it up and turned to my right—and spotted another skull. And another. In all, I found seven buck skulls (one a button buck) and five doe skulls in that less than a quarter acre.

Why had so many deer died in that small an area?

From the thickets at the edge of my land to the graveyard was an open area about 150 yards wide. That abandoned Jeep trail was the only easy entrance into the mixed pine and hardwoods that had shaded out most of the understory. I figured the deer had been shot on the neighbor's land, injured fatally, but had managed to flee that far before lying down. They had fled to the woods, and the old Jeep trail was the easiest entrance into the woods and to cover.

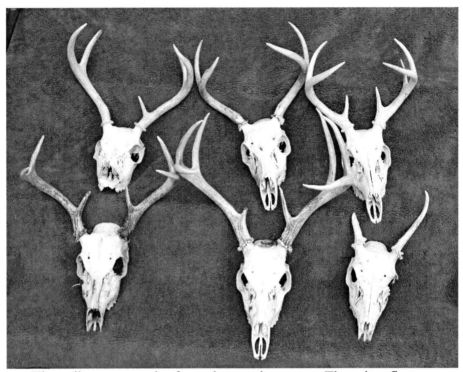

The spike seems to be from the previous year. The other five were fresh kills, with some skin remaining on the back of the skulls. The bucks were definitely not *throwaways*—who would dump a middle Georgia whitetail with these racks?

All antlers had hardened and had not bleached white, so I knew they had died since Labor Day, when local bucks shed their velvet. And probably before deer season ended on January 1.

Three rib cages, still attached to the spine, lay in an almost direct line, nearly touching each other. Bones showed teeth marks where predators had fed. My hunters reported coyotes in that area and a lot of shooting across the line.

Had they been shot? If so, by whom and where? And why would they all come here to die?

After pondering for two days, I decided:

> First, they had all been shot by a hunter off my land.
> Second, they had not been killed instantly.
> Third, they had all run in the same direction.
> Fourth, they had all been shot *at the same location.*

As a scientist said, it follows that for so many bucks to be shot at the same location in one deer season, they had to be there for a reason—a good meal.

Come next season, my rangers will be after the culprits. I only hope their punishment costs the bad guys more than the corn they used to bait the deer.

They were not the first deer to seek refuge on my land. They brought to mind Ole Crip, the buck I watched for almost two years as his injured leg healed.

In my youth, as the Great Depression slowly yielded to the production era of the World War II, the poor in the neighborhood felt that the (not necessarily wealthy) landowner would not lose much if they slipped a little corn from the barn or poached fish and game. In fact, some neighbors caught all the fish from our goldfish ponds, and we often missed feed from the barn that we knew would be turned into bootleg.

Some folks said it's the economy, that these men need food for the family. But the poacher invests too much in vehicles and equipment to be forced to hunt illegally to feed his children. He is driven by ego, not starvation.

With cradle-to-the-grave care by Big Brother, no one now needs to poach to feed his family. Today poachers are simply criminals.

I shall keep on pursuing and prosecuting them. After all, I do have a reputation to keep up.

MY REPUTATION

One afternoon when I was in the sporting goods store to purchase some shotgun shells, the owner called me by name. A young male customer came over to me and asked me if I were "The Susan Lindsley."

"I don't know anybody else with my name," I said.

He held out his hand. "I've heard about you for years. I've always wanted to meet you."

I shook hands with him. "I hope it wasn't all bad."

He laughed. "From what I hear, it's bad for the poachers. I'm glad to meet you. My dad started me hunting several years ago, and it's the most exciting thing I've ever done."

Twenty years since that afternoon, but I still remember that barely-out-of-boyhood fellow and his kind words.

My good friend Phyllis Humphrey referred me to Eddie, a neighborhood hunter who sought only trophy bucks. He said almost word-for-word the same thing that youngster had so many years ago. And added he also heard: **If you poach on Susan Lindsley's place and survive, you will go to jail.**

I wonder if these fellas ever knew I rode around with a .12 gauge, and chased poachers with my headlights off, or that in the dark ages of communications in the mid 1980s I had managed to find a two-way radio-telephone for my vehicle. The bad guys who didn't know soon learned.

I hope today's bad guys hear about my reputation and stay away from my part of the county.

MY POSSUM COPS

From the first ranger I knew through the years into the 21st century, the possum cops were vastly different and unbelievably alike.

They knew what dangers they faced each day (and night) on the job. The only unarmed culprits they faced were fishing, not hunting. But, unafraid, they went into the woods. One told me the best weapon he had was his radio, which he wore strapped to his shoulder, inches away from his mouth for easy access to backup.

They were often called to help find missing persons at Lake Sinclair or to help out when non-wildlife crimes were committed.

When new in a county, they had thousands of acres to walk and miles of roads to drive. Each ranger had to carry a map of the local geography in his head—and oft times he was called upon to help out in another county.

Their wives had to be special. They didn't complain about the 3:00 a.m. phone calls. Each trusted her man and knew he was working when he was out most of the night and not playing hanky-panky somewhere.

In the early days, rangers did not earn overtime. They had no time off during hunting season, and put in seven-day weeks, and often twenty-hour days. Vacation couldn't be scheduled when normal folks traveled—summer meant enforcing boating and fishing regulations on Lake Sinclair, the largest man-made lake in the state.

They were all dedicated to the job and to the wildlife.

But in spite of the long hours, they had fun, not just on the rare times they did get a day off, but also on the job.

The stories they told me about their cases would fill another book, but one of the best adventures they had involved a state-wide poacher operation consisting of several groups or teams, each team with special assigned duties. One team scouted out the deer alongside the road; another pair came along and shot the deer; another pair came along a half-hour later, with no firearm or spotlight, to pick up the deer. They had a refrigerated truck parked in the woods and running on a generator. When a deer was delivered one man would field dress and skin the animal in record time—less than two minutes. The gut pile would be hauled off into the woods to feed foxes, buzzards and other predators.

The carcasses would hang in the cooler for several days, until enough deer had been collected to make a trip upstate.

The driver for a major meat packing company delivered his company's meat from Atlanta to middle and South Georgia. Once his truck was empty, he picked up the poached deer and delivered them to mom-and-pop barbecue sites throughout middle and north Georgia on his way home to Atlanta. The various poaching groups stayed in touch with CB radios.

The wardens, with their many sources, learned of the operation and began listening to the CB. The groups talked in a semi-code, and once the rangers figured out their secrets, they called in help—federal vans with a rotating dish on top, that pinpointed the location of the CB talkers. The game wardens caught them, broke up the operation, seized the refrigerated truck, and ensured that the meat-packing driver lost his job as well as joined the various group members at the jail house.

Two of my rangers would stop by the house on their way to work some evenings and warm their backsides at my fireplace before they headed for the cold hours of a stakeout. They told stories about their recent adventures. One told of his attempts to learn to mosey, amble or stroll up to a culprit. Another would speak of learning how to pretend he was lost. They enjoyed their own antics at approaching a poacher.

Because no matter when I called for help, day or night, I never saw a sloppy ranger, I at times wondered if perhaps they all had a coat hanger under the jacket and slept hanging on the clothes rod in the closet.

As a landowner, I've never felt I was in physical danger when I approached a trespasser or poacher, but I learned from the rangers how to introduce myself to the poachers. Be polite and discuss hunting or firearms, and you meet on equal footing and have time to judge the situation.

I've asked many a poacher to let me see his firearm, and he handed it to me. I've also asked them to wait for the ranger, and most did so. Those who ran usually got caught down the road.

I've heard many a tall tale from hunters, but the best I've heard was told by a ranger. When he did have some time off, he would go hunting. His club held a supper at season's end, and if you had shot at and missed your deer, you lost your shirt tail.

Well, Ranger Carl had missed one. But he had gone to extreme measures to ensure that no one knew. Darkness was falling when he shot at a big-racked buck—and knew he missed. He cussed himself for not using his bolt action rifle that day. The automatic ejected the empty shell into the approaching darkness. He got down from his stand and began to search for the empty shell. He couldn't find it. On hands and knees, he felt through leaves and vines and mulch. No luck.

Back at camp, fellow hunters wanted to know where his deer was. "I didn't shoot," he swore. "Somebody else shot. Just off the lease. I don't know who."

Somehow, they figured he must be lying. While he slept the night away, someone went to his stand with a metal detector and found the empty shell. No one said a word. Ranger Carl returned to that stand the next morning, and rather than hunt deer, he hunted that shell. No luck.

But at the banquet, someone produced the shell. Off came Ranger Carl's shirt tail. Years later, he told the story on himself and laughed so much in the telling it was almost impossible to understand his words.

* * *

No matter what happened, my possum cops never gave up on the job. A ranger pulled one of my stunts and got lost. He began his search for a poacher on a neighbor's land, but somehow got turned around and wound up on my place. Norman was perched in a stand and saw this fella in a red vest but no firearm wandering his direction.

Norman called, "Can I help you?"

"What's the best way to get to Highway 212?"

"You lost?"

"Yep."

The ranger walked closer and Norman gave directions.

"Thanks for the help." The ranger grinned. "By the way, do you have a hunting license?"

Even lost, a ranger does his duty. And yes, Norman produced his hunting license, and the two men laughed at the situation.

* * *

One of my favorite stories is about an unusual event during deer season. A hunter on his way home from middle Georgia to metropolitan Atlanta noticed a number of Game and Fish law enforcement vehicles up and down the expressway. He wasn't concerned until one tailgated him and flipped on the "I gotcha" lights and siren.

He pulled over.

"What's the problem, officer?" he asked in all innocence.

"We wonder where you have the turkey," came the response.

It wasn't near turkey season. "I don't know what you mean."

Before the first ranger answered, a couple more law enforcement trucks pulled in behind the first truck.

The first ranger explained. "We know you have a turkey in your truck. Where is it?"

Again the man insisted he didn't know what the ranger was talking about. The ranger explained:

"You killed a hen in (such and such) a county. We know she is in your truck. She was in a wildlife study and carries a tracking device. There is no way she has been running up the highway at seventy miles an hour. Where is the turkey?"

The "I gotcha" lights told it all.

* * *

Rangers are determined, dedicated and persistent men and women. They can mosey along, sneak and amble. They can be slyer than Brer Fox and pretend to be as passive as Brer Possum. All are delightful story tellers and make wonderful friends.

I am fortunate to have known the best and to be able to call each one a friend.

APPENDIX I
SPEECH ABOUT HUNTING DEER OVER BAIT

Good afternoon, Gentlemen. I'm Susan Lindsley

I represent: 3 landowners who also hunt and 200 people who hunt my land:
> These folks are a cross section of rural and urban Georgia
counties
>> Gwinnett,
>> DeKalb,
>> Fulton,
>> Douglas,
>> Baldwin,
>> Bibb.
> Also: Florida and Alabama

> Men and Women in many occupations:
>> office personnel
>> professional people, doctors and attorneys
>> factory workers
>> independent business owners
>> retirees
>> law enforcement personnel
>> government employees
>> politicians, e.g., county commissioner & legislators

I myself:
> Have hunted for 30 years
> Brought just one reference (point to antlers)
> Am also a wildlife photographer
> Am NOT an animal rights activist
> As a landowner I pay taxes by leasing to hunters

Let's talk photography:

I hunt over bait to take pictures.
> (show samples)
>> hunt over bait here in GA
>> hunted over bait on extensive TEXAS shoot

I don't hunt for the freezer over bait and I could get my limit annually if I did not pass up deer.
I try to kill deer selectively to benefit the herd over time.

I have killed a deer at 300 yards with one shot between the eyes; how easy would it be for me to kill this or any buck from my front porch if it were feeding in the yard?

Give me three weeks and feed and I can train any deer herd or any turkey flock to be where I want it when I want it there.

If I were feeding and you hunted next to me, you wouldn't get either a deer or a turkey—in fact, I could keep you from even seeing game.

Hunting deer over bait will:
> Provide extra income for those who produce and sell grains such as beans and corn and peanuts.
> Are these the people WHO WANT THIS BILL?

Hunting deer over bait will
> Allow some landowners to have guaranteed hunts for large fees
>> Hunting fees pay my taxes now but my hunters have no guarantee of success

>> My hunters help both me and the wildlife
>>> Help keep off poachers
>>> Help prevent fires
>>> Help meet any emergency I have

>> My hunters bought two decoy deer for Rangers.

BUT MY HUNTERS HAVE NO GUARANTEE OF A KILL.

Hunting over bait will destroy the challenge of hunting:

Hunting means *seek*, use skill in the woods and knowledge of animal.

Hunting is not defined as *tote feed every week*.

Hunting over bait will provide deer to those who can consistently provide feed and will deny hunting pleasure to those who can pay a lease fee but do not feed.

It's perfectly legal to hunt over planted crops, and it's a only a small challenge to be at the planted field when the animals feed. Don't take away even that little challenge.

If we allow killing deer over bait, we turn the deer herds into feed-lot animals but charge a fee for what we call a hunting license and a big game license.

If we are going to allow people to legally shoot deer over bait and if we decide to turn the deer into a feed-lot animal, then we should charge the same hunting fees to everyone who kills cattle at the slaughter house.

What's the difference?

APPENDIX II
MORE ABOUT GETTING SHOT AT IN 1983

In 2016, I learned that about 1,000 people are shot by hunters annually in the United States and Canada combined. I was fortunate not to be one of the statistics in 1983.

My letter to the editor about the incident came out a few days after the event. I usually said *red* instead of *blaze orange* for the vests.

Union-Recorder
November 2, 1983

To the Editor:
A shotgun is powerful noisy when it fires only yards away at you.

Our local young men who deer hunt on lands of another—who poach—are no better than a bank robber; both use firearms to commit crimes.

I wonder how many parents or wives know where their men are hunting. And how many poachers ever know whose land they are on?

The man who almost shot me violated several laws:
—Hunting without permission
—Hunting without red vest
—Trespassing across lands of several people
—Shooting without properly identifying the target
And the greatest crime of all—shooting without knowing who or what was in front of his shotgun.

There is no such thing as a *hunting accident*. The killer is always violating the law when he shoots what he cannot see.

Wives and mothers: Is the hunter in your family a criminal in camouflage?
Susan Lindsley
Milledgeville

* * *

The local paper also ran a news article about the event:

Lindsley finds orange hunting vest vital
By Nita Birmingham
Staff Writer

Susan Lindsley thought the state law requiring deer hunters to wear fluorescent orange vests wasn't necessary for hunters on their own property, but that was before she was fired at Monday evening.

"I really credit that red vest for saving me yesterday," Lindsley said Tuesday as she recalled the incident that occurred the prior day.

Lindsley was deer hunting on property owned by her family off Georgia 212 between 5 p.m. and 6 p. m. Monday. She was "still hunting"—taking a few steps, then stopping and listening for sounds of deer.

She heard a deer to her left. The deer snorted three or four times and then Lindsley heard two shots.

The shots came from a hunter who was trespassing on Lindsley's property and shooting at deer from a tree stand she built.

"The deer was between me and the poacher. I was in the line of fire. I could tell from where the pellets landed," Lindsley said.

Lindsley ran in the direction of the fire and the trespasser ran in the opposite direction. She wasn't able to catch the trespasser.

Lindsley called Georgia Department of Natural Resources Conservation Ranger Sgt. Marion Nelson, who then investigated the incident.

Nelson said he was unable to apprehend the trespasser, but the investigation is continuing.

Nelson said there haven't been any serious problems reported in Baldwin County since deer season opened October 22.

Lindsley has been hunting since 1964 or 1965*, but Monday was the first time she has been caught in the line of fire.

"I've caught poachers, trespassers and night hunters, but I have never been shot at before," she said.

_____
*I began hunting poachers in 1964 and hunting deer in 1966.

"They (illegal hunters) don't know what's in front of that gun. They just point it and pull the trigger," Lindsley said.

Several hunters have already been shot since deer season opened because people didn't know other hunters were in the area or someone wasn't wearing fluorescent orange, Nelson said.

"Last year we investigated or had reported to us approximately sixty hunting-related or firearms-related casualties in the state. Of those there were about a dozen fatalities last year," he said.

Nelson said hunters should make sure they comply with the state law that requires hunters to wear fluorescent orange.

The law requires hunters to wear a total of 500 square inches of daylight fluorescent orange above the waistline.

"We do encourage a person to ensure they have permission from the landowner (to hunt).We have had some problems in the county with people hunting without permission," Nelson said.

It is a violation of state law to hunt on private property without the landowner's permission. If the property is posted, a person must carry with him written permission to hunt from the landowner.

The Turn In Poachers project that is coordinated through the Georgia DNR offers a reward to persons who can provide details of wildlife law violations, Nelson said.

If information provided by a person is used to convict a violator, the informant can receive a $100 reward.

APPENDIX III
LETTER FROM REX BAKER ABOUT T.I.P.

I am proud to have received this letter from Rex Baker, Chairman of the T. I. P. program. He wrote, on April 11, 1985:

Dear Susan:

I'd like to thank you for the pictures you sent me.

I'd also like to thank you for your interest in our T. I. P. Project. With supportive people such as you behind us, we are able to continue our endeavors to eliminate poachers more effectively.

Again, as Chairman of Turn in Poachers, Inc., I appreciate your conscientiousness.

Good health,

Rex Baker
Chairman

APPENDIX IV
POACHER ARTICLE FROM LOCAL PAPER

In spite of all the publicity the local paper gives the rangers and me to help combat poaching, the crime goes on. Somehow many people do not consider poaching a serious violation. In Maine, the *minimum* fine for killing a deer at night is $1,000.00 plus jail time. In Georgia, that is the *maximum* fine. I will be delighted to see such punishment for poaching in Georgia.

If the deer herds diminish in numbers, poaching will increase. Because of the costs to insurance companies who pay for damage when deer and car collide, some of these companies will be glad to see a decrease in deer numbers. So will those who have lost both vegetable and flower gardens to the neighborhood deer.

The article below ran in my local paper in December 1986. The dead deer in the photograph with Tom Hicks was killed in a large field in sight of the highway. Her hindquarters were taken—the rest was left to feed the scavengers.

The story ran on the front page. The one-line header read:

Despite efforts, few poachers of deer are apprehended

By Robert Morris
Staff Writer

Poaching deer is a temptation too strong to resist for some hunters, according to a conservation ranger of the Department of Natural Resources.

And despite the illegality of the practice, odds are a poacher won't be caught.

"Many hunters are opportunists," said Sgt. Marion Nelson. "They don't necessarily leave the house with the express purpose of illegal hunting."

Hunters are susceptible to falling into the tempting trap of taking a deer illegally, especially after several unsuccessful deer-

hunting outings, he said.

"When an opportunity presents itself in an isolated area, the hunter knows relatively well the chances of others observing him are small," Nelson said. "A large number of hunters are tempted beyond their ability to withstand the temptation."

Despite the combination of the lack of success and a tempting opportunity, poaching is illegal, he said.

Nelson defined poaching as "any type of illegal deer-hunting activity." All game in Georgia is the property of the state and cannot be sold. Any illegal hunting or selling of game is considered theft by taking, a misdemeanor, and carries a maximum fine of $1,000 and a 12-month prison sentence.

Reports of poaching are frequent, Nelson said. Often people hear gunshots at night, see hunters after sunset or observe them involved in other illegal hunting activity. But the reports are difficult to track down.

Susan Lindsley/For The Union-Recorder

James T. Hicks of the Department of Natural Resources inspects a doe killed illegally

"Most reports involve incidents that have already happened. It could be days or weeks after the fact," he said. "Unless it is a recurring violation, there is little chance of a fruitful investigation."

In one case that did result in charges being filed, rangers in

November charged three men with hunting at night, hunting from a public road and hunting from a motor vehicle.

Poaching methods used by hunters vary.

Unlawful hunting on someone else's property tops the list, Nelson said.

"Rather than risking being turned down (by a property owner), they will attempt to slip on another's property," he said.

Susan Lindsley manages about 3,000 acres of wooded land in Baldwin County that she leases to hunters. Although she's been a successful deer hunter since 1966, she said she'd "rather lock up a poacher than get a deer." She spends many hours a week patrolling the roads, looking for illegal hunters in a citizen-organized "Poacher Patrol."

In a seven-week period Lindsley turned up 13 deer carcasses illegally shot within a two-mile radius of her home, she said.

Susan Lindsley/For The Union-Recorder

Bones of poached deer are bleached white by the sun

Lindsley said she's found evidence of decapitating deer for antlers and quartering deer on her property.

"A man gets a new firearm and he's got to go out and kill

something," she said. "If a little housewife can go out and kill a deer legally, why can't these men do it."

Hunting deer at night is illegal, and when it is combined with trespassing, the danger multiplies. Deer hunting is allowed 30 minutes before sunrise and 30 minutes after sunset, Nelson said.

"There is a safety factor to discharging a gun into a darkened area," Nelson said. "Houses and other properties have been struck by projectiles (from guns)." Sometimes, when hunters are too close to the highway, they hit vehicles, he said.

But all hunting at night is not illegal, Nelson said.

"A shot at night doesn't necessarily mean there is something illegal going on," he said. The law allows the hunting of raccoon, fox, possum and bobcat at night because they are primarily nocturnal animals. Smaller-caliber weapons are used to hunt these game.

Another method deer poachers use is hunting after sundown with a light.

"Deer fall easy prey to hunting at night," Nelson said. "They will venture into open areas where there are few opportunities to escape."

Despite an overpopulation of deer, which is dramatized by crop damage and accidents with motor vehicles, enticing deer with a lure or bait is illegal.

"It's an unfair advantage for the hunter. Some species (of game) are susceptible to decimation by baiting. You could create a situation of wholesale slaughter rather than random selection," Nelson said.

A liberal deer-hunting season that allows both-sex hunting in the late season is part of an attempt by the state to reduce the deer population. Nelson estimates there are about 15 to 20 deer per square mile in the northern region, which includes Baldwin County.

A three-deer limit is enough to satisfy most hunters, but the bag limit could be enough enticement for hunters to fudge on their kill—and poach.

When an individual bags a deer, the hunter is required to tag it with a form attached to the big-game license. The hunter is required to keep the tag attached until the deer is processed for consumption. Then the tag is mailed to the Department of Natural

Resources. The tags help the DNR project the next deer-hunting season.

Nelson said only a few hunters make it their intention to poach.

"It's a relatively small group that prefers to take his game illegally. He plots and contrives his hunting activities and knows before he goes," he said. "They spoil the pie for others."

Others are not tempted at all and are compelled to obey the letter of the law, he said. Rangers don't arrest all suspected poachers. There are borderline cases, Nelson said.

"The enforcement program is flexible in minor infractions where a mistake is made on a technicality, and it doesn't significantly affect wildlife, life or property," he said.

APPENDIX V
TWO LETTERS RE HUNTING SEASONS

These letters are re-typed because the carbon copies, if scanned, would not be legible. I have excluded addresses. These are only two of the many letters I wrote during the flap over deer season.

Date: February 21, 1985

To: Howard H. Rainey,
    Chairman, Game and Fish Committee

Dear Mr. Rainey:

You are in the best position to put an end to the squawks of the special interest groups attempting to interfere with the biologists of Game and Fish Division who are responsible for our deer herds.

I am opposed to any change in deer seasons other than those insisted upon by our biologists.

I do not favor our legislature setting hunting seasons because of the political football such a situation could become. Our herds would suffer.

As it is, if the special interest groups get their way and the season is cut by two weeks, a lot of people will suffer: The disabled, those who have pre-set vacations, those who own and operate businesses that cater to the hunters, and on and on.

A few, a *very few,* will gain, and that gain will only be a personal desire fulfilled; the State of Georgia will gain nothing.

A lot of hunters who don't know what's happening right now are going to appreciate your efforts come fall and hunting season when they learn it was your committee that helped keep things as they have been and kept politics out of game management.

* * *

February 27, 1985
To Thomas Murphy
  Speaker of the House

Dear Mr. Murphy:
   Enclosed is a copy of a letter I sent to Leonard Ledbetter, Commissioner, DNR, when I first learned of an attempt to change deer season.
   I have just learned (from a member of the Georgia Wildlife Federation who does *not* want any change) that several bills have been presented to our legislature to control not only deer season but other aspects of hunting and trapping.
   Don't you feel it would be a grave mistake to take control of our wildlife from our biologists—the men and women hired to protect them—and put the future of our game and fish in the hands of lawmakers?
   Our legislators are good people, I do not deny, but they are not biologists; and traditionally, lawmakers are slow to act when conflict presents itself from the people. But our Game and Fish biologists can act immediately, and THEIR ONLY INTEREST IS CONTINUED CARE AND PRESEVATION OF WILDLILFE.
   They will *not* yield to special interest groups—I know from personal experiences. I felt I needed to reduce the deer herd on my plantation—Westover—in Baldwin County. But the biologists removed our doe days just as my herd peaked because the rest of the county's herd had suffered losses for a couple of years. Since I did not have a commercial crop being damaged or destroyed, these biologists would not allow me to kill does on my property.
   But suppose I had gone to friends across the State who could put political pressure on their friends in the legislature. Could I have gotten a special law passed to allow me to remove 15 does regardless of the conditions in the rest of the county?
   That is a law we do not need, *not even for my own personal wants.*
   Can't you see the future of our wildlife with such laws that cater to the special interests?
   Some groups will want to harvest game and fish for the marketplace, and will lobby for that law to be changed.

Some people will want an open season on all game from Labor Day through February 28, and will lobby for that change.

Just as some people today who don't want to hunt when it's warm are lobbying to prevent anyone else from hunting then.

And just as the hunters did not want to give up shooting the passenger pigeon, no law was enacted to save that bird.

All law-maker bodies are slow to act, wanting feedback from the people; only in time of great emotional crisis will a legislative body unite—as Congress united to push Jack Kennedy's proposals through immediately after his death.

We should not yield to politics what has been removed from special interest pressure, especially when it could lead to greater and greater complications for us all.

Perhaps it's hard to see how enacting one or two simple laws can create havoc for our game, but once people learn that our legislature will cater to special interest groups and thereby interfere with our game regulations, then more people will ask that their special interests be covered by a law.

Do you remember the nightmare a few years ago when a man had been arrested for night hunting deer and his vehicle and firearms were confiscated? He was a friend of Culver Kidd, and he apparently pressured Mr. Kidd to introduce a bill to get his vehicle back and to remove vehicle and firearms confiscation from part of the penalty for night hunting from a vehicle (retroactively). That bill died quickly, but that is an example of what political pressure can do.

I know you are interested in our game and fish. You just last week helped move a resolution easily through the House, to commend a group of private citizens who are dedicated to helping enforce our laws and regulations—Bobby Parham's resolution on Project T. I. P.

For your help in that, I thank you. You and the House showed real interest in our wildlife and in the people who support our Rangers with their time and energy.

Please extend this helping hand even further and don't let special interest groups pressure the legislature into passing special laws to suit their emotional fancy.

Please help keep the welfare of our wildlife solely in the hands of the experts, our wildlife biologists.

Sincerely,
Susan Lindsley

Carbon copies to:
Howard Rainey, Game and Fish Committee
Jack Crockford, heading a committee on control of deer season
Leaders of DNR and Game and Fish:
    Leonard Ledbetter, Leon Kirkland, Terry Kile

APPENDIX VI
SPEECH IN HOUSE CHAMBER

I'm Susan Lindsley.

I'm a deer hunter. I know you're not used to ladies who hunt, so I brought my references with me.

I pointed to the antlers in a row on the front of the Speaker's podium. One pair, not mounted on a board, was wide enough to wrap around a 300-pound man's waist. (See: The Sky-High Stand.)

The men applauded.

The clock ticked away precious seconds.

I stood silent until they quieted.

I took a breath and began to speak.

I'm also a poacher hunter—I drafted the original version of House Resolution 253 supporting the Turn in Poachers Project.

Today, I am speaking on behalf of

        —1,000 Georgia members of Deerhunters United, a national hunting organization based in Macon

        —more than 1,600 signers of a petition, including my local Representative in the House

I turned to Joe Kurz and handed him the stack of petitions.

We want the deer season to remain as it is for FIVE reasons:

I. GAME BIOLOGISTS are the best qualified to make decisions.

More applause. More time lost.

(They are)   Best informed about herd size and health

More objective about needs of both deer and the hunter

2. BUSINESS will be hurt if one or two weeks are cut from the season.

DEER COOLERS will have to turn down business—they can't handle an upsurge in volume of a shortened season.

        LOSS ON GAS alone will exceed $135,000

                Lost business dollars equal lost government revenue

        THINK of loss on basics— stuff hunters take to the camp

beyond home use:

    Bread and snacks

    Bacon, sandwich meats

    Colas, beer, milk

    Restaurant losses

    3. **LAW ENFORCEMENT** problems will increase with two opening days.

    We have 220,000 hunters in the Northern Zone

If ½ of 1 % WHO NEVER POACHED decide to hunt during these two weeks of closed season,

    Another 1,000 people would be poaching

    4. **SEVEN-WEEK SEASON** gives **EVERYONE** a choice of weather conditions.

    ANYONE who wants to hunt in the cold can wait for the cold

    We little old ladies and the disabled and elderly can hunt in the early weeks while it's still warm.

Laughter rippled across the chamber. I had to pause again.

If you say old folks have no business hunting, remember, you'll be old someday yourself if you live long enough.

    Christmas week is time for those who can't get time off

        Teachers

        Students

        Out-of-state hunters

    5. **THE BIG FLAP about TEMPERATURE, snakes, ticks and poison ivy is JUST A FLAP.**

    The TEMPERATURE argument is BASELESS.

    Nov 7 is ONLY 2 degrees colder than Oct 20

My group of hunters killed more bucks per hunter in 1984 than in any other year

SNAKES, TICKS AND POISON IVY are not a problem if you use common sense.

    KNOW the plant and animals

    USE physical barriers

        Snake leggings

        Tape around pants legs to stop ticks

    USE chemical barriers— repellant

I've killed and photographed deer while I used repellent, but NEVER while using a HAND WARMER in cold weather.

A man told me recently: "I don't want to hunt in October, and I'll do ANYTHING I have to, just to be sure no one else goes hunting and gets my deer before I'm ready to hunt."

CAN WE LIVE WITH OURSELVES IF we let this selfish man dictate deer season?

CAN WE LIVE WITH OURSELVES if we let snakes and ticks dictate deer season?

"Times up," Joe interrupted.

"Well, Joe, they interrupted me twice with applause. I have only a couple of sentences left."

I continued to speak.

If snakes and ticks close down two weeks of deer season, they will close down
> **all of Georgia's outdoor activities all summer**
>> **—close the trout season and fishing seasons**
>> **—close the public parks and public campgrounds**
>> **—and of course, close down turkey season.**

I wobbled toward my seat.

The men applauded.

My legs shook, my hands trembled, my stomach churned. I grasped the back of seats for support as I stumbled up the aisle. *Thank God that's over.*

A man behind me reached over, touched my shoulder and, when I turned, said, "Thank you. I sure do agree."

I only muttered, "Thanks."

The next speaker rose when his name was called and announced from his seat: "I don't have anything to add to what the lady said. I agree with her."

Many of those who agreed with me simply dittoed my words. Some took the podium and gave many of my reasons to support the game biologists.

Most of the opposition, however, did speak. They didn't get much applause.

I shook and sweated the duration of the talks, but delight pushed my fear aside when the session was over and many of the men came up to me to thank me for speaking as I had. My ego swelled.

APPENDIX VII
SPEECH AT THE MACON, GA HEARINGS

I'm Susan Lindsley and I'm a landowner, a deer hunter, and a professional wildlife photographer. I brought several deer pictures as my references.

(I pointed to the pictures which faced the audience.)

Tonight I represent

9 landowner families in Baldwin County

8 hunt clubs with some 100 members from 4 states and 15 Georgia counties

More than 1900 signers of this petition.

I'll turn in the petition now as part of my presentation.

(Handed it to Joe.)

We all support the recommendations of Game Management because they

—reduce law enforcement problems

—provide the best overall hunting for the most people

— are OBJECTIVE and do not cater to special interests.

TO OPPOSE THEIR RECOMMENDATIONS IS TO OPPOSE SOUND GAME MANAGEMENT.

HAVE YOU EVER BEEN SHOT AT? I don't mean in war time.

I mean by a POACHER IN YOUR DEER STAND.

WELL, I HAVE, AND I DON'T LIKE POACHERS.

Most of the poachers on my place have been BIG CITY boys

From Clark, Clayton, Cobb, Douglas, and Gwinnett counties.

Most poachers are just "GOOD OLD BOYS" trying to prove their manhood to

THEMSELVES

THEIR BUDDIES

THE WOMAN BACK HOME.

In 1982, these good ole boys left a DOZEN dead deer along my roads.

If we have two opening days,

220,000 people won't be able to hunt in the Northern Zone while everyone hunts in the Southern Zone.

Some of them will poach.

Do you want them riding your roads, hunting your leased lands for two weeks before you hunt legally?

I DON'T.

BIOLOGISTS DON'T.

RANGERS DON'T.

WHO AMONG US HUNTERS IS MORE KNOWLEDGEABLE THAN OUR BIOLOGISTS?

Who has better information on herd size? On sex ratio? On age? On disease? On habitat?

Who among us hunters can be totally objective about the season?

Can you meet the needs and desires of the hunter and preserve quality hunting for future years?

Do you want to vote on hunting?

I could easily get a thousand signatures in a WEEK to STOP ALL HUNTING IN GEORGIA.

STOP DEER SEASON.

STOP TURKEY SEASON.

EVEN STOP FISHING.

IF WE TAKE GAME MANAGEMENT FROM OUR BIOLO-GISTS, WE'LL ALL LOSE.

We lost the passenger pigeon before biologists took over.

Biologists saved the pronghorn antelope.

Biologists saved the desert bighorn.

We could lose our whitetail deer in Georgia AGAIN if we take control away from the biologists.

When your grandson asks you "Grandpa, why don't we have deer in Georgia?" will you have the guts to tell him the truth, that in 1985 it was you who put personal preference ahead of game management?

APPENDIX VIII
TWO LETTERS RE CONTROL OF REGULATIONS

I have included only two of the dozens of letters I wrote to Georgia's governors, members of the state legislature, and leaders in the Department of Natural Resources over the years. These two illustrate my stance on numerous matters.

January 12, 1987
To: Governor Joe Frank Harris

I'm enclosing petitions and ballots from Georgians who are concerned about wildlife management in Georgia.

For several years, a few people have asked legislators to remove certain management responsibilities from Game and Fish Division, DNR, and place these in the control of legislators.

I've circulated a petition and obtained 4,272 signatures from 141 counties requesting that responsibilities for Game and Fish regulations be left in the hands of the game biologists. These petitions are enclosed.

Also enclosed are 480 ballots (from 93 counties) of the 3,000 sent to known deer hunters: Attendees of the 1986 Buckarama who registered for a drawing and Georgia members of Deerhunters United, a national hunting organization. Note that *only two* of the 480 persons indicated that legislators, not biologists, should control our wildlife. Total return of the ballot was high: 480 of 3,000 (16%) indicates high interest in the matter among hunters.

On the basis of this response, I feel sure that you would quickly veto any bill to reach your desk that would go counter to the wishes of Georgia citizens who are concerned about the future of our wildlife.

Susan Lindsley
Milledgeville

Carbons to:
Speaker of the House
Chairman, Game and Fish Committee
Members, Game and Fish committee
Representative Bobby Parham
Representative Birdsong

January 31, 1987
To Governor Joe Frank Harris

I was shocked to learn the contents of House Bills 391 and 392. *Either* bill, if passed and signed into law, can cause the loss of one of Georgia's major economic and natural resources: Our deer herd.

To allow anyone suffering "damage" by deer to kill the deer without first obtaining a permit from Game and Fish Division, DNR, would also eliminate the effectiveness of our game laws: Poachers would be delighted—we could no longer prosecute those hunting out of season because the poacher's defense would be that the deer ate the tomato plant in the yard.

With one-half million gardens in Georgia, each gardener would have to kill *only two deer* to eliminate the herds. The deer seeking safety in the timberlands would be wiped out by timber growers whose excuse for killing deer would be that the deer were nibbling on seedlings.

I can personally speak to the issue from every side: I'm a landowner; I have lost shrubs, crops and timber seedlings to deer; I am a deer hunter; I am an avid supporter of our game laws and have organized a "poacher patrol" to help our rangers in Baldwin County; I depend on rental income from deer hunters to help pay taxes on my farm lands; I have friends whose businesses depend on income from hunters in the fall (butchers and storeowners).

I know we have too many deer in some areas of the state. In fact, my land is overstocked with deer right now. Our game biologists gave us double the either-sex days in 1986 compared with 1985; and we have more than doubled the number of does killed. I have asked the local, regional, and state-level biologists about plans for the 1987 season and have been told the number of doe days will again be increased. With more doe days earlier in the season, we'll be decreasing the overall herd quite dramatically in the Piedmont.

Any farmer or landowner can reduce the deer on this lands under our present laws: He can himself hunt during doe days and kill only adult does that would throw two or three fawns next spring; he can invite guests to hunt; he can *increase his income* by $1.00-10.00 per acre by leasing hunting rights.

Let me stress that I know the frustration of too many deer, and that I could have illegally reduced the herds on my lands to the levels I wanted and never been caught. But our wildlife conservation laws and regulations are designed to provide the next generations with quality outdoor experiences, and what I personally want for my property would not necessarily provide that experience for the next generation of my family. So I have yielded to those with more knowledge—our Game Biologists.

Susan Lindsley
Milledgeville

APPENDIX IX
LETTER RE HONORARY MEMBERSHIP IN GWF

February 27, 1994

Dear Susan:

We are happy to present you with a Life Membership in the Georgia Wildlife Federation. These memberships have only just begun to be offered on a widespread basis, so your newly assigned Life Membership number is #066. In the years to come such a low number will certainly set you apart as one who, early on, was concerned with the future of our wildlife and the environment of our great state of Georgia.

There is a great deal yet to be done to ensure the wise use and management of our wildlife and other natural resources. Be assured that the GWF will make the best use of your contribution (land) in our educational and wildlife conservation work. It is the policy of the GWF to raise money through such activities as our trade show and other sales programs in order to cover the overhead and administrative costs of operating the GWF. This allows us to use contributions such as yours for conservation work and not to pay rents, salaries, etc. We believe that this is how members would wish their contributions to be used. It is our pledge to you that we will use your contribution wisely to accomplish projects and programs that are consistent with your high conservation resolve.

Thank you again for joining with us. Please keep in touch with us concerning any suggestions you might have about ongoing or planned programs.

Sincerely,

THE GEORGIA WILDLIFE FEDERATION
Tommy Gregors, Jr.
Chairman of the Board

APPENDIX X
COMPLETE LETTER TO SENATOR KIDD, 1987

Dear Mr. Kidd:

I'm writing in response to your letter in the *Union-Recorder* asking for ideas on how to improve the deer situation. I'm a landowner who leases to deer hunters, who deer hunts and who is an activist in matters relating to deer herd management and deer hunters. Your concern over the crisis we face with the deer herd of Central Georgia is appreciated.

The deer problem is complex but stems basically from four factors which reflect attitudes stemming from ignorance of the facts and from the attitudes from the Depression era and from stories of Robin Hood that poaching is honorable to feed the family.

1. Underreporting of kill, caused by legal hunters not bothering to report their deer, and by the poacher and road kill never being known. Therefore the figures Game and Fish uses for its kill estimates are skewed to the low side.

2. Poacher kill. Poachers include not only the well-known road hunter but the teenager who slips onto the neighbor's land to kill a buck only for the antlers. Poachers include the otherwise legal hunter who borrows tags from a friend or his wife or even buys a second or third set of tags so he can keep on killing and tagging his deer without ever reporting any of them. Poachers include the hunter who, on doe days, kills every deer he sees and then picks out the two or three he wants and leaves the rest. (I've had people tell me of doing all of these acts.) Such actions certainly lead to imperfect statistical reporting to our game biologists, which in turn leads to imperfect deer seasons and bag limits.

3. Hunter desire for a trophy. Some hunters seek only a trophy set of antlers to hang on the wall. Many of them have little if any knowledge of game management and the necessity of keeping the

deer herd well below the carrying capacity of the land to produce
trophy bucks. These hunters often refuse to kill a doe because to
do so is sissy, or not good hunting practice (they believe).

4. Landowner attitude. Nonhunting landowners sometimes
refuse to allow hunting on their farms but complain about the
number of deer or the poaching on their property. They don't
want hunters to kill Bambi. They don't want slobs trashing their
lands. They don't want the danger of high-powered rifles fired
near their homes. These attitudes need to be influenced with a
combination of education and exposure to reputable, careful
hunters.

We can effect changes in all these factors:

Better reporting of kill,
Better license control,
Better hunter attitude,
Better landowner attitude.

I hope these changes can be effected without our legislators
having to become involved with setting seasons and bag limits
because, as you know, we have some fine biologists in our DNR
who are seeking to provide the best possible hunting experience
for the largest number of hunters while considering the needs of
the nonhunting public and seeking to protect the farmers' crops.

True, it's usually not a hunter who smashes into a deer with
his car—as Judge Joe Duke will testify, having hit two of *my* deer
on Georgia Highway 212 recently.

Any law we put on the books should be based on consideration
for the Rangers who must enforce them, but a drastic change in
our license could help the Rangers and also help improve the
reporting of the deer killed.

Today, the license is a single copy, given to the hunter. No
record is kept by DNR. This needs changing. The license should be
issued for three, four, or five years; it should be coded with the
owner's drivers' license number. It should contain his photograph.
It should show his home address. The license should also have
space to show that big game tags have been issued and space to
show the kill for each year. Anyone claiming to have lost tags
should be required to apply for new ones on a form on which he
swears under penalty of perjury that the tags were lost, not used.

The application for the license should require under penalty of perjury, that the hunter provide information for encoding into the DNR computer, including a list of all, if any, game and fish violations in the past three years. It should inform the hunter that failure to report deer kills will also constitute perjury by omission.

True, such perjury would be difficult to prove, but such an oath would keep the otherwise honest hunter from failing to report and from scrounging extra tags. The multi-year license with ID would make enforcement easier, especially with the hunter information encoded into a computer and verifiable by a Ranger in the field.

Conviction of violating a game law should result in stiff punishment by the local judge, plus mandatory loss of hunting license for at least one full calendar year for the first conviction, two years for the second conviction, and at least five years for the third conviction. Local judges should be encouraged to levy high fines for life-endangering offences (e.g., road hunting, night hunting, hunting without permission, hunting from a vehicle) and a minimum fine of $50.00 for any game and fish offence.

With a strong, verifiable license system and stern punishment for violations, the biologists would have much firmer information on which to base their population estimates, to set the seasons, and to set the bag limits.

True, some deer would get killed illegally and some would go unreported, but the reports would be more accurate.

(NOTE: I failed to suggest that all railroad conductors be required to report all train kills.)

To determine the road kill, we need to encourage all law enforcement officers to submit a monthly report of deer killed in their jurisdiction, including deer sex, location of kill and age if the enforcement officer is able to age the deer. Location information would be important to prevent duplication of reporting.

All auto insurance companies should be required to report every claim for deer damage to cars, giving DNR the exact day, time and location of the accident, including whether or not the deer was killed, the sex of the deer, and if known the age of the deer.

Both road kill and hunter kill information can be verified somewhat by requiring coolers—both those that butcher and those that simply provide temporary cold storage—to provide a list of hunters by name, license number, date, and sex of the deer to DNR. Of course, if the deer is a road kill, the report will so indicate.

In the long run, such a system of reporting and computer verification will serve to help Game and Fish have a better count of our deer herds.

Meanwhile, however, we need a herd reduction NOW to prevent more road accidents, and to prevent the loss of habitat from the deer overeating their food supply. Anyone who receives income from hunters does not want the herds to eat themselves out of food because then the individual deer are smaller and less healthy, and hunters will lose interest and no longer bring their dollars here to spend—they'll go elsewhere in the state or even out of state.

Game and Fish does not want to increase the bag limit because we'll have another 100,000 hunters in Georgia by the year 2000. That many hunters would eliminate the deer, and once the bag limit is increased the average hunter will want it to stay increased. Also, most hunters don't kill but one deer—few kill three (according to the reports, which we know are low).

But a temporary increase of an additional doe tag to hunters who have already killed and reported killing two does would help. Such a system would have to function through the local Game Biologist, to whom the hunter would have to report his kill and turn in his tags.

Another temporary measure is to issue landowner/leaseholder permits (tags) to kill a certain number of does above those for which the hunters already have tags. These permits could be handled somewhat like the summer crop permits, but be in the form of the honorary tags now issued to landowners. The tag should be filled in to show the land on which they were to be used (owner or hunting-lease holder).

Local game biologists already know many of the areas that are overpopulated and would not have to do a survey to issue permits.

At this time DNR has special doe days on their Wildlife Management Areas (WMA)—sometimes these doe days have been in counties that were closed to doe hunting except on the WMA, and more recently they have been held two-three weeks before the rest of the county was open to doe hunting. The game management techniques that apply to a WMA could also apply to the surrounding lands. Therefore, when a doe hunt is held on a WMA, the rest of the county should be open to doe hunting.

Education is the only answer I can see for the hunter who refuses to kill does and for the landowner who objects to hunters.

We need to support the Georgia Wildlife Federation in educating the hunter about game management. We need to encourage local and statewide newspapers and magazines (e.g., *Georgia Outdoor News*) to publish articles by state biologists on how to have trophy deer and on the need to kill does to keep a healthy herd. We need to encourage the Georgia Public TV to run specials on deer herd management.

As we change the attitude of hunters about herd management, we need also to educate the landowners about hunters' willingness to pay to hunt, to keep the lands neat, to refrain from putting nails in trees, and to observe common sense and safety laws while hunting.

The education of those opposed to killing Bambi as well as the hunter who wants Bambi only as a trophy will be a long-term project for all of us.

Let me stress that any changes in season and bag limits should be temporary. If written into law then they must have a sunset clause to protect both the game and the hunter (from himself!).

May I suggest that whatever solution you recommend to DNR be a recommendation only, so that their biologists can draft any legislation you and other legislators feel we need. Then the DNR can iron out details to best serve the needs of our wildlife, our hunters, and our general populations.

Sincerely,

Susan Lindsley
Milledgeville

APPENDIX XI
REPORT OF DEER HARVEST, 1989

This letter to Game Management is one example of my attempts to increase the legal number of deer per hunter. Middle Georgia land can support about thirty-five deer per square mile. The statistics at the end of the letter show that the hunters were culling more than fifty per square mile for several years.

Joe Kurz/Dick Whittington
Game & Fish Commission
State of Georgia

Dear Joe and Dick,

Here's our report on our deer kill for the l989 season on the same TWO square miles I've been reporting on for several years:

EAST side of OUR HWY:

  Area: 600 acres
        Hunters: 16 total including 7 weekend guests
          Archery hunters: 6

Deer Killed. Note that some were not recovered and would therefore not have been reported as killed; this total includes ones we know died either because of finding them later or from sign when shot, e.g., gut contents on arrow.

	ARCHERY: total 9	FIREARMS: total 26
Mature does,	4	5
6 month does,	1	4

Button bucks,	2	2
4-point buck,	1	6 (2 ten-pointers)
sex unk, 6 mo (not recovered)	1	

BONUS week 9 mature does, with 12-13 embryos. Five had one embryo each, 3 had two each (total 11). One Ranger Nelson called a "hoss" was gut shot and the uterus was torn, but very large, so we thought she probably had two embryos, for a total of 13.

We did not age many deer this year; some does were aged at 3-5 years.
Found dead (we know we did not shoot):
               2 mature does
               1 6-mo doe
               2 spike bucks

TOTALS EAST SIDE:

  Overall total   40
           Bucks total 13
           Does total   26
           Sex unk (6 mo) 1

WEST SIDE OUR HWY (Campbell's): Area: 670 acres

   Hunters: 35 plus or minus; some guests

Limits, one antlered deer per hunter, but some known to violate regulation.
    Also some hunters were believed to kill deer not reported to Campbell who guesses probably as many as five more should be added to his total.

TOTAL reported to Campbell: 62 (estimated 67)
    29 bucks (4 buttons)
    33 does

Largest buck was 8 point with 13 inch spread; several 4,5,6 pointers, more 5-pointers than any; spikes larger than last year (e.g., 6 inches long instead of 1-3 inches) but some of the spikes were 4 ½ years old.

TOTALS for BOTH SIDES: 102 deer killed on 2 sq. miles.
        (107 if add 5 estimated on WEST side)
    Bucks: 42
    Does: 59
    Unk: 1

In spite of the extreme overpopulation (last day of season one hunter on WEST side saw herd of 9 deer) the deer seemed to be in better condition this winter than last. Both sides have heavily planted food plots, WHICH ARE PROBABLY THE ONLY REASON WE DON'T HAVE STARVATION.

Total kill for both areas by year since 1986:

    1986: 113
    1987: 100
    1988: 86
    1989: 102 (or 107)
        AVERAGE KILL/year: 100 deer or
        50 deer per sq. mi. per year for 4 years

        Sincerely,

        Susan Lindsley

APPENDIX XII
LETTER TO LEDBETTER RE NELSON, 1985

Dear Commissioner Ledbetter:

A large group of landowners, deer and turkey hunters and conservationists would like to thank one of the state's Wildlife Rangers for his high level of efficiency over the years.

Sergeant Marion R. Nelson, Macon District, has demonstrated the same dedication to the preservation of Georgia's wildlife whether he was protecting fish from netters, deer from night hunters, or turkey in newly stocked areas.

This Ranger is serving in his home county and has had occasion to come face to face with violators who were long-time friends or associates. Sergeant Nelson charges his friends with violations with the same objectivity he shows with total strangers: A violator is a violator and wildlife protection is his purpose in life.

In spite of local politics in some of the small rural counties under his jurisdiction—one fine for killing a doe out of season was only $5.00—Sergeant Nelson persists with enthusiasm and dedication. He frequently has worked 36 hours without sleep to stake out an area, make the arrests, and follow up with the necessary paperwork and legal procedures. If the good ole boy he arrests is a special friend of local political leaders and he knows the case will be *nol pros*, this ranger goes ahead with his job.

One aspect of his situation that demonstrates his dedication is his being locked in to his present rank. His next promotion would be logically to District Captain, but Sergeant Nelson is in his home county, living on family lands, with no desire to move. But the District Captain, Asa Pippin, has no plans to vacate his job, so Sergeant Nelson's efficiency results from dedication to his job, from the satisfaction of doing it well, not from ambitions to be bucked upstairs.

Without the support of an understanding and devoted wife, no Ranger can perform effectively. Harriett Nelson loves the wildlife of Georgia and has given her husband support, not just by not objecting to his long hours away from home, but also by taking messages and helping callers obtain quick help when her husband is not available.

Therefore, we of Central Georgia recognize Sergeant Marion R. Nelson as an exceptional Guardian of Wildlife and extend to him our appreciation.

Sincerely,

Susan Lindsley

APPENDIX XIII
SEASONS AND BAG LIMITS
A Brief History

Deer hunting became legal in my home county in the mid-1950s, with a bag limit of one buck until 1964, when the bag limit was raised to two bucks. That year the state introduced the first archery season, which ran a month before the firearms season. Previously, anyone could hunt with bow and arrow only during firearms season.

My first year to hunt deer was 1966, when the season lasted two weeks, with a beginning and ending weekend, for a total of sixteen days. Our limit was two bucks, and each had to be tagged immediately after it hit the ground. Untagged, illegal deer were seized. And when he confiscated the deer, the ranger took a tag and gave a ticket.

Archery season provided the hunter with two tags, but his seasonal (annual) limit was two deer. Archery tags were a set; firearms tags were another set. They were not interchangeable.

Does were like the Pope—holy and not to be disturbed.

The seasons were set by region in most of the state, and in some locations, by county. Over the years some regions were merged. In 1978, the state was split into two zones. My county was in the Northern Zone. These zones have been in effect since then.

The regulations discussed here relate to my county and my zone, not the entire state.

The season changed in 1967—to run from November 4 through November 27. We still had only two tags, but one could be used for an antlerless deer, that is, any deer without antlers; it might be a doe or a buck that had dropped his antlers or a young buck that had not yet sprouted his first set. But we had only one doe day, November 27, the last day of the season—a Monday when most hunters were back at work.

For several years, the limit remained the same, but the season was extended to run from the first weekend in November through the first weekend in December.

Then came the week-long bonus hunt, in 1972. That year, it began on Christmas Day, which meant many men were gone from the family gathering to the woods. Not many families were happy to have Daddy gone on Christmas day, so the next year and thereafter, the bonus hunt began on December 26 and ran, as previously, through January 1. But doe days were limited to end-of-the-hunt days—the last day of the regular season and the last day of the bonus hunt.

When the blaze-orange vest requirement came in 1973, everyone complained. The deer would see the orange as a solid blob of one color, and with the sun on it the orange would look white—the danger signal for the deer. But the regulation remained, and probably saved a few lives.

By 1975, the deer population was expanding, and biologists began to increase the number of doe days: We had five doe days that year, but still had the limit of two deer. One could be a doe.

A new law took effect in 1977. A child under sixteen could not hunt alone, but had to be under the *direct* supervision of an adult at all times.

We saw a big jump in doe days in 1978, but were still limited to two deer: Both could be does. We had twelve doe days.

The bag limit finally increased in 1980, up to three deer, and one must be antlerless—either a doe or a buck with a *bald head*. But we had fewer doe days.

Turkeys became legal game for us in 1985. The limit was two gobblers, and that remained the limit until 1993, when it was increased to three gobblers. The state at this time (2015) does not have a hen season.

Joe Kurz, game manager, had been to my home lands twice. One year he hunted the doe day at the end of the season—a full day of seeing no deer because the understory had been winter-killed and offered the deer an almost endless view through the woods.

He returned at my request to count deer in late February 1991.

As a result of the head count I was able to convince him that we needed more doe days and a higher doe bag limit. That was the year he took my suggestion to allow the use of archery tags during firearms season.

Doe days now came earlier in the season, so hunters had a better chance to have natural cover while hunting.

The next year brought another change. Deer killed on a Wildlife

Management Area that required check-in and check-out would be tagged with a WMA tag. These deer would not count against the hunter's bag limit of antlered deer or against the season's five-deer limit.

The State realized the population was about to exceed the carrying capacity of the land, thirty-five deer per square mile.

In 1998, the biologists made the change that Guy Stancil and his friends had wanted in 1985: The three-week early December break was eliminated and the season ran from October 24 through January 1.

The herds continued to increase, and some counties voted themselves "Quality Deer Management," which limited legal bucks to certain antler configurations.

Two years later, the bag limit rose to eight total, with only two antlered.

In 2002, the bag limit reached twelve total. Only two could carry antlers. In 2006, the entire season was open for doe days.

The State also recognized Quality Deer Management counties and listed them in the published regulations. Some county's restrictions differ from those of the state: In Georgia now, a hunter may take one-of-any-bucks, but his other buck must have at least four points on one antler. My county (Baldwin) does not have quality deer management beyond that of the state.

I encourage my hunters to harvest does—our herds are too numerous for the land, and a browse line is visible even from my home. Note that the deer have eaten all the browse (leafy material) they can reach while on all fours.

Although coyotes kill deer, they have—so far—not affected the population enough in my area to allow the understory to recover.

In the 1960s, deer sightings were uncommon, but today I may see as many as twenty-five deer feeding in my fields or on their way to persimmons or oaks.

Deer have broken into glass-fronted stores, not just in Milledgeville but in some of the larger towns. They seem to want to cross a road when a vehicle approaches, and insurance companies see them only as costly pests.

I read a book by a lady who lived in the far north, who fed an injured deer one winter and he returned the next year when the snow was deep. He also brought company, and over the years his herd grew. One foggy night when she went to the barn, one deer stuck his nose in the flashlight beam that looked solid in the fog and sniffed at it. She realized then that the deer did think a light beam was solid, and I wonder if deer that jump into the side of a car think that when the light passes, the danger has passed so they leap, and hit the car broadside.

I hope the deer do not multiply beyond the hunters' ability to keep the population under control and that the ever-increasing numbers of coyotes do not pull down the size of the deer herds.

INDEX

I have indexed only the names of people since subjects can be located from the table of contents.

Arrington, Sheriff 160
Baker, Rex, 180, 194, 405
Baker, Robert, 16
Baldwin, G. S., Jr., 2, 3
Barnes, John Wayne, 109, 110, 209, 289, 292-296, 299, 361, 365, 367,
Berra, Yogi, 268
Birdsong, Representative, 421
Billy (Herbert's son), 148, 149,
Birmingham, Nita, 403
Blanks, Pat, 278, 333, 337
Bramlett, LaVerne, 380, 381 (photograph)
Bramlett, Russ/Rusty, 244, 264, 265, 270, 271, 380
Bramlett, Thulia, 271
Brown, Tom, Jr., 21, 22
Bryson, Willie Mae, 216, 325
Busbee, Governor, 58
Cabisius, Gail, 211, 334, 337- 339
Campbell, Merle, 57, 94, 95, 97-101, 286, 350, 358, 360
Campbell, Rachel, 97
Chapman, Tony, 108
Crockford, Jack, 189, 190, 414
Darnell, James R., 222, 225
Dennis (Livingston), wildlife ranger, 130
Duke, Judge Joe, 426
E. D., see Harrison, E. D.
Gardner, Milton, 322
Giacometto, Lawrence, 252
Giacometto, Ron, 252
Goldstein, Sonny, 322
Green, Bob,   227, 315-319, 321, 322
Greg (see Smith, Greg)
Hamm, Keith, 265
Harris, Governor Joe Frank, 185, 198, 200, 420, 422
Harrison, Annelle, 20

Harrison, E. D., 19, 20
Harrisons, the family, 8, 10, 315
Hartzell, Randy, 82
Haslam, Ruth, 334, 337, 339
Held, Steve, 255
Hicks, Tom, 406, 407
Hough, Jean, 247, 249, 250, 255
Humphrey, Phyllis, 394
Hunsucker, Jeff, 295
Hunsucker, John, 58
Jackson, Vernell, 57, 288, 301, 321
James, Will, 249
Jimmy (Fowler), 16, 106, 107
Key, Richard, 208, 209, 262, 354, 368
Key, Shelia, 261, 262
Kidd, Culver, 68-71, 205, 413, 425
Kile, Terry, 190, 201, 414
Kirkland, Leon, 190, 226, 414
Knight, John Alden, 59, 64
Kurz, Joe, 65, 67, 123, 192-195, 206-210, 415, 417, 418, 430, 436
Langford, Robert (Bobby), 82
Larry (Herbert's son), 47, 48, 120, 122, 147, 148, 370
Ledbetter, Leonard, 190, 198, 225, 226, 412, 414, 433
Maruta, 300
McCollum, Jerry, 201, 202
McEuen (family/ranch), 248, 255
Melanie, 196
Mitchell, Kent, 189, 190
Morrison, Jim, 70, 190, 197, 201
Murphy, Thomas, 190, 193, 198, 412,
Nelson, Harriett, 433
Nelson, Marion, 39-41, 83, 225-227, 321, 403, 404, 406, 407-410, 431, 433, 434
Palmer, Eddie (see Woot)
Parham, Bobby, 179, 180, 198, 413, 421
Payne, Mark, 260
Peterson, Jerry, 174
Pippin, Asa, 433
Prissy, 196

Rainey, Howard H., 190, 411, 414
Reynolds, Burt, 256
Riner, Trish Bass, 337-339
Rithmire, Doug, 201
Rob (a visiting hunter), 25-28, 45, 62
Salten, Felix, 11, 231, 366
Sanders, Cindy Key, 292, 326, 327
Scarlett, 196
Sills, Howard, 81
Simpson, Mr. Elmer, 106, 107
Simpson, Norman, 37, 39, 46-52, 72-75, 103, 104, 119-122, 129, 130, 132, 134, 135, 137, 169, 170, 209, 263, 264, 271, 282-284, 289-292, 296, 297, 314, 320-322, 365, 367, 370, 377, 380, 397,
Sires, Bob, 256-260, 387
Skeeter, 312, 313
Smith, Greg, 262-264, 271, 272, 296
Smith, June Kitchens, 334, 337, 339
Sonny (Fowler), 15, 16, 106, 107
Stancil, Guy, 189, 190, 195-198, 200, 201, 437
Steve, TV reporter, 333
Stevens, Keith, 249, 250
Stewart, Calvin, 184-187
Tanner, Joe, 69
Tartar, Buzz, 249
Texotic Game Ranch, 234
Thompson, Hugh, 288
Thompson, Jim, 158
Triple 7 (777) Ranch, 234, 228
Turn In Poachers Hotline, 81
Waller, David (Dave), 95-97, 358
Watts, James (Jimmy), 160, 318
Wayne (see Barnes, John Wayne)
West, John, 94
White, Ranger Steve, 57
Whittington, Dick, 67, 164, 430
Woods, Stuart, 279, 280
Woot (Eddie Palmer), 330-341
Wordsworth, William, 12
Y. O. Ranch, 234

ABOUT THE AUTHOR

Photograph by Roy Davis, Milledgeville, Georgia

Susan's writing has won numerous awards, including a national first from the Northern Colorado Writers for this book and the Independent Publishers Award for best in Regional Fiction for her second novel *When Darkness Fell*. Several of her books have been nominated for Georgia Author of the Year, and *The Bottom Rail* was ɑɑmi finaliɑt in 2013. Several chapters in this book are also award winners.

Daughter of college professors, Susan was reared on a 2,500-acre plantation in middle Georgia, among herds of horses and cattle. Susan began writing stories in childhood in between adventures horseback riding, driving cattle in for market, breaking the foals and yearlings, and playing Roy Rogers.

Tenants on the plantation included cattle rustlers, moonshiners and murderers. In later years, the farm became a "poachers' paradise" until she began pursuing the poachers.

Susan worked as a reporter and feature writer for a daily paper in Georgia. In the Boston area she wrote for Raytheon Manufacturing and edited research papers at MIT. She returned to work as writer and editor at the Centers for Disease Control. Her work has been translated for use in Africa and Asia.

Her stories, poetry, articles and editorials have been published in several anthologies as well as in local, state and national magazines, including *Southern Living* online magazine. Her nonfiction subjects have ranged from *Gone With the Wind* to wildlife management. She has nine other published books.

Other Books by Susan Lindsley

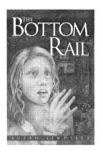

The Bottom Rail, trade paperback, $14.95, ThomasMax Publishing. Susan Lindsley's debut novel, winner of the 2013 ThomasMax "You Are Published" award and honorable mention for Georgia Author of the Year in first novel category. Seeking a future, the Carter families move from their home in the mountains to middle Georgia. By 1946 they expand their bootlegging enterprises to include murder, cattle rustling, election fraud and interracial affairs. Kindle/Nook, $4.99.

Susan Myrick of* Gone With The Wind*: An Autobiographical Biography, hardcover with dust jacket, $34.95, ThomasMax Publishing. The story of Susan Lindsley's aunt, Susan Myrick, who served as technical consultant for Southern authenticity in the making of the movie "Gone With The Wind." Contains letters, including correspondence between Myrick and Margaret Mitchell, clashes with David O. Selznick, Myrick's diaries and dozens of photographs. Also available on Kindle for $9.99.

Margaret Mitchell: A Scarlett or a Melanie? Trade paperback, $14.95, ThomasMax Publishing. Susan Lindsley presents works by her aunt, Susan Myrick, in answering the title question and also explores other articles by Myrick, including three feature stories about survivors of the War Between the States. Also available for Kindle or Nook for $4.99.

Blue Jeans and Pantaloons in Yesterplace, Trade paperback, $16.00, ThomasMax Publishing. A slice of rural life in the "Old South," Yesterplace inhabitants included Flannery O'Connor, Susan Myrick, cattle rustlers, shady politicians, world-renown scientists, murderers and a conjure woman. With neither TV nor telephone, Susan and her sisters made up their games and songs, rode horses to the picture show, and played at Roy Rogers and Jesse James. Kindle/Nook, $5.99.

Christmas Gift, Trade paperback, $10.00, ThomasMax Publishing. Lindsley has created a classic collection of family-friendly Christmas poetry with illustrations, including "A Deer with Funny Feet" and twenty other poems. Kindle/Nook, $3.99.

Myrick Memories, Trade Paperback, $10.00, ThomasMax Publishing. Learn about race relations, including interracial marriages, in the early 1900's. Explore courtrooms and visit an old-fashioned prom. Learn about housekeeping and child care in the late 1800's. Read Susan Myrick's only published short story. Kindle/Nook, $5.99

When Darkness Fell, Trade paperback, $14.95. Winner of Independent Publishers Award for best regional novel. Buck Steele, a black soldier, returns to his middle Georgia home because he loves Molly, a white girl. He and Molly are terrorized by the local KKK members and protected by a 12-year-old white girl and her family. Kindle/Nook, $4.99.

All books shown are currently in print and available virtually everywhere books are sold. If your favorite bookstore doesn't have a copy, ask them to order it for you. Also available through Amazon.com and other online book sellers, including Barnes & Noble, Books-a-Million, and many other websites. To purchase autographed copies and see or purchase other works by Susan Lindsley, contact the author through her website, yesterplace.com or via email at yesterplace@earthlink.net.

CPSIA information can be obtained
at www.ICGtesting.com
Printed in the USA
FFOW02n2006200317
33573FF